City of revolution

In memory of Mary Neighbour
18 September 1914–11 October 2000

City of revolution
Restructuring Manchester

EDITED BY

JAMIE PECK AND
KEVIN WARD

Manchester University Press
Manchester and New York
distributed exclusively in the USA by Palgrave

Published by Manchester University Press
Oxford Road, Manchester M13 9NR, UK
and Room 400, 175 Fifth Avenue, New York, NY 1000, USA
www.manchesteruniversitypress.co.uk

Distributed exclusively in the USA by
Palgrave, 175 Fifth Avenue, New York, NY 10010, USA

Distributed exclusively in Canada by
UBC Press, University of British Columbia, 2029 West Mall, Vancouver, BC, Canada V6T 1Z2

British Library Cataloguing-in-Publication Data
A catalogue record for this book is available from the British Library

Library of Congress Cataloging-in-Publication Data applied for

ISBN 0 7190 5887 2 *hardback*
    0 7190 5888 0 *paperback*

First published 2002
10 09 08 07 06 05 04 03 02   10 9 8 7 6 5 4 3 2 1

Typeset in Fournier
by Koinonia Ltd, Manchester
Printed in Great Britain
by Bookcraft (Bath) Ltd, Midsomer Norton

Contents

CONTENTS

List of plates and figures

Plates

Figures

List of tables and boxes

Tables

Boxes

List of contributors

ALLAN COCHRANE is Professor of Public Policy at the Open University. He has researched and published widely in the fields of urban policy and politics, most recently in the context of Berlin's reunification. He is the author of *Whatever happened to Local Government?* (Open University Press, 1993), joint author of *Re-thinking the Region* (Routledge, 1998) and joint editor of *Managing Social Policy* (Sage, 1994) and *Comparing Welfare States* (Sage, 2nd revised edn, 2001).

IAIN DEAS is a Lecturer in Planning at the University of Manchester. His research interests centre on urban policy evaluation and urban and regional governance. Current research focusing on Manchester includes a three-year project funded under the ESRC *Cities* programme to explore competitiveness and social exclusion, an evaluation of the work of Moss Side and Hulme Partnership, and an exploration of inter-agency collaboration in the New Deal for Communities area of East Manchester.

PETER DICKEN is Professor of Geography at the University of Manchester. His research interests focus on global economic change as reflected in his book *Global Shift: Transforming the World Economy* (Sage, 3rd edn, 1998). He is currently directing a major ESRC-funded research project on global production networks in Britain, East Asia and Eastern Europe in collaboration with colleagues at the Manchester Business School and the National University of Singapore.

BENITO GIORDANO is a Simon Research Fellow in the School of Geography at the University of Manchester. Before that he was a Research Associate, also at the University of Manchester, on an ESRC project comparing economic change, urban governance and social exclusion in Manchester and Liverpool. Giordano's research interests are in regionalism and regional governance in the European Union, and he has written numerous articles on Italian regions. He is currently working on a project comparing sub-national devolution in England and Italy, specifically focusing on the city-region dynamic in the two countries.

DEAN HERD is a researcher in the School of Geography, University of Manchester. His research interests include the political economy of welfare reform and the dynamics of urban poverty. Having enjoyed two spells as an Honorary Fellow in the Department of Geography, University of Wisconsin-Madison, he recently completed his Ph.D. thesis – *Connecting Spaces: Transatlantic Welfare Reform and the Re-Regulation of the Urban Poor.*

ADAM HOLDEN is a Lecturer in Geography at the University of Durham, having previously completed a Ph.D. (1995–99) on the politics of entrepreneurialism in Manchester, and worked as a researcher in the Centre for Urban Policy Studies, University of Manchester. His research interests are in urban and regional change, state theory and urban regeneration.

MARTIN JONES is a Reader in Human Geography at the University of Wales, Aberystwyth. Author of *New Institutional Spaces* (Jessica Kingsley, 1999) and numerous journal articles, his research interests are in regional and local economic development. He is currently undertaking research, funded by the ESRC, on the impacts of UK constitutional change on economic governance.

GORDON MACLEOD is a Lecturer in Human Geography at the University of Durham. He has published widely on regional economic development, the changing political geographies of the state, institutional change and regional identities, and urban and regional theory. He is currently working on a study of urban renaissance and homelessness in the city of Glasgow.

ROSEMARY MELLOR died shortly after completing her contribution to this volume. She was a very valued member of the Department of Sociology at the University of Manchester for over twenty years. She wrote widely on issues of urban redevelopment, urban inequality and the evolution of urban sociology as a sub-discipline.

TERRY PATTERSON is an Associate member of the Manchester Economy Group. He is an experienced welfare rights and housing practitioner, trainer, researcher and author. His writings on social entitlements and equality issues span over twenty years and range from *Survival Guide to London for Young Homeless People* (Centrepoint, 1981), to 'Welfare Rights Advice and the New Managerialism' in *Benefits* 30, 2001 and 'From Safety Net to Exclusion: The Ending of Social Security Benefits in the UK for "Persons from Abroad"' in Cohen, S., Humphries, B., and Mynott, E. (eds), *From Immigration Controls to Welfare Controls* (Routledge, 2001).

JAMIE PECK is Professor of Geography and Sociology at the University of Wisconsin-Madison, having previously been at the University of Manchester for twenty years. Author of *Work-Place: The Social Regulation of Labor Markets* (Guilford, 1996) and *Workfare States* (Guilford, 2001), his research interests are in urban political economy, labour studies, and economic governance. He is currently working on a study of contingent labour markets in US cities.

BRIAN ROBSON has been Professor of Geography at Manchester University since 1977 and before that taught at Cambridge. He is director of Manchester's Centre for Urban Policy Studies (CUPS) which has undertaken a wide range of research projects on urban policy, deprivation and regeneration for government departments, local authorities, research councils and other funders. He was a member of a working group of Lord Rogers' Urban Task Force and was awarded the Founder's Gold Medal by the Royal Geographical Society for his work on urban policy.

STEVE QUILLEY lectures in Urban and Environmental Sociology at University College Dublin. Having completed doctoral research on the political economy of regeneration in Manchester, he is now researching contemporary patterns of urbanisation in Ireland. He also has developing interests in a number of areas including: cultural constructions of nature in relation to leisure and tourism; animals and society; environmental history and socio-biology.

ADAM TICKELL is Professor of Geography at the School of Geographical Sciences, University of Bristol. A decade-long resident of Manchester, he has research interests in urban politics and global finance. He is currently working on ESRC-funded research projects on the politics of English devolution and the reframing of global financial norms.

LAURA TWOMEY, now a civil servant, was previously a Research Associate working on the ESRC-funded project 'Economic Competitiveness, Urban Governance and Social Cohesion in Manchester and Liverpool' at the Centre for Urban Policy, University of Manchester.

KEVIN WARD is a Lecturer in Human Geography at the University of Manchester. Author of numerous journal articles, his research interests are in urban and regional governance, urban regeneration and labour geographies. He is currently working on issues of urban entrepreneurialism, the negotiation of the work/ non-work divide in urban Britain and on a study of the globalisation and urbanisation of the temporary staffing industry.

GWYNDAF WILLIAMS is Professor of Urban Planning and Development at the University of Manchester. He is joint author of *Metropolitan Planning in Britain: A Comparative Review* (Jessica Kingsley, 1999) and author of numerous articles on strategic planning, urban regeneration and urban governance. He is currently writing a book on city centre regeneration – *The Enterprising City Centre: Manchester's Development Challenge* (Spon Press, 2002).

Preface

The plan for this book, which had been the subject of a lot of talk but not much action for several years, was finally hatched in the Manchester Bar, New York City, in the spring of 1999 and it was (almost) completed in the offices of the Department of Geography, University of Wisconsin-Madison two years later. Despite these transatlantic entanglements, this book is very much a local affair. Originating in a seminar series that the two of us organised at the School of Geography, University of Manchester, during the 1997–98 academic year, it represents an attempt to make sense of the changing political economy of the city of Manchester. Then, as now, we were concerned with what to make – cumulatively – of the plethora of very 'real' changes that were happening around us in Manchester, in the city's institutions, in its economic and social conditions, and in its politics. Many of these developments were, it seemed to us, being misrepresented or rendered virtually invisible amidst the froth of self-promotion and 'partnershipspeak' that had become such a conspicuous feature of the 'new' Manchester.

A book on the changing political economies of Manchester would, we hoped, shed some light on the complex nature of Manchester's (partly) home-made reconstruction, while also raising critical questions about the parallel transformations that are under way in other British cities. While Manchester may be a place in which these transformations find an especially sharp focus, they are certainly not unique to this city. At the same time, Manchester can never be 'just another case study', because in a sense it has always been a city on the cusp of change and – let's be frank – it has never had a reputation for modesty. So this is an account of a city under transformation, a city that has done its best to shed its manufacturing past while aggressively seeking to remanufacture a new urban future. In *City of revolution*, a wide range of contributors – all of whom have lived in, worked in or worked on this city – have been brought together to explore a number of different facets of Manchester's political-economic transformation, including the changing patterns of economic restructuring, partnership and governance formation, planning strategies, social policy and urban politics. As questions of urban policy are (finally) rising up the political agenda again, this examination of the limits and possibilities of Manchester's make-over seems especially timely.

Now the book itself is of course not just our product, nor simply the sum of the contributors' parts. Its production has, in a not entirely trivial way, been a social process, and a great number of individuals have helped along the way. The following have all been involved, in one form or another, in shaping ideas set out in this book, although they are of course exempt from blame for its remaining inadequacies: Huw Beynon, Mike Bradford, Allan Cochrane, Ian Curtis, Peter Dicken, Adam Holden, Bob Jessop, Martin Jones, Gordon MacLeod, Rosemary Mellor, Brian Robson, Steve Quilley, Adam Tickell and Darren Wisher. We are especially grateful to Andy Wood for his careful and constructive review of the text, and to Nick Scarle and Graham Bowden for demonstrating once again their cartographic skills. The staff at Manchester University Press, especially Matthew Frost, were enormously helpful, professional and (most importantly) patient during the production of the book, which was completed despite rather more modest (but nonetheless unsettling) transformations in both our work circumstances during 2000. Finally, we remember Rosemary Mellor whose untimely death during the final stages of this book deprived Manchester of one of its most enthusiastic urbanists and fascinating characters.

Jamie Peck and Kevin Ward
Madison and Manchester

Abbreviations

—■◆■—

CMDC	Central Manchester Development Corporation
DEA	Department of Economic Affairs
DETR	Department of the Environment, Transport and the Regions
DoE	Department of the Environment
DTI	Department for Trade and Industry
GLC	Greater London Council
GMC	Greater Manchester Council
GMLPU	Greater Manchester Low Pay Unit
GONW	Government Office for the North West
MCC	Manchester City Council
MCCTF	Manchester City Centre Task Force
MIDAS	Manchester Investment and Development Agency Service
MM	Manchester Millennium Ltd
MMTF	Manchester Millennium Task Force
NRDA	Northern Regional Development Agency
NVQ	Non-vocational qualification
NWBLT	North West Business Leadership Team
NWDA	North West Development Agency
NWRA	North West Regional Association
OECD	Organisation for Economic Co-operation and Development
RDA	Regional Development Agency
SRBCF	Single Regeneration Budget Challenge Fund
TEC	Training & Enterprise Council
UDP	Unitary Development Plan

I

Placing Manchester

JAMIE PECK AND KEVIN WARD

MANCHESTER has always been a city of extremes, a city of hard edges. The city has a gritty vibrancy, even on its (many) rainy days. There is here a spirit of dogged independence, sometimes expressed in the form of arrogant exuberance, sometimes as downright indifference to what the rest of the world thinks. Mancunians will always tell you that it happened in Manchester first, though only rarely will you find them patiently attentive to the counter-arguments. The city has always been on a hurried path to (some kind of) improvement, and has little time for those who would put obstacles in the way or get distracted by temporary setbacks. Always a city on the move, it has been in an almost perpetual state of restructuring, right back to its early stirrings as the crucible of industrial capitalism. Talk of revolution, like the drizzle, is nearly always in the air.

But the twentieth century was a hard one for Manchester. Being first proved to be a double-edged sword. The first industrial city was the first to experience large-scale *de*industrialisation – the absolute decline in manufacturing capacity and employment – which from the 1960s onwards started to pull the guts out of the place. Industry had not only been a source of jobs but also of cultural identity for a city that had long prided itself on the tradition of no-nonsense graft and money-making. For the working-class men of the city, in particular, the factory and the football ground were the fundamental co-ordinates of an uncompromising lifestyle which was dealt a hammer blow by the collapse of industrial employment. In 1959, well over half of the Greater Manchester workforce was employed in manufacturing. Today, less than one in five of the conurbation's workforce are employed in factories. Approaching four-fifths of the city's workers are employed in services of one kind or another – some in the financial sector, but the majority working in

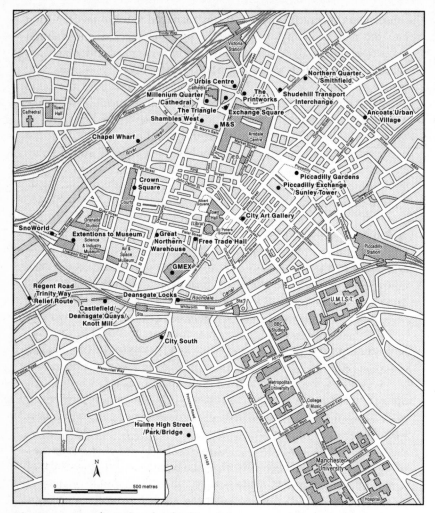

Figure 1.1   Manchester's redevelopment map

relatively low-paid retail, clerical and personal-service occupations. And now slightly over half of the workforce are women. Manchester is a different kind of city from the one it once was. The place has been changing, and in ways which fundamentally challenge its political-economic role and cultural self-perception.

In this context, perhaps the fundamental question is whether Manchester's is a story of decline or transformation. Is this a city on a slow-motion slide into the post-industrial sludge of low-wage service work and under-employment? Or has it, after a decade or two of conspicuous underachievement, finally managed to make the transition into the new economy of high-tech, financial services and cultural industries? These are the questions that in a range of different ways animate the contributions to this book. And perhaps not surprisingly there is no simple answer. Contemporary Manchester exhibits a perplexing mix of both ongoing decline and dynamic transformation. While the narrative of success is certainly the dominant one in the city, only its most zealous advocates would claim that the work is done, that the deep-seated processes of decline have been arrested and reversed. In essence, the regeneration and restructuring of Manchester remains a work in progress. Certainly, there have been some high-profile achievements – think of the airport, the redeveloped city centre, the vibrant culture-economy – but these sit often uneasily alongside reminders that all is not well in this place. Problems of localised deprivation, of endemic low pay in many parts of the economy, of political and social alienation, of crumbling public infrastructure remain very real ones, even if they figure only fleetingly in the city's boisterous narrative of successful urban transformation. Making some kind of sense of this complex *and partial* transformation is the central objective of *City of revolution*. This locus of the industrial revolution is now desperately trying to catch the next wave. Whether it will make it is perhaps the single most important question facing the city.

This is more than a matter of local interest, moreover, because Manchester has in a sense always been located at the leading, or bleeding, edge of change. To be sure, many of the shifts, surges and slumps in the city's recent political-economic history that represent the focus of this book – the decline of manufacturing industry, the narrow obsession with city-centre regeneration, the (re)emergence of elite decision-making networks and privatised governance, the can-do entrepreneurialism of local agencies, the search for 'joined up' responses to social exclusion – all of these have been features of urban restructuring across the United Kingdom and in continental Europe too. Yet while not wishing to exaggerate the uniqueness of Manchester's experience, it is difficult to deny that these (cumulative) trends and developments have been especially intensely experienced in this city. More than this, though, Manchester really has led the way – for good or ill – in a number of areas. On the negative side, the scale of the jobs collapse in this once-paradigmatic industrial capital has been extraordinary, even if this now tends to be palmed off as a 'natural' development, leaving the city languishing near the bottom of many league tables of labour-market vitality (see Turok and Edge 1999). And, not surprisingly, many social, health and housing indicators tell a depressingly consistent story (see Griffiths 1998). But on the positive side, the city-centre face-lift has been remarkably successful in physical and promotional (if not social) terms, reflecting the conspicuous skills of Manchester's ruling elite and the cadre of (quasi)public-sector professionals in playing the 'regeneration game'. As Jonathan Glancey (2001) has enthused:

> Manchester, especially now it has its successful tram network, upbeat Chinatown and buzzy nightlife, does have the air, on a good day, of a confident European city. Each weekend, some 140,000 visitors come to indulge in the city's boozy nightlife. Huge sums have been spent on rebuilding the centre, smartening up the Canal Street quarter, building a major new sports complex on the edge of the city, lining the canal with yuppie apartment blocks, stretching the investment down to Salford Quays, the bombast of the Lowry Centre and the explosion of ideas that give form to Daniel Libeskind's Imperial War Museum North.

Similarly, the much-vaunted 'cultural revolution', while drawing on very deep and long-established roots, has been mobilised effectively in recent years as an urban asset, as what began as a series of counter-cultural movements has been appropriated as a cultural 'industry' (see Haslam 1999).

But while comparative dimensions of Manchester's recent transformation – partial, contradictory and incomplete as it has been – form one of the subtexts of this book, much more explicit and direct is its unapologetic concern with the city itself. Focused squarely on the city's political economy, the book seeks to provide a multi-faceted review and critique of Manchester's tales of transformation, identifying key moments and turning points, and attempting to separate the structural shifts from the ephemeral movements. Maybe it has always been this way, but the velocity of urban restructuring in Manchester does seem to have been accelerating in recent decades. This city, which has never had much patience for nostalgia or tradition, seems again to have trampled over its past on the way to a new future. It is still too early to say what this future will hold – as conflicting images of urban progress and dystopia continue to define Manchester – but characteristically there are few who are looking back. The occasional backward glance can, however, be revealing.

Manchester had more manufacturing company headquarters than any other British city at the turn of the twentieth century, but at the turn of the twenty-first has hardly any. Places like 56 Oxford Street reflect the changes. Once the home of Tootals textile company, a fixture on the city's industrial landscape since 1799, the building has since become the base of operations for a host of initiatives aimed at 'regenerating' the city – the Central Manchester Development Corporation (now defunct), the Manchester 2000 Olympic bid committee (since failed), the Training and Enterprise Council (now replaced), the Chamber of Commerce (seeking a new role), Marketing Manchester (still going, just), and so forth. Number 56 has again become a decision-making centre of sorts, many of them made in the name of the business community and many of them supplanting functions once dispensed from the Town Hall, just the other side of Albert Square. But the proximity is also revealing. The City Council continues in many ways to be a key player in the schemes and dreams to regenerate the city, but in contrast to the old model of committee-based decision-making, municipal control and public-sector delivery, today the talk is all about 'working in partnership'. More often than not, the 'partners' include key figures from the business community – the self-styled 'Manchester Mafia' – and senior people from the plethora of regeneration agencies which now share the job of trying to turn the place around. Typically, these are the people who claim the credit for having 'got Manchester working again'.

Although there is no shortage of self-congratulation about in such circles, some of it justified, there should be no doubt that the underlying task of regenerating and sustaining a city like Manchester is getting harder, not easier. While the centre of the city has been comprehensively reconstructed, both physically and culturally, in ways that would have been hardly imaginable 15 or 20 years ago, many of the city's underlying social and economic problems have been displaced rather than solved. This is not to dismiss Manchester's city-centre regeneration as some wafer-thin veneer, below the surface of which lies nothing but social division and economic decline. But rather it is to make the more subtle point that for all the manifest progress which has been made in turning around the city centre, and for all the ringing endorsements that one hears (including, and this *is* a change, outside the city) of Manchester's new spirit of partnership and purpose, the effect of all this activity on the socio-economic 'fundamentals' has been extremely modest, if it is visible at all. The consequences of Manchester's much-vaunted 1990s 'transformation' are easy enough to see – indeed difficult to miss – in the city's political institutions and its material form. Indeed, it has often been said that an appropriate index of Manchester's revival is the number of cranes that dot its skyline.

Too often though, such 'concrete' measures are mistaken for reliable indicators of economic and social progress, when they are in fact

Plate 1   Urbis, Manchester's museum of the modern city takes shape

nothing of the sort. Stare as hard as you like at indicators of poverty, social exclusion and dislocation, political alienation, 'real' unemployment and wages and the striking thing is that the lines during the 1990s hardly bent at all, and most continued to track steadily in the wrong direction.

For all of the hard work and genuine commitment which has been going into the regeneration of Manchester, most on the front line will tell you that the battle is far from won. Manchester has learned how to be very good – some would say one of the best – at the political theatre of regeneration, with its set-pieces and carefully staged cast, but the very effectiveness of the city's agencies and networks in these terms shows just how difficult it is to grind out results in the infinitely less glamorous world of implementation. If there is a feeling in Manchester that the city is 'winning' the regeneration game, more often than not this is framed in terms of winning funds rather than actually turning around entrenched social problems, let alone long-standing economic problems. While Manchester quickly adjusted to the post-1997 discourse of 'tackling social exclusion' – and, more than this, could be considered in many ways to have engineered a 'proto-Blairite' policy stance by the early 1990s (Hetherington 1999) – it must also be recognised that silences on economic policy continue to hurt this city.

It is easy to get carried away with the creativity and energy that Manchester shows in responding positively (and often aggressively) to its 'external' policy environment. But much of this activity is reactive and limited in scope. Manchester may have been successful in its bids for the Commonwealth Games and for countless urban-regeneration and place-promotion competitions – efforts which have earned it the reputation of a reflexive, entrepreneurial, 'can-do' city – but in some respects this represents a drop in the bucket relative to the scope and depth of the policy challenges facing the city. Yet the rules of these competitions are established in London and Brussels and elsewhere, not in Manchester. Materially much more important in a city like Manchester would be measures to protect low-paid workers, a comprehensive childcare strategy, a phase shift in spending in areas like environmental clean-up and public transport, an industrial policy, and so forth, but in the UK at least, these issues remain beyond the reach of 'urban policy'.

So accounts of Manchester having 'turned the corner' from unmitigated deindustrialisation and decline to a new era of post-industrial/ cosmopolitan revival must, at the very least, be qualified. Most would accept this, even – in their more candid moments – those members of the political, economic and cultural elite who have most invested in (and most to gain from) such stories of transformation. There is no such consensus, however, about where the strategy might be leading in the longer term. On the one hand, the most ardent advocates of the current entrepreneurial approach will invoke an urban version of 'trickle-down' theory to justify the glitzy make-over of the city centre: poor residents of the peripheral council estates will not feel the effects immediately, but they will reap the longer-term rewards of a restructured economy and a concretely pro-business climate. And anyway, this has been the only game in town since the 1980s, so as a city we might as well make the most of it. On the other hand, critics will often voice the concern that the long-run consequences of these policies are likely to take the form of an increasingly 'Americanised' city: economic and social polarisation will have become perversely underwritten by a set of policies which

Plate 2 Manchester's stadium for the 2002 Commonwealth Games and beyond

effectively legitimate the transfer of funds from social safety-net programmes into the subsidisation of speculative accumulation, zero-sum competition and middle-class consumption. While the new Manchester script has it that the new schemes and initiatives are bringing 'new money' into the city, the fact is that success in one area usually means losing funds elsewhere, so the cumulative outcome is a form of regressive social redistribution.

What seems certain is that twenty-first-century Manchester will be *both* more cosmopolitan and heterogeneous *and* more unequal and divided than before. Even apologists for the current policy of entrepreneurial development will usually accept this, albeit in their view as a price worth paying for the city's ongoing restructuring and (post)modernisation. The contributors to this book adopt a range of positions on this fundamental question of the long-run implications of Manchester's recent 'transition'. What all agree on is that something happened during the 1990s that seems to have nudged the city towards a qualitatively different development trajectory. Whether it will all end in tears, or with a bustling café-bar on every street corner, nobody really knows for sure, but it has become abundantly clear that Manchester's future will look, and feel, very different from its past.

Tales of transformation

The question of urban transformation, however, raises a paradox. Manchester has always been a restless city, one with scant regard for sentimental attachments or customary niceties. It has always been a revolutionary city in the sense that waves of social, economic and political change, while not always made in Manchester, nearly always yield particularly vivid expressions and/or responses here. Episodes of path-altering, revolutionary change punctuate the history of Manchester, and more often than not these have a real, extra-local significance. One thinks of Engels' accounts of the world's first urban-industrial prole-tariat, the radical importation of American capital and mass production methods into Trafford Park at the beginning of the twentieth century, and the waves of cultural and artistic innovation over the past twenty-five years. To be sure, lapses into arrogance and hyperbole have played a part here, but the city has had an uncanny ability to live up (or down) to the rhetoric. What for historian Asa Briggs (1963) was the 'shock city' of the mid-nineteenth century has largely retained the capacity to surprise, appal and occasionally inspire. For one reason or another, the city has nearly always figured in public discourse around issues of political, social and economic change, having spawned its own school of free-trading economics in the nineteenth century and having sought to stay at the forefront of public-sector reform movements in the twentieth century – whether building council houses and civic facilities or tearing them down. Despite their manifestly different roots, such phenomena speak to Manchester's long-established role as a city of innovations – discursive, institutional and material. As Redford (1934: v–vi) pointed out some time ago, 'the traditional cocksureness of the Lancashire men, and the boast that they said to-day what England would say to-morrow, were often justified; on many questions of public policy the Manchester merchants gave a lead which the country followed, for good or ill'.

The industrial buccaneers of the nineteenth century have since been replaced by a rather more circumspect and heterogeneous urban elite – of local politicians and public-sector entrepreneurs, of business leaders with interests in redeveloping the city as a site for advanced services, leisure and consumption, and of the unruly captains of the cultural industries. Meanwhile, the people of Manchester are negotiating their own paths – out in the sprawling suburbs with their own 'edge city' business parks and retail developments, or in the juxtaposed pockets of brash gentrification and entrenched poverty in the central city. They all have their places in the Manchester script, either as its celebrated 'successes' or as part of the residual 'policy problem'. Indeed, a tell-tale feature of Manchester's 'transition mindset' in recent years has been the subtle and not-so-subtle tendency to bracket out different aspects of the city's policy-economy in terms of a simplified binary history: factories, hard manual labour and the dour-and-grimy image are associated irredeemably with 'old Manchester', while the 'new Manchester' is about consumption, services and an optimistic outlook. In fact, these phenomena are not sequentially ordered; they exist side by side in a continuously-changing Manchester that is altogether more complex and contradictory.

In some respects, this was always the case. When Alexis de Tocqueville visited Manchester in the 1840s, he was moved to liken the city to a 'filthy sewer' from which nevertheless flowed 'pure gold'. This was a place where the respect for wealth was 'enough to make one despair', while the 'evident lack of government' suggested an apparently institutionalised indifference to industrial squalor and social polarisa-tion: 'Here humanity attains its most complete development and its most brutish; here civilisation works its miracles and civilised man is turned back into a savage' (Tocqueville 1958: 107–8). Likewise, for contempor-ary visitors to the city, many of the most striking images are of polarisa-tion and division, exuberance and (again) indifference. For example, when Eric Schlosser, editor of the respected American serial the *Atlantic Monthly*, visited Manchester 150 years later – then in search of the spirit of the Haçienda, rather than the essence of urban-industrial capitalism – he encountered a disturbing mix of hedonism and alienation:

> The city today has a surreal, highly charged atmosphere. Its plight says a great deal about what has happened lately in the 'other' England – the great northern industrial cities that rarely appear in British tourist brochures. Amid long-term unemployment and some of the worst urban poverty in Western Europe, the 'dark Satanic' mills of Manchester deplored by Victorian social reformers are being turned into tapas bars and discos … Despite a century of decline and eleven years of Margaret Thatcher, despite the lousy weather and even lousier prospects, despite the grim housing estates, the boarded-up buildings, the shallow obsessions of club culture, the drugs, the gangs, and the garbage in the streets, Manchester still feels alive. That is an accomplishment, however long it lasts. The place survives

through small acts of defiance. In and around the ruins of an empire, kids are dancing. (1998: 22, 34)

Echoing its dubious distinction as the 'shock city' of the industrial revolution, Manchester continues to attract the perverse gaze of the urban voyeur. Then, as now, the symbols of socio-economic polarisation are there for all to see; many of them inscribed into the urban landscape. But while some themes recur, the times – and the place – have certainly changed.

In Manchester, history has its echoes, but it is not repeated. As Rosemary Mellor argues in her chapter, the processes that simultaneously generated industrial might and urban squalor in the early nineteenth century would subsequently necessitate major rounds of social reform and municipal reorganisation. Through a century or more of slow, but generally progressive, reform, housing and working standards were improved immeasurably, absolute destitution was all but abolished, and real standards of living rose. In the process, Manchester went from a factory city to a public-sector city, as central government in London – so long the enemy – gradually assumed new and far-reaching roles in economic planning and regulation, in social welfare and municipal governance. By the late 1980s, in fact, public administration and services was already the biggest single 'sector' in the Greater Manchester labour market, employing more than manufacturing, banking and finance or retail distribution. The fact that the public economy is now also shrinking in real terms – Manchester City Council, for example, has shed over a third of its workforce since the late 1980s – raises the prospect that a wave of 'demunicipalisation' will compound earlier job losses due to deindustrialisation.

The decline of public-sector employment in Manchester is but another manifestation of the wider pattern of state restructuring and retreat in the city. As Mellor points out, many of the central-city zones targeted for redevelopment in recent years – like the Hulme crescents and Piccadilly bus station – are more than just symbols of a shabby Manchester that had to be erased, they were also very concrete reminders of forms of municipal interventionism that have now been abandoned. The new Manchester is now engaged in airbrushing its own history. The ongoing roll-back of the welfare state, which Herd and Patterson describe in their contribution to this volume, has not only redefined the rights and entitlements of the city's poor, it has also involved the systematic erasure of public-sector and welfarist symbols from the urban landscape. In its stead, public policy is now focused on the creation and sustenance of what Rosemary Mellor calls a 'cosmopolitan circuit of work and play', a means of accessing the discretionary spending of the middle classes in the hope that some of the benefits will trickle down to local residents in the form of burger-flipping and cocktail-shaking jobs. Whether the economics of this dualised service economy will work in cities like Manchester must remain to be seen. The aggregate trends in terms of jobs and wages, it must however be said, are far from encouraging (see Peck and Emmerich 1992; Giordano and Twomey, this volume). The economy of low-waged private services, which is held out as the successor to the old industrial core, is not compensating in either quantitative or qualitative terms for the collapse of the factory economy. Many of the jobs in manufacturing were dirty, but they were better paid and usually more stable than their modern-day equivalents in the service sector. And certainly as far as Mellor is concerned, the space-economies of the residualised poor on the one hand and the new cosmopolitan elite on the other show little sign of becoming integrated. The poor are being edged out of the public spaces on which they had come to depend – to catch a bus, claim social entitlements, sup a pint, or just watch the world go by – while in labour-market terms many young men in particular are falling into the widening chasm between welfare and work; excluded from both, too many are fashioning an existence in the cash-and-crime economy. This is not just the stuff of *Manchester Evening News* headlines, but speaks to the underside of the city's much-celebrated 'transition'.

Hence the wider significance of the entrepreneurial turn in Manchester politics since the 1980s. Manchester City Council's abandonment of municipal socialism in favour of a pragmatic strand of interventionist neo-liberalism – which can be summed up as talking up, making over and trickling down – was as much a consequence as a cause of the social and economic shifts that were already under way in the city. The deindustrialisation and impoverishment of Manchester were not caused by its local authorities, but by the same token, effective strategies for dealing with the current situation seem to be beyond the reach even of the most entrepreneurial of local agencies. As Steve Quilley explains in his chapter, the City Council's embrace of municipal entrepreneurialism during the 1980s must be seen in part as a tactical response to the loss of local-government power and the centralising neo-lialism of the Conservatives nationally. Having once talked about working with comrades in the socialist cities of Liverpool, London and Sheffield, from the late 1980s Manchester City Council went to work on reinventing itself politically, as a friend of central government and local business.

Plate 3   The Hulme Crescents demolished as part of the area's City
Challenge initiative

Eschewing the strategy of fighting the Tories in central government to
the last municipal breath, Manchester City Council opted instead to take
an 'entrepreneurial turn', and to make sure it did so *better* than anyone
else. This meant learning to work, both pragmatically and imagina-
tively, with local business and central government. This was not simply
about 'selling out', more fundamentally it was about establishing a new
modus operandi for local politics. 'Shorthand' forms of communication
between members of the city's newly empowered elite would begin to
displace the formal decision-making structures of council committees;
cappuccinos and designer cakes at meetings in café-bars replaced lukewarm tea and biscuits at the Town Hall. The City Council remained a
central player in this process, but the nature of its power and influence
had changed, perhaps permanently, and with consequences that were
not easy to predict.

The city's Olympic bids were key moments in this process of 'governance restructuring'. As Cochrane and colleagues (this volume) argue,
the 2000 Olympic bid galvanised an emergent network of public and
private sector elites. For a short period they had a common goal: to
achieve regeneration *through* the bidding process. More than just a bid
for a two-week sporting event, the *process* of networking for the Olympic
Games united cultural, economic and political elites behind the single,
overarching objective of securing Manchester's future. This period of
rapid-fire partnership-formation and strategic repositioning set the

context for how Manchester has subsequently approached the challenges of social regeneration and economic development. These distinctively 'Mancunian ways' (Robson, this volume) were honed and developed in the regeneration of Hulme and Moss Side and in the Olympic bids. The focus was placed on *opportunities* for growth, investment and development, rather than licking the wounds of employment decline and public-sector budget cuts. Sidestepping such thorny but in many ways fundamental issues, the new elite partnerships formulated a city centre-centric programme for redevelopment. Underlying this policy prescription was the belief that what was good for the central business district was good for the whole conurbation, what was good for Canal Street was good for Hyde Road. Although the benefits might take a little longer to reach some parts of the city, they would – it was fervently hoped – get there eventually (Herd and Patterson, this volume).

Even in the face of widespread socio-economic adversity this 'Manchester model' of regeneration showed no signs of collapse, and on the contrary registered some successes in the form of new (mostly public) investment and streamlined decision-making (Robson, this volume). There are few more vivid illustrations of the capacity of the city's new governance structures than the rapid and comprehensive response to the IRA bomb of June 1996. Couched again in terms of the language of 'opportunity' (Holden, this volume), the bomb (re)galvanised partnerships and networks that may have otherwise begun to show signs of post-Olympic fatigue or even sclerosis. The vigorous response to the bomb invoked a strong sense of Mancunian pride: *our* city would not be beaten. While many reacted with dismay at the damage done to the 'heart of the city', local politicians quickly went to work with property owners and business leaders to fashion a programme of rebuilding (in every sense of the term). The 'Manchester Mafia' stepped into the breach. Hardly had the alarms stopped ringing before plans were being hatched to redevelop large swathes of the city centre. Institutional innovation went hand-in-hand with physical redevelopment. Manchester Millennium Ltd Taskforce was established to manage the work. The unpopular Arndale Centre was retained, but given a facelift; the space previously occupied by the under-used Shambles Square was given over to the recently completed Marks & Spencers (Williams, this volume). Connecting with other 'prestige projects', such as the Bridgewater Hall, these initiatives marked a new phase in the redevelopment of the city centre, envisioned in twenty-first-century terms. This culminated in the opening of the Triangle development in the summer of 2000. While the city may now *look* better, this institutional and physical transformation has not come without costs. So the business of regeneration continues.

At the regional level Manchester's aspirations to become 'capital of the north' have not gone uncontested. Many in neighbouring Liverpool remain sceptical about, even dismissive of, Manchester's would-be renaissance. Briefly united in their shared antipathy to Thatcherism in the mid-1980s, the two cities seem almost as divided as ever. Indeed, when Manchester was soundly defeated in its attempt to stage the 2000 Olympics, the cheers that went up in Sydney certainly had their echoes on Merseyside. And these entrenched intra-regional rivalries are also being played out in institutional terms. As Martin Jones and Gordon MacLeod point out in their chapter, the formation of the North West Regional Development Agency in 1998, while marking a significant moment in regional institution building, certainly has not laid these local tensions to rest. In many ways, the continuing fragility of regional institutions in the region stands in stark contrast to the united fronts that have been constructed at the city level. In this context, Manchester occupies an ambiguous position. While the city has resisted the centrally-imposed restructuring of local government boundaries, it has also actively pursued its own forms of local imperialism (Deas and Ward, this volume). Buoyed by its successes and frustrated by the apparently limited aspirations of neighbouring boroughs, the city of Manchester has sought – unsuccessfully so far – to expand its boundaries. An enlarged electoral and funding base would, so the argument goes, give Manchester City Council the institutional and financial clout to match its manifest political clout. It might even allow the city to jostle for position with other 'global cities', albeit a couple of divisions below the premier league (see Dicken, this volume). In this company, however, Manchester still has a *lot* to prove, for the boosterist rhetoric and brash self-confidence count for much less on the international stage. But one thing is for sure, as the city seeks a more secure place for itself in a highly competitive global economy, distinctively *local* tensions will intensify. As the task of 'reglobalising' the city begins in earnest, governing Manchester is going to get harder not easier.

As Peter Dicken explains in his chapter, the place of Manchester in the global economy has come full circle. From being a founding *globaliser* during the nineteenth century it has during the twentieth century found itself on the receiving end of new and ostensibly more intense forms of global economic restructuring. Having established many of the basic principles for global trade, the city has since been well and truly *globalised*. Once a global player, the city is in many ways now just another potential investment site in the global economic system. As

Dicken argues, this is a kind of 'a new world economic order ... in which transnational corporations [are located] at the power centre'. No longer an imperial capital of manufacturing, the city's future economic well-being has come to rest with the service sector. Yet as Benito Giordano and Laura Twomey argue in their chapter, while the service sectors are growing robustly, they are providing neither the same quantity nor the same quality of jobs as those lost under deindustrialisation. Part-time, precarious work is no replacement for the relatively secure forms of employment that were associated with the factory economy. The period since the early 1970s, when the oil crises struck and deindustrialisation began in earnest, has been one of dramatic restructuring in Manchester's labour market. During the period 1971–97, more than one in four jobs were lost in the City of Manchester, establishing a trend of almost uninterrupted decline in aggregate employment. In the same 26-year period, the Greater Manchester conurbation as a whole lost just under one in eight jobs. Hence, job losses in the City of Manchester accounted for two-thirds of the jobs lost across the whole of the Greater Manchester conurbation. Employment change is consequently creating the kind of 'doughnut' pattern witnessed in many American cities, adding another layer of complexity and contradiction to the central-city's claim to 'represent' Greater Manchester – economically, socially and politically.

Compared to other British cities, only Liverpool has fared worse in terms of overall labour-market performance (Turok and Edge 1999), underlining the paradoxical relationship that exists in Manchester between the political narratives of success and the economic realities of decline. These paradoxes are especially exposed in the area of welfare-to-work policy, where the city's can-do attitude to programme delivery sits uneasily with the ongoing weaknesses of local labour markets. The New Deal 'client group', disproportionately composed as it is of multiply-disadvantaged, working-class young men, symbolises the long-run consequences of manufacturing decline in the city: having first been economically disenfranchised, this group is now being forcibly rotated through substandard jobs by a government determined to secure their economic 'independence' (Herd and Patterson, this volume). If Manchester's 'entrepreneurial turn' has a dark side, it is the scant regard that is often paid to the *economic* plight of the poor. This is a city in which 94 per cent of all Job Centre vacancies and 89 per cent of all full-time jobs are paying less than the benefit level for a couple with two children. This is not simply a problem of *social* exclusion; more fundamentally, it is a problem of economic dislocation. And while initiative after initiative tends to its social consequences, the underlying economic causes of poverty and under-employment have been danger-ously overlooked.

True, much of this may be beyond the reach of local policy, but at the same time, a local policy process that focuses so insistently on short-term deliverables and positive messages is doing little to draw attention to these untended problems. Instead, the prevailing – and ultimately complacent – view seems to be that the Manchester strategy, a decade or more in the making, has worked. As a recent assessment of the city's progress concluded, 'the hype is working' (Wainwright 1999: 17). In this, a city that has long prided itself on its gritty realism, it is no time to start believing the hype.

2

Global Manchester:
from globaliser to globalised

PETER DICKEN

O UTSIDE the inner circle of the 'Manchester booster industry' – those concerned with projecting the image of contemporary Manchester as a city of world (or, at least, European) status – few today would include Manchester among the world's global cities. A century or more ago, of course, the situation was very different. In 1835, 'Manchester was without challenge the first and greatest industrial city in the world' (Hall 1998: 310). By the early nineteenth century, not only was Manchester 'a centre of trade of a whole region, linked with a whole world' (Briggs 1963: 105) but, more significantly, it was the innovative focus of several of the most important developments of the newly industrialising world economy. In terms of industrial organisation, for example, Manchester was not only the archetype of the system of factory capitalism itself but also, as the synergistic financial and merchandising centre of the cotton textile industry, the organisational nexus of a highly integrated, regional division of labour whose highly specialised structure was the basis of the city's (and the country's) world industrial leadership. Around and within the city-region's cotton textile complex developed the highly significant related industries of machinery manufacture and engineering and of chemicals.

International markets were vital for the growth of these new industries and it is hardly coincidental that the political drive for free trade, expressed specifically through the movement to repeal the Corn Laws, was also a Manchester-based movement, led by Richard Cobden and John Bright. As Chaloner (1962: 137) explains:

Although the doctrines of Free Trade did not originate in Manchester ... the successful campaign against the Corn Laws of 1828 and 1842 was conducted by an organisation, the Anti-Corn Law League, which had its headquarters in Manchester ... the Corn Laws became symbolic of the whole obsolete tariff structure, and the vital part played by Manchester men and Manchester ideas in the struggle against tariffs on imported foods and foreign manufactured goods received ... recognition ... in 1846, when Disraeli put the phrase 'the Manchester School' into general circulation.

In a very real sense, therefore, Manchester helped actively to shape and to mould the newly emerging global economy of the nineteenth and early twentieth centuries. Such a formative role was reflected in the city's global position, in its key headquarters functions, and in the scale and quality of its scientific and artistic life. At the turn of the century, 'the ten largest cities in the world were, in order of magnitude: London, New York, Paris, Berlin, Chicago, Philadelphia, Tokyo, Vienna, St. Petersburg, and *Manchester*' (King 1990: 369, emphasis added). In 1907, five of the twenty largest manufacturing companies in Britain were headquartered in Manchester (Davenport-Hines 1990). Such economic dominance was reflected in an extraordinarily vibrant cultural life, much of it underpinned by migrant entrepreneurs, scientists and professionals from continental Europe (many of them Jewish). The Hallé Orchestra, founded by one such migrant in 1858, Charles Hallé, remains today as the oldest professional symphony orchestra in Britain. It was no coincidence that it was able to attract the most famous conductor in the world, Hans Richter, to be its Principal Conductor in the 1890s (Kennedy 1960). Of course, the most tangible material legacy of this era of world status remains in the scale and variety of the city's monumental Victorian architecture (Beesley and De Figueiredo 1988; Canniffe and Jefferies 1997; Dyos and Wolff 1973; Parkinson-Bailey 1996).

Today, Manchester is no longer a global city in the sense defined by the current generation of global city scholars such as Friedmann (1986, 1995), Knox and Taylor (1995), or Sassen (1991, 1994). By this criterion, indeed, London is the only UK city to rank as a global city. Manchester's position in the global economy is very different from that of a hundred years ago, just as the global economy itself is very different. From driving global economic growth, then, Manchester is now something of a second-class passenger, being led rather than leading, having less influence on its own direction. This, of course, is a fate shared with other comparable cities in today's more complex and more deeply integrated global economy (Dicken 1998). Indeed, a widely shared view in much of the global literature is that the forces of globalisation have not only emasculated the vitality of local economies but also that they have rendered the national state virtually powerless (Ohmae 1995).

According to this argument, the 'global' has triumphed over the 'local' (and the 'national'). In fact, this is a very misleading depiction of reality (see for example Brenner 1998; Dicken 1998; Dicken, Peck and Tickell 1997; Kelly 1999).

Without doubt, globalising processes are immensely powerful. But they operate in a highly uneven manner both spatially and temporally. First, they are not simply uni-directional, from the global to the local; rather, the 'local and the global intermesh, running into one another in all manner of ways' (Thrift 1990: 181) Second, because economic processes are *multi-scalar* in their operation, it is a mistake to focus only on the two extremes of the spatial scale – the global and the local – at which economic activities occur. It is more productive to think of *interrelated scales* of activity (for example the local, the national, the supra-national, and the global). As Neil Brenner (1998: 7–8) observes more generally:

> states do not simply disintegrate in the face of globalization and … cities remain tied to their host state's territory in significant ways … [T]he geography of contemporary capitalism can be viewed as a polymorphic, multi-layered 'jigsaw puzzle' in which multiple forms of territorial organ-ization – including cities, inter-urban networks and territorial states – are being superimposed and intertwined ever more densely.

In one sense, then, 'as a place of production, consumption, admin-istration or culture, the city is embedded in a global economy … All cities today are world cities' (King 1983: 7, 15). In that respect, Manchester remains a world city in so far as it is tightly integrated within the world economy. Neither its past, its present nor its future can be understood fully outside that broader structural context: 'the form and extent of a city's integration with the world economy, and the functions assigned to the city in the new spatial division of labour, will be decisive for any structural changes occurring within it' (Friedmann 1986: 70). However, this is not to argue that global economic forces *per se* are totally deterministic in shaping Manchester's economy. At the same time, Manchester is deeply embedded in its specific *national* (United Kingdom) and *supra-national* (European Union) contexts. It is also, of course, enmeshed in its immediate *metropolitan* and *regional* context (North West England), a highly contested and politically sensi-tive issue from Manchester's perspective, an issue which has recently been given a sharpened edge with the creation of the Regional Develop-ment Agencies in 1999 (Deas and Ward 2000).

Figure 2.1 captures the essence of this exceedingly complex situation

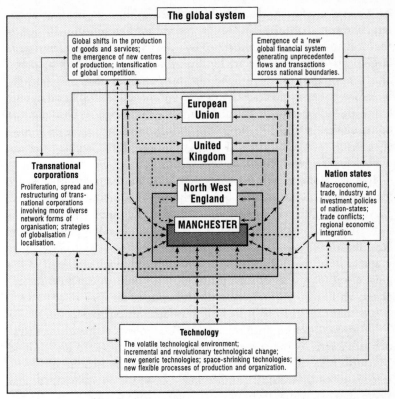

Figure 2.1   Manchester's embeddedness in a multi-scalar political-economic system

and is used to organise the remainder of this chapter. I focus on three components of major significance for the Manchester economy: the shifting nature of global competition, the international political environment, and the competitive behaviour of corporate enterprises. Figure 2.1 positions Manchester at the centre of a multi-scalar, highly interconnected, system. As the arrows suggest, not only is each of the major elements connected with each of the others but also with each of the scales within which Manchester (like all UK cities) acts to *refract*, in highly complex ways, the processes operating at each of the other scales. Organisationally the Manchester economy consists of a *mélange* of firms of various sizes and types (Dicken and Lloyd 1978). The majority, in numerical terms, are very small, single-plant firms engaged in a bewildering variety of manufacturing and service sectors and connected within and outside the local economy through ties with suppliers and customers. However, decades of increasing business concentration, largely through acquisition, merger and inward investment, have led to the local economy being dominated by a relatively small number of very large firms. Some of these are locally-owned companies with branches and subsidiaries spread around the metropolitan area and outside, including overseas (firms such as Paterson Zochonis, CIS, Boddingtons – or even Manchester United plc). Others are firms whose headquarters are elsewhere in the UK, predominantly in the South East, or abroad (like AstraZeneca, Siemens, Kelloggs, Procter and Gamble, and the major financial services companies).

In fact, Manchester's economy has been substantially affected by foreign direct investment throughout the twentieth century (Dicken and Lloyd 1976). This was especially evident in the development of Trafford Park in which foreign – particularly United States firms – played a very significant role. In a polemical study published in 1902, McKenzie wrote graphically of the 'American invaders' and paid much attention to the giant electrical machinery company, Westinghouse, which built a state-of-the-art factory in Trafford Park. It is often forgotten that the very first automobile plant built by Ford outside North America was also in Trafford Park before Ford relocated to Dagenham. A huge concentration of American and some European firms developed in and around Trafford Park in food processing, chemicals, household products, mechanical and electrical engineering. Chemical, pharmaceutical and electronics companies from Europe, notably Ciba Geigy, Bayer, BASF, Philips, Siemens and others established plants at various locations within Greater Manchester. More recently, Japanese firms such as Sharp and Brother have become major players in the local economy.

The contemporary local economy consists, then, of a variable mixture of domestic firms and transnational corporations, both foreign and British-owned or controlled. Whether directly or indirectly, the firms and institutions which make up the Manchester economy are subjected to the shifting forces of global competition. These, in turn, are driven primarily by the interlocking processes of:

- the competitive behaviour of business enterprises (especially transnational corporations) and their restructuring strategies at various geographical scales;
- the actions of national governments (including the UK government) attempting to compete with other national economies through their regulation of economic transactions, together with the activities of supra-national institutions;

- the volatile processes of technological change which are shrinking time and space and transforming products and processes.

See Dicken (1998) for a comprehensive treatment of each of these elements.

Shifting global competition

Differential trade performance between nations and regions is the clearest indicator of shifting global competition. Unfortunately, there are no data to indicate the trade performance of cities and regions in the United Kingdom. However, national trade figures provide a clear measure of the massive changes which have occurred in the position of the UK (and therefore of Manchester) in the global economy. The international division of labour which existed when Manchester was a city of world rank was relatively simple. Britain, in particular, exported manufactured goods to the rest of the world whose major function in the international division of labour was both to act as a market for such products and also to supply raw materials and agricultural produce to the industrialised core. For Manchester, as for all other major British cities, the state of the country as the leading world colonial power was extremely important for the precise way in which this international division of labour was articulated. Hence, as King (1990: 36) observes,

> The extent of the specialised industrial-commercial role of Britain in the world economy, and especially as head of its imperial urban hierarchy is measured not only by the size of London, but by the fact that five of the world's nineteen largest cities in 1900 were in the United Kingdom, each of them connected, not simply to the 'world economy' in general, but specifically to a colonial mode of production. ... The size of Manchester, for example, must be seen in relation to the structural transformation of the Egyptian economy as it was integrated into the world capitalist system producing cotton as a consumption commodity.

Elsewhere, King makes a similar point regarding the nature of colonial economic integration: 'the question is whether the real development of London or Manchester can be understood without reference to India, Africa and Latin America ...' (King 1983: 12). Put simply: their history is, to a degree, also Manchester's history. One tangible legacy of that particular mode of economic organisation, as King observes, was the subsequent large-scale in-migration of people from the former colonies, particularly from South Asia, Africa and the Caribbean, seeking jobs in cities with which they were already connected in a vicarious sense. Such connections demonstrate that the geography of nineteenth- and early twentieth-century global networks in which Manchester was embedded was very different from that of today.

In contrast, the international division of labour of today is far more complex. Particularly dramatic changes have occurred in the past thirty to forty years. National boundaries no longer act as watertight containers of the production process. Few, if any, industries now have much 'natural protection' from international competition whereas in the past, of course, geographical distance exerted a strong insulating influence. The locus of industrial production has shifted to new locations, both between and within nations. The relative positions of the older industrialised countries have shifted as competitive fortunes have waxed and waned. During the 1960s and 1970s, Japan rapidly emerged as the major new competitive force in the global economy. A small number of newly industrialising economies (NIEs) have appeared as global players. The economic growth of the East Asian economies in particular has been spectacular, notwithstanding that region's financial crisis of 1997–98. Overall, the structure of the global economy is now *multi-polar*. Three major regional blocs dominate: North America, the European Union, East Asia. This triad, to use Ohmae's (1995) term, sits astride the global economy like a three-legged colossus. These three regions dominate global production and trade. They account for more than four-fifths of both world exports and manufacturing production (Dicken 1998).

The nature of global competition has not only shifted geographically but also it has intensified markedly. International trade flows are no longer based on relatively simplistic geographical exchange of manufactured goods and raw materials between a global core and periphery. The international division of labour has been transformed into a highly complex, kaleidoscopic structure involving the fragmentation of many production processes and their geographical relocation on a global scale in a process that slices through national boundaries. The sectoral composition of international trade has itself become far more intricate. For the industrialised countries, at least, most trade is now intra-industry trade based upon a high degree of specialisation and product differentiation.

The position of the UK and its role within this volatile and intensely competitive global economic environment has obviously changed substantially. In 1870, the country produced almost one-third of total world industrial output; by the mid-1990s its share (of a vastly larger total, of course) was 4.1 per cent. From being the leading world industrial nation it now ranks fifth as a manufacturing producer and sixth as an exporter. There has also been a particularly marked shift in the geography of UK trade. The dominant component of the United Kingdom's trade network today is Western Europe. In the mid-1990s, 60 per cent of the UK's merchandise exports and 61 per cent of its merchandise imports were with Western Europe (WTO 1995). But this is neither a new development nor simply the result of EU membership. As Rowthorn and Wells (1987: 168) show:

> In 1913, Western Europe was the UK's principal trading partner. However, between then and the late 1940s … UK trade with Western Europe underwent a significant decline. Meanwhile, Britain's trade with the White Dominions and with the countries in her formal and informal Empire in the Third World expanded somewhat. However, after the Second World War, Britain rebuilt and expanded her trading links with Western Europe to the point where, by 1983, Western Europe was even more important as a trading partner for Britain than it had been in 1913.

In comparison, Britain's trade with the United States, Japan and the East Asian NIEs is far less important. Yet a popular view is that one of the causes of Britain's relative decline as a world economic power (and, by extension, of Manchester's reduced economic status) is a flood of cheap imports from the newly industrialising economies (NIEs), as well as of high quality imports from Japan. There is some truth in this but such import penetration is highly selective sectorally. In aggregate terms, for example, in 1985 less than 5 per cent of the UK's total manufactured imports came from the NIEs (OECD 1988). In certain sectors, however, NIE import penetration is extremely high. Initially, the most penetrated sectors were clothing and textiles, footwear and other simple manufactured consumer goods. More recently, penetration has increased in such sectors as electrical machinery, telecommunications and sound recording equipment, office machines and data processing equipment.

These sectoral shifts exemplify the extent to which the East Asian NIEs in particular have become increasingly sophisticated technologically. Some of the affected sectors, notably textiles, clothing, electrical machinery, represent important components of the Manchester economy. Local manufacturers have certainly experienced much intensified competition from NIE producers. But the picture is actually more complex than this. In the textile and clothing industries, for example, the nature of the competition varies by specific market segment. While import penetration from NIEs and from other developing countries has been a major factor in the price-sensitive, mass market segments it has been far less significant in the fashion segments. Here, the major competitive pressures are not so much from developing countries as from countries such as Italy, Germany and France.

The intensification of competition at a global scale and, especially, the relatively weak performance of the UK during the 1970s–early 1990s period have contributed to the country's substantial trade deficit in manufacturing industry, a situation unprecedented until just a few years ago. This has greatly affected major manufacturing centres such as Manchester. Conversely, the generally healthy external trade balance in services and 'invisibles' tends to benefit London and South East England disproportionately because of the heavy concentration of such activities there. However, in so far as Manchester's growing service sector relates to the internationally-traded goods and services sectors its economy certainly benefits.

Geopolitical environment

A most important element in explaining the changing competitive position of Manchester in the global economy is the influence of inter-national political actors, notably nation-states. In an increasingly inte-grated and interdependent global economy, states are locked into intensive economic competition with other states: to enhance their international trading position and to capture as large a share as possible of the gains from trade; to create and attract productive investment which, in turn, enhances their competitive status (for contrasting views on the issue of the 'competitiveness of nations', see Krugman 1994; Porter 1990).

Historically, the most important component of such inter-nation competition has been the operation of various types of discretionary trade policy. Some form of trade protection runs like an unbroken thread through the history of the global economy: from the mercantilist policies of the north-west European states in the seventeenth century, through the bitter trade wars of the 1920s and 1930s to the current resurgence of neo-protectionism and the adoption of strategic trade policies. Manchester, of course, was at the centre of the fierce arguments over free trade in the early–mid nineteenth century. In a later period, the UK's international trading relationships were greatly affected by the existence, on the one hand, of high tariffs in Western Europe and, on the other, by the existence of an Imperial (later Commonwealth) Preference System which created a large protected market for British producers. That system is now long gone. Today, the most important factors in the UK's, and Manchester's, international trading environment are: (1) the nature of the international trade regime in general, institutionalised in the World Trade Organization; (2) integration within the evolving European Union.

Two countervailing trends have characterised the international trade regime since the end of World War Two. One is the sustained fall in tariff barriers, which has occurred through the various negotiating rounds of the General Agreement on Tariffs and Trade (GATT). As a result, the average tariff on the import of manufactured goods into the industrialised countries has fallen from 40 per cent in 1947 to less than 5 per cent. Tariffs on imports to developing countries remain substantially higher but in many cases these, too, have been falling. In one sense, therefore, international trade has become increasingly liberalised during the past four decades. However, as tariff barriers have fallen a whole new battery of non-tariff barriers (NTBs) has emerged. NTBs are extremely diverse, and often very subtle. Currently, there is heated debate over the future of the WTO-regulated international trade regime. Attempts to initiate a new 'round' of international trade negotiations in Seattle in late 1999 broke down in chaos involving both the official delegates themselves and an eclectic alliance of protest groups. The acrimonious nature of current trade negotiations reflects an increasing degree of international trade tension. Overall, therefore, the international trade regime is presently in a volatile and uncertain state.

Clearly, what happens to international trade negotiations, and to the international trade regime in general, is of great significance to the Manchester economy and to the UK as a whole. But the more proximate international trade environment is the European Union. As we have seen, trade with Europe dominates the UK trading position. Despite more than thirty years of development, however, the EU has remained fragmented in many respects. National and sectional interests have often prevailed over Community-wide interests. It was concern with such fragmentation, and the belief that it created a major source of competitiveness for the Community and its member states and firms, which led to the drive to complete the single market by the end of 1992. Although the predicted effects of the single market have been exaggerated in some respects – particularly the idea that the outcome will be a single *uniform* market – its implications for the Manchester economy are potentially very great. Assessing such implications has been made more complex by the current political transformations occurring within Eastern Europe. Although these economies face enormous problems of transition to market-oriented economies they undoubtedly pose a potential economic threat (as well as an opportunity). By the start of the new millennium, no fewer than thirteen countries were involved in serious negotiations to join the EU. At the same time, of course, the European Union is, itself, experiencing considerable change with the establishment of the single European currency in January 1999 (adopted, at the time of writing, by 11 of the 15 EU members, excluding the UK). Although it is, as yet, far too early to assess the full implications of these developments on specific local economies like Manchester, there is a broad consensus that increasing integration within Europe is likely to lead to greater geographical unevenness in economic development; a reinforcement of the core's dominance over the peripheries. As Dunford and Kafkalas (1992) have shown, Manchester lies outside Europe's major growth axis, while Martin, Tyler and Baddeley (1997) argued that the North West region of England was one of the most vulnerable in terms of the ability of its labour market to respond flexibly to the new European currency regime had Britain been a member in the first stages of EMU.

Two factors will be particularly important in determining Manchester's competitive position within such an enlarged European economic space. One is internal to the United Kingdom itself: the extent to which an adequate transport and communications infrastructure is developed quickly to provide rapid and straightforward connection to the centre of the new Europe. This is a political matter which, so far, has been inadequately addressed. Certainly, massive infrastructural investments are needed if the Manchester economy is not to be further peripheralised within Europe. The second factor is that of the response of businesses to the new European situation. This is part of a much broader issue of the competitive behaviour of corporate enterprises and their strategies of international restructuring and is the subject of the next section of this chapter.

Changing corporate strategies

Where does Manchester figure in the corporate strategies of business enterprises? The evidence of the 1970s and early 1980s was that large numbers of manufacturing firms either closed down entirely or voted with their feet and relocated elsewhere. During the 1970s and 1980s in particular large-scale corporate restructuring led to a huge wave of redundancies in the Manchester and North West economies (Lloyd and Shutt 1985). Manchester, of course, was far from unique in these respects. Acquisition and merger often removed control from formerly locally-owned enterprises and transferred it elsewhere, either to the corporate headquarters concentrations of South East England or overseas. Some leading local companies, while remaining in Manchester, effectively transferred their major decision-making functions to the London area to be 'closer to the action'. For example, one of the city's emblematic textile firms, Tootal, relocated its corporate headquarters from Manchester to London in 1991 – and was taken over subsequently by Coats Viyella (Peck and Dicken 1996).

At the same time, Manchester's relative lack of assisted area status (particularly compared with Merseyside) meant that it did not attract the major manufacturing branch plants either of domestic or foreign companies. And yet Manchester did retain a larger headquarters population than Merseyside and it also maintained a more vibrant population of small firms in a wide diversity of industries. Although Manchester, in common with the North West region in general, has recently been less successful than Scotland, Wales or North East England in attracting large numbers of new foreign investments it has, as already noted, a substantial number of long-established international companies, both domestic and foreign and some new foreign investments have certainly occurred, in both manufacturing and services. Again, however, our aim here is to address the broader global context of corporate behaviour. What are the major current trends in the global organisation and reorganisation of international firms?

The practice of establishing production and other related facilities overseas goes back at least one hundred years (Dunning 1983). British firms, in particular, have a lengthy history of international direct investment, a propensity that has intensified over the years. Indeed, compared with United States, German or Japanese firms, British firms on average tend to use international investment as a means of penetrating foreign markets to a greater extent than exports. The growth of foreign direct investment (FDI) in the world economy as a whole has been especially rapid since the mid-1980s (UNCTAD 1998). At the same time, the geographical origins of such FDI have greatly diversified (Dicken 1998). Firms from all the industrialised countries, as well as from the leading NIEs, are increasingly internationalising their operations. The geography of these massive flows of investment is very complex. So, too, are the underlying processes. There has been an oversimplistic tendency to attribute the upsurge in foreign investment to the search by industrial country Transnational corporations (TNCs) for cheap production locations at a global scale, particularly in the developing world. This, it was argued, provided the basis for a new international division of labour (Fröbel, Heinrichs and Kreye 1980). However, since three-quarters of total international direct investment flows to the industrialised, rather than the developing, countries processes other than low labour costs are clearly involved (Dicken 1998). Indeed, the predominant global pattern is one of complex cross-investment between the industrialised countries. The major exception to this is Japan whose inflow of foreign investment is still a minute fraction of its outflows, although there are signs of change in that position as Japan attempts to restructure its economy in the face of the recession of the 1990s.

These shifting geographical patterns, within a rapidly growing volume of international direct investment, reflect complex strategic decision-making processes. These, in turn, reflect the close relationship between the political environment and business decision-making. Although, without doubt, some international direct investment is motivated by production cost considerations, it is often difficult to disentangle these from questions of market access. In economic terms, however, this is rarely now a question of transport costs but, rather, one of being close to markets in order to monitor and understand customer preferences and needs. But there is also a strong political dimension to this question. Discretionary trade policies, which restrict market access via imports, encourage access via direct investment. Historically, this was true of tariff barriers; today it is equally, if not more, true of non-tariff barriers. There is no doubt, for example, that much of the upsurge in Japanese investment in Europe (including the United Kingdom) in the 1970s and 1980s was stimulated by voluntary export restraint agreements in industries such as automobiles and consumer electronics, by the introduction of antidumping legislation and, more generally, by the fear of being excluded from the single European market. Similar apprehensions also generated a renewal of interest in Europe by United States companies, although there is already a huge volume of long-established American companies throughout Europe. Indeed, Europe continues to be the major destination for United States FDI. Within Europe, there is intensive competitive bidding for internationally mobile investment projects using various subsidy and incentive packages. These may well tip the balance between alternative European locations although the effectiveness of such incentive packages remains a matter of some controversy, as does their compliance with EU regulations.

On the one hand, then, the volume and the geography of international investment have changed, a matter of great significance for cities such as Manchester. On the other hand, and equally if not more important, the qualitative nature of that investment, and of international production in general, is also changing. The stereotype view of international production is one of transnational corporations, headquartered in their home countries, establishing regional offices, R & D laboratories, production units and sales offices in a variety of countries, each being organised within a rigid, centralised hierarchy of control. Such organisational forms certainly exist. Within them, the tendency has been for the higher-order functions to be geographically concentrated in specific types of location and for the lower-level production units to be more widely dispersed. It is this kind of structure which led to the emergence of branch-plant economies, both at an international and a sub-national scale. Within the United Kingdom, the branch plant syndrome tended to be particularly characteristic of the peripheral regions although, within the North West, Manchester has been rather less affected in this way than Merseyside.

However, it is now apparent that the organisation of international production is actually far more diverse than this stereotype suggests. Even within such hierarchical corporate structures there is great variation in the degree of autonomy of individual units, a matter of great importance for such critical decisions as the sourcing of inputs from local suppliers. Certainly, there are differences between TNCs from different home countries in the ways in which they organise and co-ordinate their international activities. In general, however, there is growing evidence of the development of 'flatter' intra-corporate hierarchies. The need to respond rapidly to local developments within a global competitive straegy is forcing TNCs to reorganise the internal relationships between the internationally-dispersed parts of their operations. But there is also increasing diversity in other forms of international corporate involvement. Many of the newer forms do not involve ownership and equity relations but are, instead, various forms of collaboration between legally independent firms in different countries. Indeed, we may be witnessing the emergence of the 'virtual' business operating across national boundaries, built around a fast-emerging 'e-commerce'. More certainly, an increasingly important mode of international business organisation has been the international strategic alliance. More and more companies are forming not just alliances with a single company but, rather, networks of alliances with many companies. More and more companies are enmeshed in highly intricate spider's webs of alliances. Such alliances usually relate to a specific function or market; in all other respects, the partners remain fierce competitors.

These diverse modes of international business organisation reflect increasing complexity and flexibility in the world of business. They make the processes of corporate restructuring – and its effects on local economies – both more intricate and more difficult to predict. Certainly the large TNC has the unparalleled capacity to restructure its operations at a global scale, to switch and re-switch its operations between alternative locations. But this may involve a whole spectrum of actual adjustments which will have widely varying local impacts. Between the two extremes of plant closure on the one hand and the opening of new plants at the other is a whole range of restructuring options, for example, the reallocation of specific corporate functions between the firm's locations, the intensification of the production process, the introduction of new technology, the subcontracting out of specific operations, collaboration with other firms, the development of network structures. Nevertheless, manufacturing remains extremely important to the Manchester economy despite dramatic job losses and reductions in firms' market shares. Although employment profiles and the physical appearance of the revitalised city centre suggest an overwhelming dominance of services (many of them locally traded), manufacturing operations – often linked into international networks, either directly or indirectly – retain a significant role in local wealth creation.

The variety of restructuring modes presents both threats and opportunities to the Manchester economy. The threats are the obvious ones of vulnerability within corporate networks which are controlled from elsewhere, although locally-headquartered international companies are by no means immune to such practices. But as more flexible forms of corporate organisation develop they may – though by no means inevitably – offer opportunities to small and medium-sized enterprises in the local economy to participate in less hierarchical and less centralised network structures. Potentially, these provide the opportunity for local firms to lock into geographically more extensive production systems and markets. Such opportunities may be especially important in the context of the single European market. Business enterprises are currently engaged in major restructuring of the geography of their European activities with major implications for cities such as Manchester.

From globaliser to globalised

Manchester's position as a 'global city' is not what it was a century ago. But although it is no longer in the global city super league it is, like all such cities, a global city in the sense that it is tightly integrated into the global economic system. The key questions, therefore, are what kind of role will/can Manchester play in the global system? Can the pioneer city of the first industrial revolution find a place in the next one? Can it carve out an economic niche in a new world economic order of complex and flexible organisational relationships in which transnational corporations remain at the power centre? Does its future lie as a regional financial and business services centre with strong international links? Can a sufficient critical mass of local business leadership develop in a situation in which most of the leading companies in the city are head-quartered elsewhere? There are some positive signs although, as yet, they are small.

Manchester clearly faces enormous problems of adjustment to the rapidly evolving global economy. Its fate lies, in large part, with the fate of the national economy and its position in the global and supra-national system and with how processes generated at different geographical and organisational scales are 'refracted' into the local Manchester economy (see Figure 2.1). But, whatever happens at those levels, Manchester has both to attract new investment and also to stimulate new indigenous ventures in activities which are both high value-adding and which also create desirable jobs. In this regard, the major environmental and infra-structure investments currently under way within the various urban regeneration schemes are extremely important, as is the continued development of Manchester International Airport. However, in its justifiable drive to create a city attractive to investment, the city must be aware of the social implications of such a strategy. In this respect, the experience of the US city of Baltimore is instructive. Baltimore has been hailed as one of the miracles of US urban revival, widely copied else-where. A major part of its strategy was the kind of massive physical regeneration to attract both outside investors and tourist trade, similar to that being pursued in Manchester at present. But, as Levine (1989: 150–1) argues:

> Baltimore was adjusting to new global economic realities, but thousands of its residents were being left behind … Cities cannot ignore the realities of the global marketplace. Standardised, mass-production manufacturing is unlikely ever to provide the urban employment base it did through the 1960s … the current 'competitive advantage' of large urban centers is in information- and communication-based economic activity, and cities can gain quality jobs by accommodating the development of these sectors … But a 'global' strategy must be accompanied by, and, if possible, linked to, a distinctly local redevelopment strategy. Growth in the 'global' sector of an urban economy is unlikely to produce tangible benefits for the urban underclass.

In a highly integrated and intensely competitive global system, Manchester, in common with similar cities (and regions) is faced with an exceptionally difficult balancing act.

3

Mancunian ways:
the politics of regeneration

BRIAN ROBSON

AT the very end of 1999 the government included Manchester as one
of its 42 'beacon authorities'. By that stage, Manchester had already
been the beneficiary of almost all of the discretionary initiatives that
formed part of the Labour government's 'zoning' policies. It had a Health
Action Zone, an Education Action Zone, some eight Single Regeneration Budget programmes, and a Sure Start programme. It was one of the
17 pilot bodies for New Deal for Communities. In so far as these can be
taken as signs of success, Manchester was riding high.

Nor can this be taken merely as reflecting the advent of the new
Labour administration in 1997. Most of the Single Regeneration Budget
Challenge Fund (SRBCF) programmes came on stream during the earlier
Conservative administrations. And many of the high-profile schemes
that had begun to transform the townscape of Manchester were funded
through that same regime. The Bridgewater Concert Hall was the product
of the Urban Development Corporation that was established in 1988
(Deas *et al.* 1999). So too was the extensive refurbishment of warehouses in Castlefield and the new residential build in Piccadilly Village
and elsewhere in the centre. The creation of the G-MEX centre in the
shell of the old Central Station was an even earlier development that
opened in 1986. The transformation of Hulme was the product of City
Challenge that started in 1992. And the large-scale plans for the huge
area of East Manchester were partly triggered by the building of the
cycling velodrome and the 2002 stadium which came through earlier
government and European funds. Planning for the Metro network (whose
first line opened in 1992) was effectively started in 1982, and it was given
formal governmental permission in 1989 when it was awarded a Section
56 grant from the Department of Transport. The role of Manchester as
one of the three City Pride authorities (the others being London and

Birmingham) was yet another signifier of the Conservative government's approval of the City Council's approach in the 1980s and 1990s. All the evidence is that Manchester had 'got its act together' in the regeneration game during the late 1980s and early 1990s and had, in terms of winning competitive resources, benefited substantially as a consequence. The then City Council Leader, Graham Stringer, often spoke of his 'crane index' as a measure of the City Council's well-being. The number of major construction sites throughout the last two decades – reflected in the cranes on the skyline – was indeed some testimony to the City's success in winning discretionary funding. And the funding was used with some imagination to begin the process of converting Manchester into its self-styled role as a post-industrial city.

The benefit of hindsight stamps on all of this an air of inevitability. Yet roll the clock back to the early 1980s and the auguries were very different. In the early years of the long sequence of Conservative administrations – a period in which the eventual shape of regeneration policy was gradually hammered out against the background of massive social and economic change in the landscape of the country – Manchester was seen in the eyes of government as one of the 'lunatic' authorities. It may not have been seen as being as recalcitrant as the trio of Lambeth, Liverpool and Sheffield, but not far short. Some of Manchester's road signs proclaiming its role as the world's first nuclear-free city still stood until recently as testament to the period that followed the 1984 take-over of the Town Hall. It was that period that saw the ousting of the previous leadership by young radical rebels – notably Graham Stringer who became leader and John Nicholson who, for a time, was the articulate and charismatic face of local socialism. The telling slogan that encapsulated their aim was 'Defending Jobs, Improving Services'.

It now seems a far cry from that attempt at creating municipal socialism to the most memorable moment of the 'new' entrepreneurial approach to partnership-building signified by Graham Stringer's standing on the steps of 10 Downing Street alongside the then Prime Minister John Major in 1991. The political tale of Manchester's recent history is the story of this transformation (Quilley, this volume).

There is disagreement amongst commentators about the degree to which the change was either a sudden one, prompted by the failure of Labour to win power in 1987; or a gradual one that evolved over the course of the 1980s and that was crafted against a background in which the 'rhetoric' of the political and the harsh realities of the economic worked asynchronously. The former view makes for a more dramatic road-to-Damascus saga; the latter is probably a more accurate interpretation.

Graham Stringer has often called in aid the 1987 election result and the inevitable inference that it was ineluctable that the City Council's strategy subsequently had to move from political opposition to central government to creating the economic context in which investment could be attracted. Yet, as Quilley (1998) has noted, whatever the rhetoric about local socialism, much of the period in Manchester between 1984 and 1987 saw a good deal of collaborative working between the political leaders of the City Council and the private sector. The senior politicians in the City Council proved highly adept at the Janus-faced task of presenting an impeccable radical left agenda alongside a readiness to work with the private sector in the interests of development within the city. The Economic Development Department, which was initially established to develop an agenda of the left, in practice always played second fiddle to the Policy and Resources Committee which was securely in the hands of the political leadership. Nor can it be said that the City Council ever developed an especially convincing process of local devolution. The fact that the creation of a Community Development arm to the Town Hall rapidly faltered may well have been because of the costs of establishing devolved mini-town-halls across the City Council, but the style of the Town Hall has consistently been one of *de haut en bas*. Community involvement was always tempered by the determination of the centre to retain control. The uneasy relations between the Town Hall and an umbrella body like Manchester Council for Voluntary Services (now Voluntary Action Manchester) suggests that the notion of the politics of a radical alliance was always as much rhetoric as substance.

It is therefore not unrealistic to interpret the 'transition' period of 1984–87 simply as the replacement of one generation of politicians by another; a period in which effective control was established at the centre by a younger cohort of 'new realist' politicians in place of the earlier old Labour generation. It was from this palace revolution that emerged the powerful combination of the Leader, Graham Stringer, and the Deputy Chief Executive, Howard Bernstein, who were to form the central cog in the process of driving the Council forward into its entrepreneurial phase from the later 1980s.

Urban visions

There have been three key elements to the city's approach. First has been the evolution of a 'vision' for the city's future role. From the late 1980s, the leading politicians embraced the arguments about competition between cities. This helped to get them in tune with what central government was demanding as the entry fee for the various competitions for discretionary resources that began from that period. The Council began to elaborate an ever-sharper rationale for its role in a post-industrial era. This was evident in its closer working with Central Manchester Development Corporation (CMDC), where Graham Stringer was a board member and increasingly subscribed to the argument that Manchester needed to compete not merely with other major cities in Britain but with its equivalents in Europe (Kitchen 1997). It was also evident in the Council's economic strategies that were based on identifying niches on which it might best capitalise. Such strategies gradually evolved from a series of analyses of the strengths and weaknesses of the city. The development of the 'vision' was partly helped, too, by the two bids for the 1996 and 2000 Olympic Games (Manchester Olympic Bid Committee 1993; Cochrane *et al.*, this volume), and by the City Pride process which reported in 1994 (City Pride Strategic Planning Group 1994; Williams 1995b). Even though the impact and the importance of City Pride was more in the process through which new partnerships were formed than in the writing of the eventual document, the need to produce a document at end of the day helped concentrate minds. The 'vision' that crystallised had a variety of elements:

- Repopulating the city centre. This was an aim that was not initially part of CMDC's strategy, but which subsequently became a central plank in its plans (Robson *et al.* 1998). It was aimed simultaneously at a number of targets: stemming the population loss and hence the rate base of the city; creating a mix of housing tenures to dilute the high proportion of council-owned property within the city boundaries; bringing in a high-spending population that could support the growth of consumer-based land-uses of the centre.
- Capitalising on the sporting prowess of the city. The Leader and Deputy Chief Executive had long been passionate advocates of football – albeit as supporters of two different local teams. But it was not merely football, but the tantalising broader promise of what the Olympic Games might bring to the city that helped to cement a sporting theme to the vision.
- Creating a consumer base to the city. This was seen in terms both of 'high' and 'low' culture – of classical and popular music, and of theatre and of street 'happenings' – and of the conscious encouragement of restaurants, clubs, cinemas, hotels and the like to the city. Again, this consciously built on the strengths of the city: its resident orchestras, its vibrant contributions to popular music in the shape of groups such

as the Stone Roses, Simply Red and Happy Mondays, its four live theatres backed by lively fringe groups.

- Encouragement of a high-tech base. This recognised the potential role that the local universities might play. It was symbolised not only in the joint creation of the Science Park (developed through a consortium initially of the Council and the three Manchester universities), but also in the (abortive) bid for a national Medical centre, the (abortive) proposals for a Medical Park in Moston and the encouragement of IT-based developments that were best symbolised in the city's leadership of the Eurocities telecities programme.

- Emphasis on the role that the airport could play in attracting inward investment from international companies. This helped lead to the development of a string of companies in the southern sector leading to the airport – including the high-profile Siemens building that houses one of the company's HQs and a major training facility. It prompted the (as yet elusive) attempt to develop a major business park adjacent to the airport at Davenport Green and the (now largely overlooked) 'South Cityside' proposals that were commissioned by the city from KPMG (South Cityside Steering Group 1996) to provide the next stage in the developments spilling out from Hulme.

The City Council has also been at some pains to proselytise this vision and to use it as a lever to attract investment and development. The creation of a marketing arm – in the form of the somewhat awkward alliance of Marketing Manchester and MIDAS (Manchester Investment and Development Advisory Service) – was fashioned to proselytise 'Manchester' as a rather elastic concept ambiguously stretched between the City itself and the conurbation more broadly, but distinctly separate from regional agencies that market the North West as a whole (Deas and Ward, this volume). Boosterism has played a key role both in trying to persuade the citizenry (in the somewhat leaden words of an early strapline from Marketing Manchester) that 'Manchester is up and going' and in altering the image of the city from its industrial past to a 'happening' future. A welter of 'promotional' materials – many badged with the photography of Len Grant – flowed from the Town Hall's Economic Initiatives Department (see, for example, Fox 1995).

Delivering regeneration

Second has been the evolution of distinctive mechanisms for the delivery of regeneration. There is now widespread recognition of the 'Manchester model' of regeneration. This was initially developed for Hulme's City Challenge in 1992, was later elaborated to tackle the physical rebuilding of the bomb-damaged city centre, and is being applied most recently in the elaboration of New East Manchester Limited which is one of the three national Urban Regeneration Companies sanctioned by central government. The essence of the 'model' is a delivery body with an executive that has an avowedly semi-autonomous arm's-length relationship with the local authority and is serviced by a dedicated team of officers usually seconded from relevant Council departments. The company owns no assets, but draws together key players from the relevant agencies that can deliver elements of the regeneration programme. It can therefore both develop strategy and provide the framework through which partners deliver specific elements of a coherent programme. Its 'commercial' ethos offers a vehicle through which private-sector interest and contributions can be pulled into the regeneration process on the basis that companies can have some confidence that a private-sector ethos will characterise the delivery of projects and programmes. Above all, the model entails short lines of decision-making that are facilitated by the involvement on the central board of key senior politicians and local authority officers.

This 'model' has produced some striking results. For example, for some two decades the future of Hulme was stalled against a background of an unholy triangular battle played out between the City Council, the then DoE and local resident groups. The advent of the government's City Challenge programme and the use of the model as the City Council's targeted delivery mechanism helped to square the circle and to ensure that redevelopment was achieved (almost within the time-span of the seven years of City Challenge) with support from all three parties and the active involvement of volume house builders (Harding 1997). Even more dramatic was the time-scale through which the rebuilding of the city centre was achieved. The IRA bomb exploded in June 1996. Inevitably, the process of rebuilding (and especially of redesigning new layouts) in a complex, densely developed city core was not simple. The redesign of the central core entailed achieving agreement amongst the five principal landowners whose buildings had been affected. Yet the major keystone of the rebuilding – the reopening of the pivotal Marks and Spencers store – was achieved on target before Christmas 1999. This was no small accomplishment. And its success owed much to the structure and composition of the Task Force that was established in the form of Manchester Millennium Ltd: with a board comprised of some of the heavy hitters in the region chaired by Sir Alan Cockshaw (then

Chairman of AMEC); and with a dedicated arm's-length team run by Howard Bernstein alongside a number of secondees drawn from key private sector companies.

A second element of the regeneration strategy has been the avowed intention to roll out regeneration progressively from one geographical area to another. This has helped to address the political difficulty that any competitive process of resource allocation is bound to favour 'winning' areas at the expense of rival claims from other areas. The sequencing of regeneration schemes suggests in part a conscious strategy of tackling areas progressively over time. The large city centre schemes (CMDC, City Challenge, and, as a special case, the rebuilding of the core) have been accompanied by a sequence of SRBCF programmes (North Manchester, East Side, Wythenshawe, Stockport Road, East Link, Cheetham and Boughton, Moss Side and Hulme) and by a range of other area-based schemes such as in the Northern Quarter, Ancoats Village and the like (Williams, this volume). This has two advantages. Not only is there an implicit suggestion that areas not yet tackled need only wait patiently until their turn comes, but it also has the undoubted merit that schemes can be relatively big and thereby increase the probability that the needs of deprived areas can be tackled comprehensively across such policy domains as housing, job creation, skills and education, crime and the like. This has been especially evident in two major schemes. First – inevitably – was Hulme and Moss Side which have been a focus for public intervention and resources over many years. The initial City Challenge programme was a seven-year scheme for Hulme. During its lifetime, the City Council successfully bid for European URBAN resources to roll out the Hulme developments into neighbouring Moss Side. Such continuation strategies, of course, can only work successfully if there are multiple sources of funding on which successive regeneration programmes can be built. The second example is the City Council's approach to its ambitions for the major redevelopment of East Manchester. This is an area – once the metal-bashing heart of Manchester, with some major heavy engineering firms – that has seen perhaps the largest loss of jobs of any part of the city. The City Council attempted to start a process of environmental tidying-up in the 1980s (Tye and Williams 1994), but the area has continued to lose jobs and population at an accelerating rate. Part of East Manchester, for example, was one of the case studies in Anne Power's work on the collapse of private and social housing markets in neighbourhoods suffering from the downward spiral of dereliction (Power and Mumford 1999). The City Council took the adventurous and imaginative decision in 1998 to

Plate 4   Post-bomb retailing in Manchester, Marks & Spencer style

bid for resources from the two separate programmes of SRBCF Round 5 and New Deal for Communities (NDC) as though they were essentially a single pot of resource. This led to a bid for a NDC pilot that was part of a wider area contained within the simultaneous SRBCF bid. That both bids were successful (and have now been further co-ordinated within a new Urban Regeneration Company for East Manchester) has provided the City Council with what is an immense challenge in terms of the scale and difficulty of tackling so large and complex an area, but equally a once-in-a-generation opportunity to reverse the fortunes of the area.

The arrangements for the Urban Regeneration Company (New East Manchester Limited) are another version of the Manchester 'model' of regeneration. The task faced in East Manchester is both to co-ordinate the multitude of existing funded initiatives (amongst which are three SRBCF partnerships, New Deal for Communities, Sure Start, and an Education Action Zone), but also to provide a masterplan framework for the transport links and housing stock for this whole quadrant of the city. The Company is a joint undertaking by English Partnerships, the North West RDA and the City Council. Its small Board is chaired by Sir Alan Cockshaw (now chairman of English Partnerships) and includes the chief executive of the RDA (Michael Shields, who was previously chief executive of Trafford Park Development Corporation), the Leader of the City Council (Richard Leese), a representative of the Business Leadership Team and two community representatives. Its Secretary is the Council's chief executive (Howard Bernstein) and its first chief executive was Marianne Neville-Rolfe (previously Director of the North West Government Office). It perfectly exemplifies the principles of the Manchester 'model': the gathering together of 'big hitters' who can be expected to deliver their organisations as effective partners in an overall masterplan; the ability to make decisions that stick; and the readiness to work to a commercial ethos tempered in this case by sensitivity to community priorities.

In this process of rolling out regeneration, one of the key dilemmas that the City Council has faced is the geography of its administrative boundaries. Greater Manchester is more highly fragmented administratively than any other British conurbation (Deas and Ward, this volume). Divided into no fewer than ten metropolitan districts, its core district of Manchester has a population of less than half a million out of a total conurbation of 2.5 million. This compares, for example, with the West Midlands where Birmingham has a population of 1 million out of a total of 2.4 million. Across the conurbations, the city's percentage of the total conurbation population (at 17 per cent) is significantly lower than that of any other English conurbation: Liverpool has 25 per cent of its conurbation's population; Newcastle has 33 per cent; Leeds has 35 per cent; Sheffield has 41 per cent; and Birmingham has 42 per cent. Manchester's boundaries are excessively tightly drawn and they exclude all of the commuter areas to the south and east. By comparison, Leeds includes generous swathes of commuter territory, as does Sheffield. Two issues have arisen from this. First is the resulting ambiguity about Manchester's dominance within its conurbation. Even though its commercial dominance is clear, the City Council is little larger than many of the other metropolitan districts; and this has fuelled the suspicions and antagonisms across the ten districts. For example, at the outset of the Enhanced Urban Programme in 1977/78, the 'partnership' between Manchester and Salford was one more in name than substance. Indeed, rightly or wrongly, Salford was long seen by central government as readier to work with the private sector than was Manchester and its early success in attracting government grants, especially for housing schemes (Bradford and Steward 1988) and for the development of Salford Quays was an early source of tension between the two neighbouring authorities. As we have seen, this dramatically changed during the later 1980s and Manchester has increasingly worked collaboratively not only with Salford, but also with Trafford and more recently with

Tameside (which four districts effectively comprise the inner core of the conurbation). Even now, however, there is considerable ambiguity about what the Council means when its advertising proselytises the claims of 'Manchester'. Its perception of 'Manchester' tends to stop at its administrative boundaries. This raises interesting issues, for example the way in which regeneration will be tackled in East Manchester – an area whose problems run seamlessly into those of neighbouring Tameside. It also prompts questions about the politics of regional devolution and the City Council's approach to the North West Development Agency and the regional chamber (both of which were established in 1999). There is a sense in which the City Council's future is inextricably bound up with sub-regional alliances and with a city-region concept rather than with the North West as a whole. This debate will doubtless be played out in the next few years – against a background of the somewhat lukewarm enthusiasm now shown by the government for regional devolution within England (Jones and MacLeod, this volume; Robson *et al.* 2000).

The tight administrative boundaries also have obvious implications for the narrow rate base of the city. This becomes an ever-greater difficulty as the City Council develops its core area as a service and consumer base. Those who use its museums and cinemas and clubs and restaurants and concert halls are as likely to be drawn as 'free-riders' from neighbouring areas as from the city itself. A crude and unsuccessful attempt was made in 1999 to propose the enlargement of the City Council's administrative boundaries – crude, since it appeared that none of the adjacent affected districts had been consulted (Deas and Ward, this volume). Even though this came to nothing, the issue remains important.

Partnership and networking

The third element is the partnership process that so critically underlies the delivery mechanisms of regeneration programmes. It has been Manchester's success in capitalising on the partnership concept that has set it apart from its rivals in the process of bidding for competitive resource. It has – either in reality or in the perception that it has created – operated more effectively than elsewhere as a series of consortia of willing participants. In practice, all cities to greater or lesser extent get things done through the efforts of a small number of key influential players. Manchester is no different. It clearly benefits (as do most big cities) from the continued ebullience of some of its professional services

– law firms, accountancy practices, insurance companies and journalism remain relatively strong within Manchester (Mellor, this volume). And to them can be added the strength of the medical professions. It is key members of some of these professions who have provided the nodes in the series of interlocking networks from which the civic life of the city draws strength (Peck 1995). Surprisingly – at least until recently – the universities have played a very minor role in this process.

The professional associations have played a contributory part in this: for example the Manchester Law Society, the Chamber of Commerce, the Professional and Finance Forum. And at a regional level, there has been a variety of loose associations that, while responding to the regional imperative from Europe, have had the incidental effect of strengthening local ties around the Manchester node. Formal bodies such as the North West Business Leadership Team and informal discussion groups such as the North West Economic Development Forum have provided contexts through which such contacts have been generated. Some of the large businesses and privatised utilities that have a local presence have also played an important role – for example, Kelloggs, the Co-op Bank, United Utilities, AMEC, Peel Holdings. Likewise, the agent of the Bank of England, whose official role is to test local business temperatures, has acted as a significant lubricator of many such relationships.

And the city still has a number of Victorian societies that play some part in providing additional cement for such networks – the Literary and Philosophical Society being perhaps the most potent, but others such as the Statistical Society or the Geographical Society have played supporting roles. Some of the local media outlets have been especially active in this process of creating local identity, notably the *Manchester Evening News* and Granada TV.

The ethnic mix of the city has also helped such processes. To the already strong presence of the Jewish community in the business world has been added the entrepreneurial activities of the more recent groups with backgrounds from India, China, Pakistan, Bangladesh, East Africa and the West Indies. Many of the international connections from such areas have been used in developing the City Council's evolving policy of targeting putative trading linkages. The Chinese connection, in particular, has consciously been used by the City Council in its attempts to encourage international trade links. So too was the link with Malaysia through its staging of the Commonwealth Games in Kuala Lumpur, prior to Manchester's role as host in 2002 (Manchester Commonwealth Bid Committee 1995).

That the volatile and enterprising mix of ethnic groups has a down-

Plate 5 Conspicuous victories … large banners adorn prominent buildings
in and around the city centre

side is only to be expected; and the press concentration on certain
stereotypes has not been helpful.

All of these networks have provided strands within the matrix
through which key individuals have transacted informal business and
have helped to embed businesses and individuals into a heightened sense
of the conjointness of their interests with those of the locality and
region. In this, a significant role has been played by both of the local
football clubs and in particular by the high profile of Manchester United
Football Club. Not only does the Club embody the localised aspirations
and pride of (at least some) Mancunians, but anyone who has been in its

Directors' box will know the number of influential local and national politicians and business figures who attend matches. The potential, during games, for transacting informal business or simply for cementing networks is clear.

It is out of this dense mesh of contacts and networks that key individuals have played significant roles as charismatic, or at the least as influential, players in local governance: Bob Scott, in his role in leading the Olympic bids; Sir Alan Cockshaw in his role as chairman of AMEC (and subsequently of English Partnerships); Terry (now Lord) Thomas as chairman of the Co-op Bank and chairman of the RDA; Robert Hough as first chairman of the Commonwealth Games Committee, deputy chairman of Peel Holdings and chairman of its major subsidiary the Manchester Ship Canal Company with its extensive land holdings across the conurbation; James Grigor as chairman of Central Manchester Development Corporation; Sir David Trippier as chairman of Marketing Manchester and the Chamber of Commerce. These are but some of the individuals who have played key overlapping roles as drivers of the City Council's attempt to modernise and regenerate itself. Equally, some of those appointed to quangos have played significant, and continuing, roles: for example, Marianne Neville-Rolfe as Regional Director of GONW (and the first chief executive of New East Manchester Ltd); and John Glester as chief executive of CMDC (and now as chairman of Hallogen, the company that operates the Bridgewater Hall). So too have individuals from the world of the arts and popular culture: for example, Tony Wilson, Mick Hucknall, David Plowright. This is not an attempt to catalogue Manchester's 'great and good', merely to list some of the significant players who have worked on behalf of Manchester during recent years. Some may have had mixed motives in that their business prosperity was tied to the city's fortunes, but all have illustrated that sensitivity to locality that has traditionally been more a hallmark of American than of British cities and out of which civic boosterism and civic involvement have drawn substance.

Turns and transitions

That the effects of such strategies have had an impact on the city cannot be doubted. The tangible physical evidence is there for all to see. New buildings and new streetscapes have been created to revamp something of the erstwhile dreary featurelessness of the city. Some of its ebullient Victorian architecture has begun to take on a new and impressive life and has been augmented by some handsome new buildings that reflect the growing confidence of a significant school of Manchester-based architects (Parkinson-Bailey 1996). Hulme City Challenge played an interesting role in this since its physical redevelopment was steered by an innovative design guide that tried to recreate a sense of urbanity to inner areas; and indeed the Guide was subsequently generalised to cover the city more broadly (Hulme City Challenge 1994; Manchester City Council 1995).

The institutional changes in governance are equally evident. The City Council has somewhat loosened its patriarchal hold on its local fiefdom – partly at the behest of national legislation, but also as part of the new civic urban entrepreneurialism. The joint companies established under the regeneration model are one example of this. Perhaps the most striking is the establishment of a housing trust in Wythenshawe which now 'owns' some 7,000 ex-Council properties in the form of the Willow Park Trust. Yet the City Council still appears to retain its determination to control and to dominate, albeit in subtler ways than when its powers were less trammelled than now. It shows a continuing impatience with critics – for example in its battles with the Civic Society over the use of 'legacy' buildings such as the Free Trade Hall or the Victoria Baths or Piccadilly Gardens. Nor has community development ever featured strongly in its priorities. However much as one may sympathise with the economic force of its case, the heavy hand of central control is not far from the surface of Council business. In this, the recent replacement of the traditional committee structure by a cabinet style of local government (accompanied by scrutiny committees) can be interpreted as modernisation and the determination to drive decisions through more efficiently and rapidly, but equally as a mechanism well suited to an authority that has long protected the power of its key senior members and officers.

The most triumphantly successful of the City Council's achievements has been to realise its aim of repopulating the central core of the city. The process was started, with public subsidy, under the aegis of CMDC, but this was much in accord with the City Council's own policy. By the end of CMDC's life-span, the process had developed a market momentum of its own. The first non-subsidised private housing was started in 1996 and subsequently a range of warehouse and loft conversions and of new build has dramatically transformed large swathes of the canal frontages within the centre. To the pioneers – Jim Ramsbottom working in Castlefield, and Tom Bloxham through Urban Splash – have now been added a slew of national volume and specialist housebuilders. The population of the central core (which had been less than 300 in 1987) has now grown to a figure for which estimates vary between 5,000 and 10,000. Overwhelmingly, the new population is professional, young and single, and is employed predominantly in the city itself (Robson et al. 1998). Few, if any, households with children have yet been attracted, but there is a significant minority of (largely transient) student households. This all demonstrates that a genuine market in central-city living has been created; and this in turn has helped to generate a local demand for a range of consumer goods and services that form the core of the city's aspiration to become a post-industrial venue. One of the most significant indicators that the process may be seen as a long-term change in the composition of the city was the recently-declared intention by the Council that it would commission a study of the potential for establishing a primary school in the city centre. Any such development would aim both to attract families with children but also to retain existing young households as they move into the family-formation stage of their life cycles.

Yet for all such successes – and as later chapters in this volume amply demonstrate – the economic and social challenges of reinventing the city have as yet been only lightly scratched. Overall employment has continued to fall, as has the city's population (although both began to reverse this trend in the final years of the 1990s). The stark facts of the continuing deprivation in Manchester have been amply recorded in the City Council's own poverty and social audit (Griffiths 1998). There is little gainsaying the city's continuing problems of job losses, unemployment, poor health, low educational and skills levels, high crime and extensive environmental dereliction. The statistics, however, have to be read in the light of the tight boundaries of the city itself. Since its boundaries map out what is essentially the inner core of the conurbation, they inevitably throw a harsher light on Manchester than were the city to be as generously defined as other of the English conurbations. This is illustrated by the fact that, while for example Manchester and Liverpool appear similarly distressed, the conurbation statistics for the whole of Greater Manchester are significantly better than those for Merseyside and rank alongside those of the two most prosperous conurbations of West Yorkshire and the West Midlands (Deas and Giordano 2000). Much of the city's prosperity continues to find its home outside its tight administrative boundaries – not least in Stockport, in Cheshire and the Peak District – and this means that the prosperity of its economic functional area is less well reflected in the statistics for Manchester than is true of other core districts of the English conurbations. Gloom about Manchester would be less justified were we to focus on the conurbation as a whole rather than only on its core district.

Nevertheless, for the city, the core conundrum remains whether it is possible to privilege the economically driven entrepreneurial agenda and yet address the growing problems of social exclusion that are linked to joblessness, poverty, poor health, low educational attainment and the social malaise associated with deprivation. The City Council began to address this when it rolled forward its City Pride agenda in 1997 (City Pride Strategic Planning Group 1998a). This was in no small part tied to the change of Leadership when Richard Leese brought with him a greater concern for the social dimension of regeneration. The decision to produce a second version of City Pride was stimulated by two prompts. First was the fact that, in its final days, the Conservative government extended the invitation to produce City Pride statements to seven other cities, and Manchester was determined to show that it was still ahead of the pack of competing cities. Second, with the election of a Labour government, the City Council faced the ironic possibility that it might be seen as the creature of the previous administration and hence wanted to demonstrate its determination to develop a civic manifestation of the New Labour agenda for regeneration. The most novel element of the roll-forward of City Pride was the establishment of a social strategy forum. This aimed to identify social issues that ran across the remits of working groups on transport, the economy and the like. This can be argued to have anticipated the national government's establishment of the Social Exclusion Unit which has begun to make significant impacts on social priorities across government departments.

This meshing of economic, social and environmental policies into a seamless agenda remains for Manchester – as for other of the big cities, and as for central government departments – the key test of success. So far, the city has been outstandingly successful in changing its image – both its self-perception and the picture it portrays of itself to the outside world. Such images have become a vitally important element in influencing the economic success of cities in a global economy in which perceptions play an increasingly important role. The major challenge now is to link whatever economic success the city can achieve to the fortunes of the poor and deprived who live just beyond the booming residential housing markets of its core. Whether the City Council is able to translate such concerns into its new rounds of regeneration programmes – not least in East Manchester – will be a key test of the plausibility of linking social and economic concerns into programmes for the reinvention of cities.

4

Economic transitions: restructuring local labour markets

BENITO GIORDANO AND LAURA TWOMEY

THIS chapter discusses Manchester's economy. It reviews employment and unemployment trends in the last thirty years of the twentieth century to provide a comprehensive commentary on the Manchester economy's transition from a manufacturing-dominated past to a services-dominated future (Peck and Emmerich 1992). The analyses of these employment and unemployment trends suggest that the hype and projected image of Manchester, at the end of the twentieth century, as a thriving and vibrant city with excellent opportunities can be challenged. The chapter begins with a brief review of the economic geography of the city and its surrounding region in order to provide a historical context for the analyses.

Manchester's economy was spawned in the wake of the industrial revolution, but has struggled against the legacy of its formation during much of the subsequent period (Lloyd and Reeve 1981). The city's economic prosperity had its roots in the textile industry (Lloyd and Mason 1977) and in the development of a network of banks, warehouses and railheads, which served the surrounding large cotton manufacturing towns. However, from a position of pre-eminence in the nineteenth century, the later half of the twentieth century saw broader processes of economic restructuring, which had a particularly severe impact on Manchester and its wider conurbation (Dicken, this volume). For example, between 1966 and 1975 Greater Manchester experienced a decline of almost a quarter of its manufacturing jobs (Lloyd and Dicken 1979).

The structure of manufacturing employment in Manchester meant that it was particularly susceptible to processes of industrial restructuring (Lloyd and Mason 1978). In particular, the city's manufacturing sector was dominated by several large firms, which were especially vulnerable to fragmentation strategies adopted during this period of economic restructuring. Thus, between 1962 and 1972, the inner core of Manchester suffered a net loss of just over 30,000 manufacturing manual jobs, which represented a decline of one-third. In addition, there was a parallel decline of employment in the smaller manufacturing firms, which further limited the potential for recovery, denying the city the necessary seed-bed of innovation and entrepreneurial talent from which net growth might have stemmed. The decline of manufacturing left an unbalanced industrial base in which certain dominant, mature and stable firms survived, but in which the volume of youthful firms was insufficient to ensure long-term survival and growth (Lloyd and Mason 1978).

Employment growth in the service sector offered one of the potential means by which Manchester could offset the decline of established manufacturing industry, and complement the partial gains accruing through new manufacturing inward investment. During the 1970s, the North West had gained fewer service jobs in the post-war period than any other UK region (Tym et al. 1981). Manchester, however, attracted a larger share of new employment in office-based services relative to other areas in the North West region (Lloyd and Reeve 1981). There was expansion of almost 33,000 jobs in the service sector in the Manchester travel-to-work area between 1971 and 1977. Building on an established tradition of office employment – part of it reflecting the presence of corporate headquarters related to the city's status as a focal point for manufacturing – Manchester benefited from the expansion of existing firms and the capture of new branches (Lloyd and Reeve 1981). High-profile gains of new firms such as the National Computing Centre, together with the expansion of Manchester Airport, ICI and IBM, helped diversify the city's economic base (Rogers 1980). Growth in particular sectors further strengthened the city's economy: employment in professional and scientific services grew by 22.7 per cent between 1971 and 1976; miscellaneous services expanded by 22.0 per cent; public administration by 14.5 per cent; and construction by 11.5 per cent (Lloyd 1980). However, these gains did not extend across all sub-sectors of service employment, and global totals for services were essentially modest when measured against national trends. Of particular concern was the loss of business service jobs in insurance, banking and finance in inner Manchester and Salford between 1970 and 1976 – a time of national expansion (Tym et al. 1981). By the mid-1970s the focus of employment growth in the North West region had shifted to outlying towns like Warrington and Wigan, both of which were well served by the regional motorway network. This meant that although Manchester performed well within the region in terms of service sector growth, the city compared unfavourably with Leeds and Birmingham.

The under-performance of Manchester in attracting service sector growth industries prompted those responsible for governing the city to act. Within the space of a few years, the city has experienced a political somersault, as under the same Labour administration it has made the transition from a citadel of municipal socialism in the 1980s to a metropolis of Olympian expedience in the 1990s (Cochrane *et al.*, this volume; Peck and Tickell 1995). Manchester is now seen to win public investment by emphasising its growth potential rather than its poverty strickenness. Despite the failure of the 2000 Olympic bid the city has achieved some successes. It was nominated as the City for Drama in 1994, won City Challenge funds for the regeneration of the inner city area of Hulme, was selected as the location for the follow-up to the Rio Earth Summit, and finally was selected as host to the 2002 Commonwealth Games. These success stories have been enhanced by hype alluding to Manchester's recovery into a dynamic post-industrial city full of opportunity. However, a closer examination of employment and unemployment trends may contradict the optimistic publicity associated with the 'Capital of the North'.

In support of these claims, Peck and Emmerich (1992) highlight the effects of the two major recessions in the early 1980s and 1990s as reinforcing the structural damage to the city's manufacturing base, which the increase in service industry jobs and the short-lived and credit-led 'booms' failed to counter. The recession of the early 1980s dealt a devastating blow to the city's manufacturing base, which the recession of the early 1990s compounded. The examination of data in the subsequent sections of this chapter lend weight to the observation of the devastating trends in both employment and unemployment in Manchester during the last thirty years of the twentieth century. This casts doubt, therefore, about the up-beat messages emerging from the City Council about employment opportunities and leaves the serious question of how to deal with Manchester's seemingly intractable problem of joblessness.

Changing employment

The 26-year period from 1971 to 1997 saw dramatic shifts in the geography of employment in Manchester. This section of the chapter deals first with structural employment change, which includes an analysis of gender shifts in the workforce and second, sectoral changes in employment.

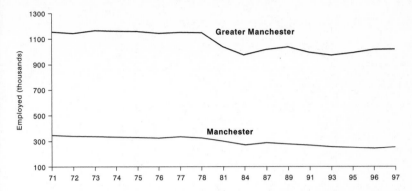

Figure 4.1 Total employment change in Greater Manchester and Manchester, 1971–97

The decline in Manchester's total employment has been pronounced during the last three decades. The number employed in the district declined by just over 90,000 jobs from a total of 344,739 in 1971 to 254,550 in 1997. This represented a decline of 26 per cent of the total number of jobs in 1971. During the period between 1971 and 1981, the district of Manchester lost almost 48,000 jobs whereas a further 42,000 jobs were lost between 1981 and 1997. As Figure 4.1 shows, the situation in Manchester has been one of more or less consistent decline in employment since 1971, apart from relatively slight increases between 1976 and 1977, 1984 and 1987, and between 1996 and 1997. On the other hand, in Greater Manchester, the situation has been more cyclical, with intermittent periods of growth followed by decline. Overall, the total number of jobs in Greater Manchester declined by 135,285 between 1971 and 1997, which represented a 12 per cent decline over the period. Therefore, the decline in the number of jobs in the city of Manchester represents two-thirds of the total number of jobs lost in the conurbation as a whole, which clearly illustrates the scale of the decline of the district's employment base during the last 26 years.

According to Turok and Edge (1999), between 1981 and 1996, there was a continued divergence between the inner and outer areas of conurbations in Britain, with inner core employment contracting by 261,000 (or 12 per cent). However, the significant point is that the contrast between employment decline in the core and growth in the outer areas has been more acute in Greater Manchester than any other conurbation in Britain. For example, core employment fell by 19 per cent while the number of jobs in the outer areas increased by five per cent between 1981 and 1996. Indeed, in comparison to other cities in

Table 4.1 Employment change in Manchester, Greater Manchester and England, 1971–97

	Male FT	Male PT	Male	Female FT	Female PT	Female	Total
Manchester 1971	191,467	9,577	201,044	98,625	45,070	143,695	344,739
Manchester 1997	109,816	14,638	124,454	79,504	50,608	130,112	254,550
Difference 1971–97	-81,651	5,061	-76,590	-19,121	5,538	-13,583	-90,189
% change 1971–97	-42.6	52.8	-38.1	-19.4	12.3	-9.5	-26.2
Greater Manchester 1971	669,096	27,999	697,095	308,753	149,046	457,799	1,154,894
Greater Manchester 1997	455,351	55,698	511,049	280,351	228,261	508,612	1,019,609
Difference 1971–97	-213,745	27,699	-186,046	-28,402	79,215	50,813	-135,285
% change 1971–97	-31.9	98.9	-26.7	-9.2	53.1	11.1	-11.7
England 1971	11,054,672	516,320	11,570,992	4,673,301	2,429,225	7,102,526	18,673,518
England 1997	8,750,856	1,198,663	9,949,519	5,263,539	4,377,095	9,640,634	19,608,149
Difference 1971–97	-2,303,816	682,343	-1,621,473	590,238	1,947,870	2,538,108	934,631
% change 1971–97	-20.8	132.2	-14.0	12.6	80.2	35.7	5.0

Source: NOMIS and authors' own calculations

Britain, therefore, Manchester has faired particularly badly in terms of its employment decline. In fact, Liverpool is the only city that has undergone a broader and deeper decline in employment terms (Turok and Edge 1999). In comparison with other urban areas across Britain, Manchester can be grouped alongside Sheffield, Glasgow and Birmingham, all of which lost between 12 and 19 per cent of their total employment between 1981 and 1996.

The data for employment change in England since the 1970s further underline the severity of the employment decline, which has taken place in both Manchester as well as Greater Manchester. The key point is that the last three decades have been a period during which, despite fluctuations, England has experienced an increase in total employment of 934,631 jobs between 1971 and 1997, which represents a 5 per cent increase during the period. The overall growth in the employment base nationally has been accompanied by important shifts in the labour market, which have witnessed the decline in the number of male full-time (FT) jobs, and a corresponding increase in female (and, to a lesser extent, male) part-time (PT) jobs. Indeed, between 1981 and 1996 in Britain, male FT jobs fell by nearly 1.5 million (a fall of nearly one in seven), while female PT jobs increased by over 1.4 million (or 38.4 per cent) and male PT jobs by over half a million (a 90 per cent increase from a relatively low level in 1981) (Turok and Edge 1999).

The trends that have taken place within the national labour market are broadly mirrored within Manchester, but with some distinct and important differences (see Table 4.1). In Manchester, between 1971 and 1997, the number of male FT jobs dropped by just over 81,000 (a 43 per cent decline), which was proportionately greater than the decline in male FT jobs nationally. Indeed, Manchester's decline constituted two-thirds of the total decline in the number of male FT jobs within Greater Manchester. On the other hand, in Manchester, as with England as a whole, there has been an increase in the number of male PT jobs between 1971 and 1997, however, the increase of just over 5,000 jobs hardly compensated for the decline in male FT employment in the city.

Overall then, Manchester underwent a decline of 76,000 male jobs between 1971 and 1997, which represented a decline of 38 per cent. On the other hand, between 1981 and 1997, the number of male jobs in Manchester declined by 41,000, or a decline of a quarter. This haemorrhage of male jobs, which was especially marked during the 1970s when over 35,000 male jobs were lost, clearly illustrates the extent of the processes of deindustrialisation that Manchester endured during the last three decades.

In terms of female employment within Manchester, the situation is still largely a tale of decline. Female FT employment dropped by just over 19,000 jobs between 1971 and 1997, which was a 19 per cent decline. However, as with male employment, the majority of this decline took place during the 1970s when there was a drop of over 16,000 female FT jobs. In fact, between 1981 and 1997, there was a decline of 2,638 female FT jobs (a 3 per cent decline) in Manchester. On the other hand, between 1981 and 1997, female FT employment increased in Greater Manchester by almost 14,000 jobs (a 5 per cent increase) and at the national level there was a 16 per cent increase. Therefore, Manchester's relative decline in the number of female FT jobs is contrary to trends both at the conurbation as well as national level.

On a more optimistic note, the number of female PT jobs increased by over 5,500 (12 per cent increase) between 1971 and 1997. Interestingly, however, the period in which there was a relatively greater expansion in female PT jobs was in the 1970s when there was an increase of almost 4,000 jobs. Yet, between 1981 and 1997, the increase in female PT jobs was relatively lower with an increase of 1,500 jobs. This again runs contrary to national trends because between 1981 and 1997 there was an increase of almost 1.1 million female PT jobs. However, between 1971 and 1981 there was an increase of just over 850,000 jobs female PT jobs in England, which was a relatively smaller increase than in 1980s and 1990s.

More significantly, in terms of total female employment, Manchester differs from both Greater Manchester as well as England because it has witnessed a decline in female employment. Between 1971 and 1997, the number of female jobs in Manchester dropped by 13,500 (a 10 per cent decrease during the period). It must be said, however, that this decline was the most severe between 1971 and 1981 when 12,500 female jobs were lost. Therefore, between 1981 and 1997 the number of female jobs declined slightly by just over 1,000, which was less than a 1 per cent decline during the 16-year period. Conversely, the female employment scenario in Greater Manchester is somewhat different. Between 1971 and 1997, there was an increase of almost 51,000 (an 11 per cent increase) and between the period 1981 to 1997 there was an increase of almost 53,000 female jobs (also an 11 per cent increase). The only period of decline was between 1971 and 1981 when almost 2,000 female jobs were lost in Greater Manchester; however, it is clear that overall this is significantly better than Manchester's decline in female employment. Lastly, when compared to the situation in England, the seriousness of Manchester's decline in female employment is underlined. For example, between 1971

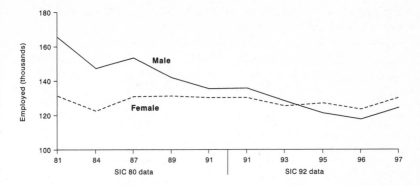

Figure 4.2 Male and female employment change in Manchester between 1981 and 1997

and 1997, the number of female jobs in England increased by over 2.5 million (a 36 per cent increase) and between 1981 and 1997 there was an increase of 1.8 million (a 23 per cent increase).

Since the 1980s, the decline in the number of female jobs in Manchester is the one that gives considerable cause for concern. Yet this decline in female FT employment in Manchester is a less well acknowledged trend that goes against the increases in female employment that have taken place both in Greater Manchester as well as nationally. In spite of this decline in female employment, it is apparent that women constitute a greater proportion of Manchester's total labour force than do men. In 1997, of Manchester's total labour force, 48.9 per cent were male and 51.1 per cent were female. Indeed, 1995 was the first year in which the number of women was greater than the number of men employed in Manchester's total labour force (see Figure 4.2). By contrast, in the labour forces of both Greater Manchester and England as a whole, it remains the case that there are proportionately slightly more men employed than women.

The increase in importance of PT jobs for both men and women in the national labour force has certainly been a trend, which has been mirrored in both Manchester as well as Greater Manchester (see Table 4.2). However, compared to both Greater Manchester and England, Manchester has proportionately less PT employment – just over a quarter compared to 28 per cent in England. Moreover, Manchester's proportion of female PT employment is also lower than the national figure. This is despite the fact that, in recent years, the city of Manchester has undergone growth in service sector employment, which has tended to favour the creation of female PT jobs. Indeed, having provided an analysis of

Table 4.2 Total number employed in Manchester, Greater Manchester and England by sex and type, 1971–97

	Manchester 1971 %	Manchester 1997 %	Greater Manchester 1971 %	Greater Manchester 1979 %	England 1971 %	England 1997 %
Total PT	16	26	15	28	16	28
Total FT	84	74	85	72	84	72
Female PT	13	20	13	22	13	22
Female FT	28	31	27	28	25	27
Male PT	3	6	2	6	3	6
Male FT	56	43	58	44	59	45

Sources: NOMIS and authors' own calculations

the changes that have taken place in the structural composition of Manchester's labour force, the next section of this chapter focuses upon the sectoral changes that have taken place.[1]

The 1960s and 1970s saw manufacturing employment decline sharply with the major conurbations of Britain experiencing declines of nearly 20 per cent in the 1960s and 35 per cent in the 1970s, representing a total contraction in numbers employed of 1.6 million (Turok and Edge 1999). This was an experience repeated – to an even more marked degree – in Manchester (and Greater Manchester) during the 1970s (see Figure 4.3). In both Manchester and Greater Manchester, the sub-sectors which experienced the largest declines between 1971 and 1981 were textiles and clothing and engineering and allied trades, as well as other manufacturing sectors. In Manchester, however, the distributive trades subsector also declined by over 10,000 jobs whereas in Greater Manchester the same sector declined by only 1,400 jobs.

While the 1970s were characterised by decline in many manufacturing sub-sectors, some areas of growth provided partial compensation. In Greater Manchester, financial and professional services experienced a net expansion of 77,000 jobs (a 28 per cent increase) between 1971 and 1981 and employment in construction 1,100 jobs (a 2 per cent increase). Over three-quarters of the increase in the financial and professional services sector comprised female employment, which expanded by over 58,000 jobs in ten years. In Manchester, however, the financial services sector was the only one to undergo an increase in employment between 1971 and 1981. The number of jobs increased by just over 11,000, which was a 10 per cent increase and over 9,000 of these jobs were female.

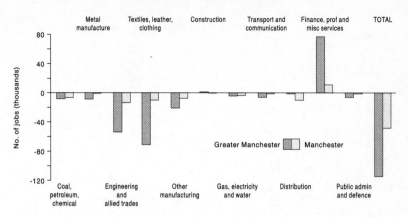

Figure 4.3 Sectoral employment change in Greater Manchester between 1971 and 1981

Thus, by 1981, female employment constituted two-thirds of the total employed in the financial services sub-sector.

The period from 1981 to 1997 saw a continuation on many of the trends evident in the 1970s (see Figure 4.4). Employment in manufacturing continued to shrink, declining by 144,000 jobs (or a 42 per cent drop) in Greater Manchester and in Manchester the decline was even starker with a drop of 39,000 jobs (or a massive 62 per cent decline). The banking and finance sector continued to grow, however, with the number of jobs increasing by 100,000 (or a 131 per cent increase) in Greater Manchester and in Manchester by 25,000 jobs (or a 65 per cent increase). The sector that had the second largest employment growth was public administration, which increased by almost 50,000 jobs (or a 25 per cent increase) in Greater Manchester but in Manchester the growth was much less significant, with an increase of only 2,300 jobs (or a 3.5 per cent increase). The only other sector to experience employment growth in Greater Manchester, between 1981 and 1997, was the distribution, hotels and restaurants sector, which increased by 31,000 jobs (or a 16 per cent increase). The corresponding sector in Manchester, however, actually declined by 1,600 jobs (a 3 per cent drop).

The overall picture of sectoral employment change between 1981 and 1997 (see Figure 4.4) reveals a scenario of decline across all but two of the sub-sectors in Manchester. Yet again this goes against employment trends in both Greater Manchester, as well as nationally, because growth occurred in three out of the nine sub-sectors, which were banking and finance, public administration as well as distribution, hotels and restaurants. Moreover, in percentage terms, the decline in employment was

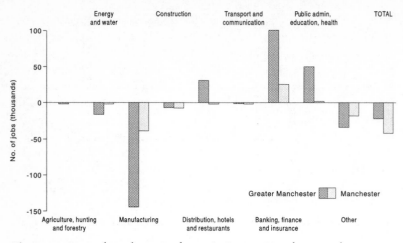

Figure 4.4 Sectoral employment change in Greater Manchester and Manchester between 1981 and 1997

relatively higher in Manchester than the declines in both Greater Manchester and England between 1981 and 1997 in the manufacturing, construction, transport and other services sub-sectors. This further illustrates the extent of Manchester's deindustrialisation and perhaps more worryingly shows that even though the district has experienced employment growth in the financial and banking services sub-sector, this has been at a reduced rate when compared to the conurbation and also nationally.

Clearly, the sectoral employment changes in Manchester have had specific impacts upon the shifts in male and female employment within the district. Most notably, the considerable decline in employment in the manufacturing sub-sector between 1981 and 1997 not only involved a decline in male but also female employment. In real terms, the decline in the number of male jobs (28,000) was almost three times as many as the decline in number of female jobs. However, in percentage terms, the relative declines in male and female employment in manufacturing were similar (male jobs declined by 64 per cent and female jobs by 60 per cent during the period). This is a trend that is repeated for both Greater Manchester and England, although the respective percentage declines in manufacturing were both lower than in Manchester.

The sub-sector in which both male and female employment increased by the most jobs, in Manchester between 1981 and 1997, was the banking and financial services sector. The number of male jobs increased by almost 10,000 (a 49 per cent increase) whereas the number of female jobs increased by 15,300 (an 82 per cent increase). However, the important point to note is that three-quarters of the increase in the number of male jobs in the financial services sector were FT jobs whereas half of the 15,000 increase in female jobs was actually PT jobs. This means that the increase in the number of female PT jobs in the sub-sector was more or less equal to the number of male FT jobs created. Furthermore, the increase in the number of both male and female PT jobs in the financial services sub-sector constitutes almost 10,000 jobs out of a total increase of just over 25,000 jobs. This illustrates the extent to which the employment expansion in the financial services sector in Manchester between 1981 and 1997 was mainly an expansion in female work.

The expansion in female employment has been particularly marked in the public administration sub-sector, which was the only other sub-sector to experience a growth in total employment in Manchester between 1981 and 1997. Male FT employment declined in the sub-sector by 3,300 jobs, while the number of male PT jobs increased by 745; however, it was the expansion in the number of female jobs that accounted for the overall employment growth. The number of female jobs in the public administration sector increased by almost 5,000, with 1,800 of these being PT jobs. Similarly, in the transport and communications sub-sector the number of female jobs increased by 3,000 of which 900 were PT jobs. However, the decline in the number of male jobs was almost 5,000, which meant that total employment in the sub-sector also declined. Indeed, male employment declined in seven out of the nine sub-sectors, and apart from financial services the only other sub-sector to increase employment was the distribution, hotels and restaurants, which had an increase of 150 male jobs. The important point to note is that in this sub-sector male FT jobs dropped by 1,600 whereas male PT jobs increased by 1,800 thus accounting for the expansion overall.

This analysis of sectoral employment change in Manchester between 1981 and 1997 reveals that the district has continued to undergo the process of deindustrialisation, which began in the 1970s. Manchester has lost proportionately more manufacturing jobs than has Greater Manchester (62 per cent in the former compared to 42 per cent in the latter). On the other hand, the story is not one of complete decline as Manchester has witnessed employment growth in financial and business services as well as the public administration sub-sector. However, this expansion has been proportionately lower than the corresponding employment growth in Greater Manchester and nationally. Second, and more important, the employment growth in the two respective sub-sectors has by no means compensated for the decline in manufacturing jobs, which has taken place in Manchester. Moreover, the employment expansion has created relatively more female as well as PT jobs whereas male FT jobs have been decimated. It seems likely that this will continue in the future with male FT employment declining even further.

Forms of unemployment

The most obvious implication of the varying difficulties encountered by Manchester in limiting the decline of employment in some sectors, and capitalising on the potential for growth in others, was the rise in unemployment levels. It is with these changes that the chapter now concerns itself. The analysis of unemployment trends in Manchester between 1983 and 1999 suggests a rough grouping into four distinct phases: *high unemployment* (1983 to 1986), *falling unemployment* (1986 to 1990), *rising unemployment* (1990 to 1993) and *falling unemployment* (1993 to 1999). Both Figure 4.5, presenting the number of people registered as unemployed in Manchester, and Figure 4.6, presenting unemployment rates, demonstrate these trends. Figure 4.5 shows that both male and female unemployment in Manchester peaked in the aftermath of the early 1980s recession between 1984 and 1986, and remained high; it reached its lowest point in 1990, but began to rise again in 1991 as a result of the recession from the second half of 1990 (Peck and Emmerich 1992), peaking once again in 1993. The total number of people registered as unemployed in Manchester has decreased by 26,199 over the last sixteen years, peaking at 45,687 in January 1986. The number of males registered as unemployed has decreased by 19,277 in the same time period from 32,318 in July 1983 to 13,041 in April 1999,

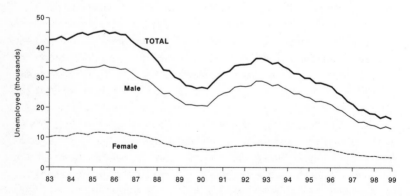

Figure 4.5 Unemployment in Manchester, July 1983–April 1999

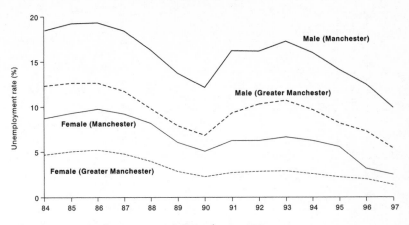

Figure 4.6 Unemployment rates in Manchester, 1984–97

peaking at 34,169 in January 1986. Female unemployment has decreased by 6,922 in the 16-year period shown in Figure 4.5.

In July 1983 registered female unemployment was 10,257, it peaked in October 1985, slightly earlier than male unemployment at 11,721 and had fallen to 3,335 in April 1999. These decreasing trends in unemployment are curious considering the concurrent decline in employment opportunities in the city.

Figure 4.6 shows that Manchester itself has experienced higher male and female unemployment rates than the Greater Manchester conurbation as a whole. In fact Manchester has tended to have the highest unemployment rates of any of the ten districts in the Greater Manchester conurbation (Stockport has the lowest). This reflects the district's status as home to much of the conurbation's traditional manufacturing base.

Part of the difficulty faced by Manchester stems from the movement of industry to the outer districts of the conurbation. Residential migration flows also illustrate the scale of the difficulty faced by Manchester. Figure 4.7 illustrates the migratory flows for Manchester based on a four-fold classification developed to explore the nature of migration patterns from the district between 1990 and 1998. The four categories are migration from Manchester to the rest of Greater Manchester; from Manchester to Merseyside; from Manchester to the rest of the North West region; and from Manchester to the rest of the UK.

Figure 4.7 shows that between 1990 and 1998 Manchester experienced a net loss of 34,757 migrants to the rest of the Greater Manchester conurbation and to the rest of the North West region, but had a net gain from Merseyside and the UK. The migration data show, therefore, that

Table 4.3 Average male unemployment percentage changes for Manchester, 1984–95

Year	Bolton	Bury	Manchester	Oldham	Rochdale	Salford	Stockport	Tameside	Trafford	Wigan
1984/85	0.8	1.2	2.3	1.9	1.8	-0.4	-1.9	-0.1	-0.4	4.7
1985/86	-2.1	-2.7	-0.2	-1.8	-1.8	-1.6	-2.1	-0.7	-2.8	3.8
1986/87	-8.9	-12.3	-7.0	-9.2	-12.2	-9.0	-11.0	-7.3	-11.3	-8.5
1987/88	-14.8	-22.1	-13.4	-18.0	-19.1	-18.3	-25.0	-19.8	-20.9	-16.5
1988/89	-19.2	-21.9	-15.3	-15.4	-16.0	-17.6	-24.6	-23.1	-17.9	-21.4
1989/90	-11.2	-13.4	-9.2	-6.6	-8.9	-10.1	-7.8	-11.2	-10.4	-16.8
1990/91	24.7	43.1	16.3	31.4	33.9	20.6	41.6	44.4	32.6	28.2
1991/92	17.5	20.1	12.8	20.9	13.1	12.5	24.4	19.6	19.7	20.4
1992/93	2.4	6.7	4.4	1.9	3.3	1.1	4.2	0.2	3.0	-1.0
1993/94	-14.5	-14.2	-7.4	-9.0	-10.7	-10.3	-11.7	-11.3	-8.2	-13.4
1994/95	-17.5	-17.3	-10.7	-15.4	-12.4	-15.3	-15.7	-13.7	-15.0	-15.5
Inter-quartile Range										
	16.2	19.7	13.3	14.2	14.9	13.2	14.8	12.5	14.4	20.3

Sources: NOMIS and authors' own calculations

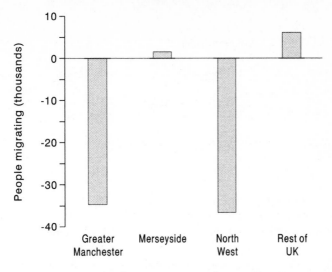

Figure 4.7 Patterns of migration in Manchester, 1990–98

Manchester has lost migrants – they probably left the city in order to exploit the employment opportunities in neighbouring districts. This is one possible explanation for the high levels of unemployment in the city because it is the unemployed that remain rather than moving away.

Unemployment rates indicate that Manchester is the district in which joblessness has been consistently the highest and most intractable in comparison to all the others in Greater Manchester. Certainly, Manchester houses a higher proportion of the conurbation's unemployed within its boundaries; indeed the proportion of the conurbation's male unemployed resident in Manchester remained in excess of one in four between 1984 and 1995. Manchester's share of the conurbation joblessness increased as numbers in unemployment in Greater Manchester declined. The city's unemployment appears to be less rapidly resolvable than in its neighbouring districts, either as a result of the characteristics of the city's skill base, or an employment structure that may be particularly susceptible to the effects of economic recession.

The overall pattern of unemployment in Manchester can be summarised by the annual percentage changes in unemployment. Table 4.3 shows these changes, with a negative value representing a decline in unemployment. However, it can also be seen that the inter-quartile range is very low for Manchester and indeed much lower than any of the other districts in Greater Manchester. This suggests that the number of unemployed in Manchester is less responsive to fluctuations as the city

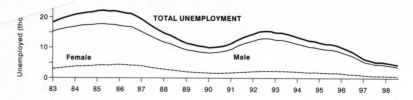

Figure 4.8 Long term (>12 months) unemployment in Manchester, October 1983–April 1999

has a larger core of unemployed residents, which has remained more or less solid. On the other hand, in the other districts there is more fluctuation in the numbers indicating a less solid core of unemployed people.

Another indication of the concentration and severity of Manchester's unemployment situation in relation to the rest of the conurbation can be found by looking at figures relating to the number of registered claimants that have been unemployed for more than 12 months. This section of the chapter now turns to consider the issue of long-term unemployment.

Manchester has the highest concentrations of total unemployment in Greater Manchester and therefore it would be expected to have similarly high concentrations of the long-term unemployed. Figure 4.8 shows the levels of long-term unemployment between October 1983 and April 1999. The total number of long-term unemployed has decreased by 14,060 in this 16-year period, falling from 18,484 in October 1983 to 4,424 in April 1999. The numbers of long-term unemployed peaked in January 1986 at 22,230. Male long-term unemployment decreased by 11,617, from 15,348 in October 1983 to 3,731 in April 1999 peaking in January 1986 with 17,876. Similarly female long-term unemployment decreased by 2,443 from 3,136 in 1983 to 693 in April 1999. However, female long-term unemployment peaked later than male long-term unemployment in October 1986 at 4,519.

Table 4.4 shows males and females registered unemployed for more than 12 months as a percentage of all registered unemployed people. The table shows that a higher percentage of all males registered as unemployed have been unemployed for over 12 months. This percentage increases in periods of rising unemployment, again demonstrating the stubbornness of Manchester's unemployed population.

Despite the trends outlined in the last two sections of the chapter

Table 4.4 The percentage of all males and females unemployed for more than twelve months in Manchester, 1983–98

Year	Males %	Females %
Oct 1983	47.6	29.8
Oct 1984	51.3	34.5
Oct 1985	53.0	36.8
Oct 1986	52.4	39.0
Oct 1987	53.2	39.2
Oct 1988	48.2	37.0
Oct 1989	44.6	33.6
Oct 1990	40.7	29.9
Oct 1991	38.2	27.2
Oct 1992	45.1	30.6
Oct 1993	46.1	32.2
Oct 1994	45.8	31.6
Oct 1995	44.6	30.4
Oct 1996	43.6	29.8
Oct 1997	35.8	23.9
Oct 1998	32.8	23.7

Sources: NOMIS and authors' own calculations

presenting an encouraging picture of the Manchester economy: one where unemployment is decreasing, this is not necessarily an indication of a healthy economy where unemployment is low. Therefore, the following section of the chapter explores what Beatty *et al.* (1997) term 'real unemployment'.

In 1997 Beatty and his colleagues published a report claiming that unemployment rates, like those presented above, based on claimant counts were misleading: they painted an inaccurate picture of the true nature of unemployment in the UK. They argue that individuals on government schemes, prematurely retired and permanently sick constitute the 'hidden unemployed' and that real unemployment was in fact much higher than that described by ordinary claimant counts. Table 4.5 shows both levels of real and claimant count unemployment in Manchester in 1991 and 1997.

Table 4.5 shows that the claimant count unemployment rates demonstrate the same pattern of overall falling unemployment in Manchester in the 1990s as seen earlier in the chapter. However, levels of real unemploy-

Table 4.5 Real levels of unemployment, 1991 and 1997

	1991	*1997*	*% change*
Claimant count	18.0	14.4	-3.6
Real unemployment	20.1	28.6	+8.5

Sources: Beatty *et al*. (1997), p. 51, NOMIS and authors' own calculations

ment (based on the methodology of Beatty *et al*. 1997) show that there has in fact been a sizeable increase in levels of total unemployment in Manchester.

The above sections of the chapter have concentrated on unemployment across Manchester as a whole. The following section looks at unemployment within Manchester.

Intra-urban unemployment

Figure 4.9 shows the percentage of change in unemployment rates between the 1981 and 1991 Censuses. It shows that the wards experiencing the greatest increases in unemployment are Ardwick, Central, Cheetham and Hulme. All of these wards are regularly associated with poverty and

Key to Figures 4.9 to 4.12				
	BNFA	Ardwick	BNGK	Woodhouse Park
	BNFC	Barlow Moor	BNFB	Baguley
	BNFE	Beswick and	BNFD	Benchill
		Clayton	BNFF	Blackley
	BNFG	Bradford	BNFH	Brooklands
	BNFJ	Burnage	BNGK	Central
	BNFL	Charlestown	BNFM	Cheetham
	BNFN	Chorlton	BNFP	Crumpsall
	BNFQ	Didsbury	BNFR	Fallowfield
	BNFS	Gorton North	BNFT	Gorton South
	BNFU	Harpurhey	BNFW	Hulme
	BNFX	Levenshulme	BNFY	Lightbowne
	BNFZ	Longsight	BNGA	Moss Side
	BNGB	Moston	BNGC	Newton Heath
	BNGD	Northendon	BNGE	Old Moat
	BNGF	Rusholme	BNGG	Sharston
	BNGH	Whalley Range	BNGJ	Withington

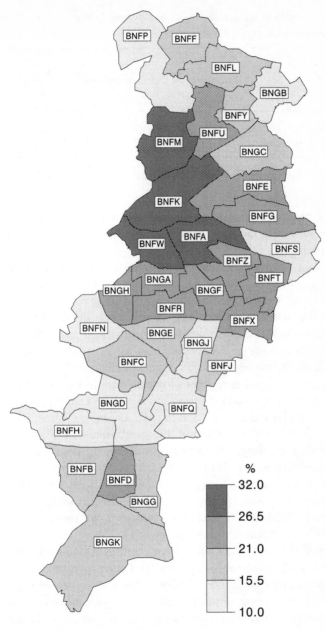

%

32.0

26.5

21.0

15.5

10.0

Source: Unemployment data:
NOMIS, Population data: NOMIS, 1991, Census: MIMAS

Figure 4.9 Map of male unemployment change in Manchester, 1981–91

Table 4.6 Index of segregation for unemployment in Manchester and Greater Manchester, 1981–91

	Total Unemployment		Male Unemployment		Female Unemployment	
	1981	1991	1981	1991	1981	1991
Manchester	0.21	0.27	0.22	0.28	0.24	0.29
Greater Manchester	0.24	0.32	0.25	0.35	0.24	0.31

Sources: NOMIS and authors' own calculations

high unemployment in Manchester and in the cases of Ardwick and Hulme subject to local regeneration initiatives that attempt to alleviate these problems.

Table 4.6 shows the Index of Segregation values for unemployment between 1981 and 1991. It demonstrates that male, female and total unemployment became more concentrated geographically within both Manchester and Greater Manchester. This would complement the maps above that show that unemployment is increasingly concentrated in the wards closest to the city centre and those findings that demonstrate that Manchester has the highest percentage of the conurbation's unemployed.

Figure 4.10 shows male unemployment rates in 1991 for Manchester. It shows that the following wards had the highest unemployment rates of between 23.5 and 29.3 per cent in 1991: Ardwick, Central, Cheetham, Hulme, with Beswick & Clayton, Bradford, Harpurhey, Longsight and Moss Side comprising a tight ring around the city centre with levels of male unemployment of between 17.7 per cent and 23.5 per cent. Similar to the pattern seen in Figure 4.10, the wards with the highest male unemployment rates are clustered around the city's centre. Burnage, Chorlton, Didsbury, Moston and Withington are the wards in which male unemployment rates were lowest in 1991.

Figure 4.11 shows male unemployment rates in Manchester in 1997. It shows a similar pattern to that seen in Figure 4.10, with the highest unemployment rates clustered around the city centre. However, the areas of lowest unemployment (between 5.5 per cent and 8.1 per cent) have become more easily identifiable in two distinct clusters. One cluster comprised of Brooklands, Didsbury and Northendon, the other of Blackley, Charlestown, Crumpsall and Moston. This would imply that male unemployment became steadily more concentrated in certain wards within Manchester. However, the two figures also show that

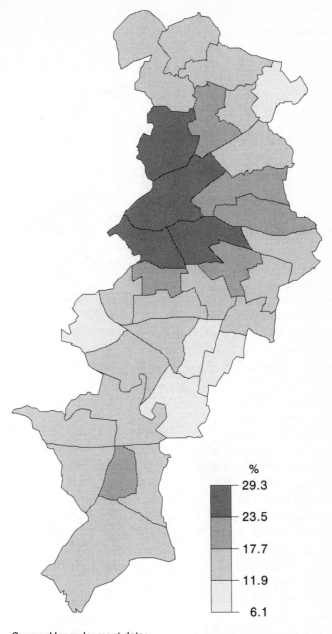

%

29.3

23.5

17.7

11.9

6.1

Source: Unemployment data:
NOMIS, Population data: NOMIS, 1991, Census: MIMAS

Figure 4.10 Map of male unemployment in Manchester, 1991

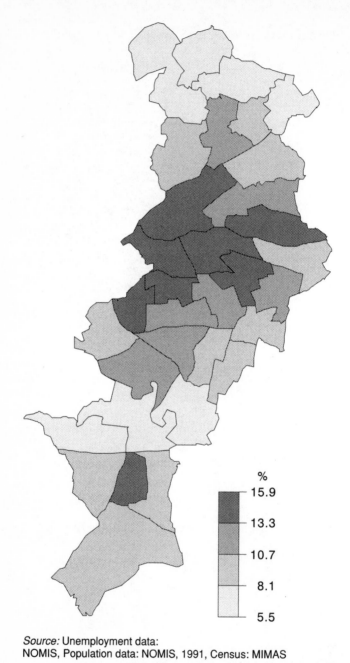

%
- 15.9
- 13.3
- 10.7
- 8.1
- 5.5

Source: Unemployment data:
NOMIS, Population data: NOMIS, 1991, Census: MIMAS

Figure 4.11 Map of male unemployment in Manchester, 1997

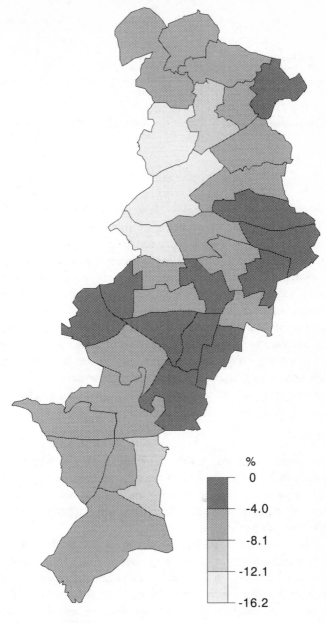

%

0

-4.0

-8.1

-12.1

-16.2

Source: Unemployment data:
NOMIS, Population data: NOMIS, 1991, Census: MIMAS

Figure 4.12 Map of unemployment change in Manchester, 1991–99

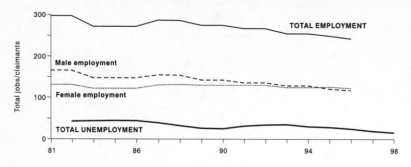

Figure 4.13 'Manchester's job gap', 1981–98

unemployment rates overall in Manchester decreased between 1991 and 1997. These changes are shown in Figure 4.12. This shows that all wards in Manchester experienced a decrease in male unemployment rates between 1991 and 1997. The smallest decreases are in the wards where unemployment has traditionally been lower, and the greatest decreases have been in those wards associated with high unemployment rates. The decreases witnessed in the city centre wards, of traditional high unemployment, could be attributed to the trends discussed earlier in the chapter put forward by Beatty *et al.* (1997). Basically, it seems that alternative coping strategies to unemployment are being utilised, for example, (especially) men are opting to register permanently sick or retire prematurely rather than continue to sign on at the Job Centre.

The 'job gap'

What is curious from this review of employment and unemployment trends in Manchester in the last 30 years is the drop in unemployment figures in a period of employment decline. This is not what would be expected. Figure 4.13 illustrates what Peck and Tickell (1997) termed 'Manchester's job gap'.

Perhaps, then, the hype and projected image of Manchester as a thriving and vibrant city with excellent employment opportunities could be challenged? The declining unemployment rates often used as a media tool to promote confidence in Manchester obscures from view that this decline may not necessarily be attributed to increased employment opportunities, but to Manchester residents choosing to claim disability allowances, move away or to take up early retirement packages. Of course, taking early retirement is not a bad thing, however, but the question that needs to be asked is why are people compelled to take up this option (or indeed others)? Declining levels of employment obviously lead to fewer opportunities, this is the real answer. On the other hand, a wide variety of employment opportunities do exist in Manchester; the fact is, however, that this is leading to the feminisation of the workforce in the city and a dependence on part-time jobs. Again, this is of course not a negative trend in fact greater opportunities for women is to be clearly welcomed. However, it is important to consider the implications of an economy that provides relatively fewer employment opportunities for men. Therefore, scratching beneath the surface of the promotional literature a different picture of Manchester's economy in the last decades of the twentieth century can be presented. One of declining unemployment claimant counts, that does not appear so impressive when compared to the rising number of people permanently sick or taking early retirement, and service sector employment opportunities, characterised by a dominance of female (and part-time) workers.

Notes

This work was conducted as part of the research for the Liverpool and Manchester Integrated Case Study funded by the ESRC *Cities: Competitiveness and Cohesion Programme* (award number L130251032).

1 In this section, sectoral shifts in two periods are analysed; the first between the 1971–81 period, and the second between 1981 and 1997. The reason for this is that the Standard Industrial Classification (sic) (adopted in 1968) was changed in 1980 and also in 1992, so it is not possible to compare directly employment data from each of the three periods (see Turok and Edge 1999). In addition, the analysis presented here uses broad industrial categories so as to allow comparison between 1981 and 1997 for nine broad SIC categories. Data for SIC '80big' were modified so as to match the nine SIC '92big' categories, which form the basis for the analysis. This modification involved increasing the number of SIC '80big' categories from eight to nine in order to match the SIC '92big' categories. Code 6 of SIC '80big' (Transport/ communication, banking and finance) was divided into two by separating out the 'banking and finance' division of the SIC80 classification (division 8). Second, the '80big' categories of 'public administration and defence' (number 7) and 'other service industries' (number 8) were modified to form categories that correspond to the nine '92big' categories. This involved removing 'education' (class 93) and 'health' (class 95) from the '80big' 'other services' category and adding them to the existing 'public administration and defence' (class 91) '80big' category to form an equivalent category that corresponds to the '92big' category 'public administration, education and health'. The remaining elements of the '80big' 'other services' category (class numbers 92, 94, 96, 97, 98, 99) form the equivalent of the '92big' 'other services' category.

5

Entrepreneurial turns: municipal socialism and after

STEVE QUILLEY

THE report of the Urban Taskforce, chaired by Lord Rogers (1999), was symptomatic of a new progressive sensibility towards urban culture and the possibilities of city-living. This partly reflects the growing appreciation of European models of urban development, apparent in cities such as Barcelona or Amsterdam. At the same time, neither the traditional British attachment to suburbia and its post-urban successor in the form of 'edge city', are compatible with the new imperatives of sustainable development. Here the argument is that it was in Manchester, under the leadership of Graham Stringer, that this new, progressive urbanism first emerged, and where the regeneration project has been most extensively and coherently developed.[1]

Although the strategic orientation upon which Rogers' vision is premised revolves around a combination of public and private investment, and the centrality of public–private partnerships in driving forward 'the vision thing', it stands in marked contrast to the ambivalent, neoliberal attitude towards 'the urban *problem*' which dominated urban policy during the Thatcher years. As Stringer himself argued, 'the trouble is that Tories don't understand cities. They regard them as problems rather than national assets. [There is no urban policy] …just a mess of "initiatives" spread across a confused web of government departments' (Stringer 1994: 26).

During the 1980s the dominant Tory approach to the cities was characterised by a continual squeeze on public investment, combined with punitive, problem-displacing initiatives targeted at successively designated social issues (e.g. drugs, crime, race, youth unemployment) or problem areas. Clearly this was not the whole picture. Politicians such as Michael Heseltine or David Trippier periodically espoused a more integrated approach. And to some extent this was evident in remit of the urban development corporations (UDCs) which were increasingly imposed on Labour-run local authorities from the mid-1980s. However, whilst the UDCs established public–private partnership as an *a priori* of urban regeneration, they proved singularly incapable of establishing plausible guiding visions, limiting themselves largely to property development. The entrepreneurial city was a Labour-driven project, arising from an accommodation between the voluntarism of the municipal left and the ideological hegemony of the supply-side, market-based strategies imposed by central government via the development corporations. It was in Manchester that the Stringer administration was able to redirect these imposed partnerships, steering regeneration onto a broader trajectory encompassing the celebratory and experiential-identity dimensions of the 'soft city' – dimensions which are so central to the new urbanism codified by the Rogers report.

In effect, the radical councils of the 'new urban left' played midwife to the new urbanism. Some accounts have emphasised the contrast between the radicalism of the early 1980s and the urban entrepreneurialism that followed in the wake of Labour's 1987 election defeat (Seyd 1990; Lawless 1990). However, the more telling contrast is between the proactive and integrated approach to local development adopted by the new urban left and the passive managerialism which characterised the municipal Labourism of the 1960s and 1970s. When Stringer left local government to become a Labour MP in 1997, commentators remarked on his 'conversion' to Blair's New Labour – Andrew Roth (1997) quipping that he had witnessed the most dramatic volte-face by an 'old-labour leftover'. In fact, the opposite was the case. Just as there are marked continuities between Manchester's early experiment in municipal socialism and the entrepreneurial project which has since blossomed in the city, Stringer's 'cut the crap and get on with it council' (the words are those of architect-cum-urban entrepreneur Nick Johnson, quoted in Wainwright 1999) practised 'joined up thinking' well before New Labour's spin doctors coined the phrase. Far from being an old-Labour hangover, Stringer was one of the first to take a new broom to old-fashioned Labourism. As will be argued in this chapter, the project of the new urban left in Manchester during the 1980s and early 1990s in many ways anticipated Blair's New Labour.

Manchester's new urban left

The emergence of the new urban left from the late 1970s and the subsequent radicalisation of Labour councils in opposition to the Thatcher government has been well documented (Wainwright 1987; Lansley *et al.* 1989; Gyford 1985). In broad terms municipal socialism can be seen as a response from the Left to the implosion of post-war consensus politics in the face of systemic economic crisis. The movement should also be seen in terms of a positive critique of the legacies of post-war Labourism: i.e. Morrisonian nationalisation, the centralised nature of the welfare state, a pervasive statism and the undemocratic and monolithic nature of the large public bureaucracies (Boddy and Fudge 1984). Many commentators have noted the importance of the 'prodigal' generation of 1968, returning to the party and filling a vacuum left by Labour's disastrous local election results in 1967 and 1968 (Gyford 1985; Wainwright 1987). Important as it was, this political transfusion simply compounded existing trends in the party which resulted from the transformation of its working-class base. The massive decline in membership (Whiteley 1983) and the changing social composition of the party, facilitated the radicalisation of the late 1970s. At the same time as there was an influx of individual members from the expanding, public-sector service class, the hegemony of the large industrial trade unions was undermined by the erosion of Britain's manufacturing base. This unbalancing 'scissors effect' gained momentum with the savage recession of the early 1980s.

Across the Labour Party as a whole the combination of these demographic and sectoral transformations fatally undermined the social basis for the traditional municipal Labourism that had dominated local Labour politics in the post-war period. In this sense, both *New* Labour and the *new urban left* can be seen as responses to similar demographic and social imperatives. Whereas the 'new realism' of the right-wing of the Party has moved steadily towards a centrist populism and the politics of middle England, the municipal left sought to create a radical alliance with a range of interests previously ignored and unrepresented by the party: women, ethnic minorities, lesbian and gay communities, disabled people, etc. Particularly in Manchester, radical alliance politics was integral to the wider formative experience of the incoming generation.

The character of the *new urban left* in different cities was highly variable and related very much to the specificities of the local economy, demographic and sociological factors, historical development and political traditions. Witness the difference between the politics of Militant on Merseyside and the 'politics of diversity' as it was expressed in London. There were, however, a number of common threads. First, the shared critique of post-war Labourism engendered an overriding commitment to constituencies outside the formal mechanisms of the Labour Party and often the trade union movement as well. This was reflected in the affirmation of participation, decentralisation and the knowledge and understanding of ordinary people and activists over and above the expertise of state officials, council officers and professional politicians. Second, they shared at least a rhetorical commitment to *socialism*, as opposed to social-democracy and the reformist compact embodied in the Keynesian welfare state. This raised the immediate practical problem of how prefigurative strategies and a genuinely transformative politics could be reconciled with the defence of jobs, services and welfare in a capitalist economy. This fundamental tension was often glossed over by discursive formulations such as 'within and against' the market (or the state), and 'restructuring for labour' (Cochrane 1988). Third, they identified the local state as a crucial strategic site. This was primarily because Labour councils controlled large municipal authorities, whilst central government was occupied by a virulently hostile Tory administration. However, it also reflected a wider democratic impulse against the centralising, bureaucratic traditions of post-war Labourism (see Wainwright 1987).

There was a genuine commitment to redrawing the division of labour between the different levels of the state. Whereas the role of local government had traditionally been restricted to the delivery of welfare services (in areas of collective consumption such as health, housing and transport), the left now sought to expand the remit of municipal intervention to include production. This coalesced around the notion of a 'local economic strategy' (Eisenschitz and Gough 1993; Cochrane 1987, 1988, 1989a). This reconstruction of the strategic rationale for local government required a profound restructuring of local state bureaucracies, which, through inertia as much as conscious hostility, remained wedded to a more limited and conservative conception of the appropriate role for local authorities. The traditional emphasis on modest environmental improvements and the provision of land for industrial development identified private-sector developers and industrialists as *individual clients*. Local authorities were little more than 'glorified estate agents' (Cochrane and Clarke 1987: 5). It was precisely to effect this reconstruction and organisational 'perestroika' that in 1981 Sheffield City Council set up its Employment and Economic Development Department with an annual budget of £2.5 million (Lawless 1990: 139). In this way the expanded role of the local state in economic development along with the widespread acceptance of the necessity for proactive local economic strategies is an enduring legacy of the early 1980s (Eisenschitz and Gough 1993; Cochrane 1995) and can be seen as a point of continuity, linking the (failed) experiments in municipal socialism with the more recent entrepreneurial economic projects with their emphasis on place-marketing and property-led regeneration.

Manchester was a latecomer to the fold of municipal socialism. The split between the Labour Party and the wider labour movement in the city, meant that the ossification of the party from the 1960s was not countered from either within the party, or by left-wing union activists. The more heterogeneous social base in the city also meant that the proliferating identity politics and the 'new social movements' were relatively more important, as was also the case in London. As a result, the City Labour Party did lose a generation of activists with the radicalisation and mobilisation of the late 1960s (Wainwright 1987). These people only began to drift back into the party towards the end of the 1970s. The effect of this was to create a sharp division between this incoming, radical cohort and the older, labour establishment.

> They were young … they came in with a new broom and were well edu-cated compared to the old guard [who tended to be working-class], manual workers [and] didn't like the white collar trade unions. The new group came in and as far as NALGO were concerned they weren't as jaundiced as the old right had been. They didn't sort of say, 'Well, you are a white collar worker so you don't count'. (Officer, UNISON [formerly NALGO] 1994)

The left took control of the City Council in 1984 after a bitter struggle with the right-wing leadership over spending cuts that had led to a four-year period of exile on the part of thirteen rebel councillors. Over this period Stringer forged contacts with a range of community activists, feminists and anti-racist groups which became the basis for the rainbow alliance strategy as it developed in Manchester. This orientation towards marginalised social groups outside the Labour traditional move-ment provided a major plank of the subsequent municipal socialist project: radical democratisation, enfranchisement and the political empower-ment of marginalised and disadvantaged groups. This experience cast the new left project in Manchester in two very definite ways. Equal opportunities and the Equality Unit became a driving imperative, moulding strategy. At the same time, the Council became committed to decentralisation and democratisation. As Stringer put it, 'We want to bring people in and open up the town hall, ask people what they want and involve them in the decision making process. We want to involve all sorts of people who are exploited in society and provide support to these people' (*Tribune*, 19 July 1985). In this way the left in Manchester developed an extra-parliamentary base which played a functionally similar role to the trade union movement in Sheffield. The nature of this alliance was reflected in the immediate priorities of the incoming Labour group: the creation of the equal opportunities committee structure; the attempt to develop decentralised neighbourhood services; the defence of the gay community in the face of police harassment and so forth (Quilley 1997). This orientation towards issues of political process and representation was given added impetus by the fact that the authority was in no position to make effective interventions in the local economy. If the economic experiments of the GLC and the local enterprise boards were ineffective, Manchester's forays into the field were doubly so because it had hardly any resources and the rate capping and cuts were beginning to bite almost as soon as the left took control. Stringer chose to concentrate on consolidating the political alliance and effecting changes in areas where it was thought policy change could have a significant and immediate impact. However, even here, the administration quickly ran into problems. For instance, the strategy of developing decentralised neighbourhood services quickly ran aground due to financial problems.

> [It became rapidly apparent] that it wasn't going to happen. It was a very expensive model of doing it ... Brand new capital ... buildings and offices. It was very expensive ... to my mind they organised it around these capital projects and ran out of money very early on and then stopped. There was no further work on having more localised or shared approaches between departments ... Even by the time they were opening the first few ... the leadership had already changed its mind. (Officer, MCC housing department, 1995)

In reality economic strategy was effectively postponed for a future Labour government. Thus although between 1984 and 1987 the leadership advanced their own version of 'local socialism', the central theme, to which all else was subordinated, was the political struggle against Thatcher. Only after 1987, when hopes of a Labour government had been dashed, did the Council reverse these priorities in favour of a serious economic strategy (see Robson, this volume).

As a serious attempt to develop local socialism, the ostensible economic project of the left in Manchester in the early years of the Stringer administration was desultory. Town hall rhetoric conflated the historic weakness of the British economy with the specific crisis in manufacturing induced by Thatcherite monetarism on the one hand, and the deep-seated global shift which was restructuring all European economies, on the other (see Dicken 1998). Predictably the main emphasis was placed on reversing the damage inflicted by Thatcherism. With the political imperative of resistance paramount, the administration was naturally predisposed to economic analyses that emphasised policy *failure* and ascribed blame. The rhetorical assumption as to the possibility of straightforward national and local responses to the economic crisis was rooted in a political rather than economic logic. Thus the sober assessment of relative economic impotence was invariably combined with a defiant voluntarism. Reflecting the political base in the public sector, this often took the form of naive assertions of local economic sovereignty and the possibility for the Council, as the largest employer, to exert leverage on behalf of the workers and the community (for example, MCC 1984c). Stringer's declaration in November 1986 is typical: 'Manchester council rejects the defeatist Keynesian and monetarist policies that would consign the city to the economic scrap heap. That is why we are developing a radical strategy for employment' (MCC 1986). Policy documents were littered with rhetorical statements about the need for local planning and the possibility of developing prefigurative models of a socialist economy at a municipal level (for example, MCC 1984c: 2). Finally the principle of *solidarity* became a prime directive as the Council emphatically rejected the logic of competition with other cities and local authorities: 'Encouraging firms to bring jobs in from another local authority area is seen as working against local government solidarity and as helping private capital to play authorities off against each other' (MCC 1984c: 2). The capital–labour relation became the axiomatic dimension of political struggle and the focus for putative economic intervention. Thus between 1984 and 1987 strategic thinking subordinated economics to politics; the overriding priority was to use the Council as a base for the wider struggle against the Tories and capitalism more generally. Until the early 1980s, even fairly left-wing councils talked about partnership in terms of a tripartite corporatism, which included the private sector. But just as the Tories rejected corporatism and redefined partnership exclusively in terms of private-sector involvement in urban regeneration (eventually marginalising even local government), so the municipal-left sought to exclude the private sector, whilst bringing in new community and minority interests. Between 1984 and 1987 the private sector was effectively abandoned as a *partner*, and redefined as the *opposition*. For example, in the strategy document *Work: A Strategy for Employment*, the section entitled 'The Private Sector' talked only in terms of giving resources to those 'fighting to preserve jobs threatened with changing work patterns' and expanding the worker-controlled segment of the Manchester economy by backing co-operatives (MCC 1986b: 2).

In terms of economic strategy, Manchester's experiment with municipal socialism achieved very little, certainly compared to Liverpool's housing programme or the more developed local strategies pursued in Sheffield. The City Council started late and had little time to build up an effective economic development department with the staff and resources to develop a strategy. It was not until 1986 that an internal reorganisation along these lines was started when Steve Machin was brought in from Sheffield as deputy director of economic development under Michael Moore. At the same time, the left-leaning economic think-tank, the Centre for Local Economic Strategies, had been established in the city. With a Labour Government in prospect, the situation looked favourable. However it was not to be.

> The vision in 1986 was for a restructuring of the economic development department along the lines of Sheffield, with a whole load of teams. The employment plan for the city [was the first step in this direction]. [It was set up] in the expectation of a Labour Government ... At the time they imagined 60-70 people coming into the department, which would have been a massive transformation in the political considerations of the city. But all of that was jettisoned when the Tories won the election. (Officer, MCC economic initiatives group, 1994)

Much general policy was developed but as elsewhere little attention was paid to restructuring the institutional mechanisms of management and implementation (see Cooper 1994). The result was policy indigestion but little action. And in fact as *economic strategy*, the various policies and reports were often not taken that seriously.

> There was a half-hearted attempt [at an economic strategy] in the early 80s, when they had this economic development department ... which failed almost as soon as it had taken off. Steve Machin went round in circles ... *It was good propaganda* ... in terms of the press. When companies were closing down there would be a blurb on it. But we never took it very seriously. (Official, GMB union, 1994)

In the end the elevation of political resistance as the overriding principle governing the agenda of the local authority meant that even service provision suffered.

> It was completely oppositional to the Thatcher government. Part of what they were saying was right but the housing service was lousy and conditions for tenants were [terrible] ... they were ill-treated. They didn't get any service or maintenance done. (Officer, MCC housing department, 1995)

Entrepreneurial turns?

It is widely acknowledged that the Conservative's third successive victory at the general election of June 1987 pulled the rug from under the experiment in municipal socialism (Lansley *et al.* 1989; see also Cooper 1994). At the same time as financial and political constraints were pushing the left on to the defensive, there was an increasing recognition that local socialism in practice had experienced serious problems. Policy indigestion and problems of 'ideological steerage' and bureaucratic diversion greatly reduced the practical import of a whole range of interventions that looked very radical on paper (see Cooper 1994). Stringer was learning these lessons in effective corporate management, but in the context of securing effective union acquiescence to a political U-turn, rather than advancing the cause of local socialism which was seen to be a lost cause. Over the next three years, the administration began to espouse a new entrepreneurial model of development (Table 5.1).

In place of outright resistance to the Tories, the City Labour Party started down the road towards critical co-operation. Eventually this was to involve active co-operation with local partners in the private sector, the acceptance of a property-led strategy of urban regeneration, co-operation with the government-imposed Central Manchester Development Corporation and Training and Enterprise Council, and participation in competitive urban redevelopment schemes such as City Challenge, City Pride and Single Regeneration Budget initiatives.

> They see that the only way forward, given the changes that have happened in the economy, given the nature of the local economic interests, and Labour's failure to deliver at national level – is to try and enter what are euphemistically called partnership agreements ... They don't express it like that ... but that is what they are doing. (Officer, MCC chief executive's department, 1994)

For left-wing critics, the most reprehensible aspect of this apparent volte-face involved the abandonment of the principle of solidarity as a prime directive. This was most obvious in the place-marketing strategy which was so central to the successive Olympic/Commonwealth bids and the *City Pride* initiative, as well as participation in the competitive bidding process associated with schemes such as *City Challenge*.

> [Graham Stringer's passion] is to get Labour ministers to admit that the word competition exists. He has had quite a hard time from within the Labour party for some of the stuff we have done. But we are willing to go into competition with other cities because you have to. It is the only way

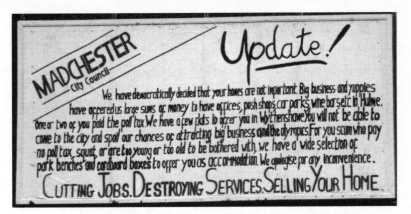

Plate 6 An alternative manifesto? Some Hulme residents make their opinions felt about Manchester's 1987 'entrepreneurial turn'

forward … Of course [there have to be losers] but unfortunately the rest of the world does it [and] unless we jump in and compete with them we are going to lose anyway. (Officer, MCC marketing department, 1995)

Where the municipal left had sought emphatically to embrace new constituencies among disadvantaged and marginalised groups in society, the effect of the emerging entrepreneurial strategy was to embrace 'new realism' by the back door (Beynon *et al.* 1993). The emphasis on partnership foregrounded the role of the private sector, whilst the emerging preoccupation with culture, leisure and the upbeat presentation of a cosmopolitan, post-industrial city appealed to the city's middle classes. The new political project, like the economic vision in which it was rooted, was essentially centrist. It amounted to the construction of a new, local consensus politics, but a consensus that is exclusive and which, at least to some extent, now denies the special claims of minority groups.

After 1987 there was much less mention of decentralising power and enfranchising the most disadvantaged. For instance the previously high profile Lesbian and Gay Sub-committees were wound up and absorbed into the powerful Policy and Resources Committee chaired personally by Stringer (Quilley 1997). Likewise democratisation and distributional issues have been progressively displaced from the strategic mindset. The new order of priorities, exemplified by the Olympic bid process can be summed up as growth first, welfare later (Cochrane *et al.* 1996).

Finally, Stringer's new project for Manchester rested on a very different and perhaps more realistic understanding of the nature of Manchester's economic crisis. In adopting the credo of the *entrepreneurial city*, the new

Table 5.1 Municipal socialism and the entrepreneurial city

	Municipal socialism	Entrepreneurial city
Relationship between politics and economics	Economics subordinated to the politics of resistance	Socialist political project subordinated to the economics of selling Manchester in the national/European economy and securing discretionary funding
Political project	Politics of radical alliance – expressed through a commitment to equal opportunities (women, ethnic minorities, lesbians and gay men, etc.)	Reorientation towards the political centre – local version of New Realism – appeal to middle classes on the basis of economic competence and getting things done ('making it happen'): cultural agenda of 'city living', emphasis on service sector, Olympic bid, flagship projects, city-centre housing projects for professional classes, etc.
	Partnership as 'class-based political alliance' organised in opposition to both the private sector and the national government	Partnership as a cross-class growth coalition rooted in a strong (chauvinist?) city identity. Acceptance of central role for the private sector
Understanding of and responses to economic crisis	Emphasis on local strategies as exemplars for future Labour government	Emphasis on local agency and economic self-determination
	Local strategies formally oriented towards developing a more self-sufficient economic base *but* substantively directed towards ameliorating the social crisis and its impact on the most disadvantaged groups	Partnership as a 'growth coalition' and a spur to endogenous economic development
		City-region competing in a European/global system, for investment (and discretionary funding)

	Acknowledgement of global/external forces beyond the control of local policy *but* down played by political emphasis on the culpability of Thatcherism.	
Orientation to urban policy	Emphasis on social aims and community development Urban policy as an extension of the welfare state, dealing with the symptoms of economic crisis Political agenda for democratisation and bringing excluded groups into the political process. Part of wider struggle against the Tory government	Urban renewal seen primarily as a vehicle to relocate the city higher up a putative European urban hierarchy: emphasis on property-led regeneration, flagship developments, the centrality of place marketing, etc. Elitist orientation to 'key player' politics (legitimacy of conflicting claims assessed according to the relative status of key players)
Orientation to manufacturing	Strong rhetorical commitment to the manufacturing base and the need for (neo-Fordist) reorganisation and modernisation. Practice limited to monitoring decline	Commitment to a 'post-industrial script' and willingness to abandon manufacturing as the necessary foundation for the regional economy
Style of decision making	Orientation towards process. Participative, strong emphasis on democratisation, decentralisation and consultation. Rhetoric of community-based policies and 'bottom up' policies	Orientation to end results and getting things done. Executive driven. Greatly increased political authority at the centre 'Charismatic' authority. New corporate slogan: *Making it Happen* replaces *Defending Jobs and Improving Services*
Relation to other cities and communities	Commitment to principle of solidarity between cities and communities.	Acceptance of institutionalised competition between cities (e.g. for discretionary funding in the case of *City Pride*) – and the inevitability of losers as well as winners

project arguably shows a more acute understanding of the 'dog eat dog' reality of globalisation; that neither local strategy nor the nation-state could be relied on to protect cities from the vagaries of the increasingly disembedded circuits of capital accumulation. The new approach to local strategy foregrounds *competition* between cities on the basis of cross-class growth (read grant) coalitions organised around particular places (Jones and Ward 1998). This mantra recurs endlessly in the Manchester script, for example, 'What attributes does Manchester possess or can develop which can attract investment, which distinguish us from competitor cities?' (MCC 1992: 5).

However, it would not be accurate to see this reorientation of the left project in Manchester as simply a product of Labour's defeat in 1987. There was a genuine feeling among both councillors and officers of policy indigestion, and that the 'panoply of Community Development and Equality Units wasn't having a great impact on people, [that the structures were not representative] ... and that they deterred ordinary people' (Officer, City Pride initiative, 1994). More generally, the desire to achieve something concrete for the city predisposed the administration to move away from their initially partisan orientation in favour of a more practical approach. As local politics became less ideological and more pragmatic, the understanding of 'partnership' was increasingly extended to include local authorities that previously had an indifferent or actively hostile attitude towards each other. The consensus around urban entrepreneurialism, which developed across the conurbation, and to some extent the region, became a vehicle through which the Manchester authority was able to exert a degree of hegemony in terms of setting the wider agenda. The most important aspect of this was an acquiescence on the part of the other authorities as to the strategic importance of the city centre. Co-operation in the City Pride initiative as well as the successive bids for the Olympic and Commonwealth games exemplified this new pragmatic spirit of partnership.

> [When I first came to Manchester in 1987] I discovered that the [Manchester–Salford Partnership] was a bit of a misnomer. There was very little contact ... and bad blood at a political level. [But since then things have got better.] It was at a time when there was a bit of a thaw politically in the relationship between the two councils. [Manchester was realising] there was little to be gained by direct confrontation ... we had to look at different strategies ... Part of that was about beginning to work with other local partners ... other local authorities but private sector interests as well. I think Manchester was becoming less ideological and less pragmatic. (Officer, MCC City Pride initiative, 1995)

Another marked change can be described in terms of an *executive shift* and a reassertion of the managerial prerogative. This transition is implicit in the change of slogan, which took place not long after 1987: from *Defending Jobs, Improving Services* to *Making it Happen*.[2] Whereas the municipal socialist project foregrounded the political process, and the importance of democratisation and questions of access ('opening up the town hall'), the new approach emphasised concrete results.

> [There is a] big change because at the start the new left was incredibly process oriented. The whole thing was about creating new channels between [the people and the Labour administration] procedures, equal opportunities ... That seems to have been thrown out. [Now it is a case of] let's get it done ... let's not go through all this process rubbish. Let's just get what it is that we want ... The emphasis has changed as the Council has become prepared to work in partnership ... in order to get things done ... So that immediately alienates and disadvantages the voluntary organisations whose culture doesn't really fit in. (Officer, MCC housing department, 1995)

This new charismatic style and the reassertion of the managerial prerogative was integral to the new economic project, which placed a premium on co-operation between local political and business elites and the achievement of a limited number of very concrete goals in the form of flagship projects such as the Millennium Stadium or the Bridgewater Concert Hall (see Table 5.1). This partly reflected a split between these flagship developments and traditional municipal initiatives entirely controlled by the Council, which 'still go through the processes with the range of consultative procedures'. In contrast the new partnership projects, which straddle institutional lines were, and are, insulated from the democratic process.

> Anything that is more within the broader city [e.g. Airport, Olympic bid etc.] ... has consultation of a different type [which] tends to be with the private sector or other public sector bodies such as UDCs. There is a very difficult line in that the council spends a lot of time getting other people to pay for things it wants to do. When it does that ... and people pay, and you have to play by a certain number of their rules ... and there are tensions, and things do get lost internally. (Officer, MCC marketing department, 1995)

Clearly there was an element of 'he who pays the piper calls the tune' in the new partnership mechanisms.

This also reflected Stringer's increasingly unassailable political position. A former senior officer implied that the democratic process was at a premium when Stringer needed the support of his local party and the unions to implement cuts in Council expenditure.

If you think about the darkest days when they were doing the cuts in expenditure in 1986 and 1987 ... when the internal processes were highly democratic ... So that is a very significant change. But it will be based upon Stringer's judgement of how safe he is within the Labour group ... I guess what you are recognising now is no more than that ... He is now safe. (Former senior officer, MCC, 1994)

The assertion of control, which accompanied this *executive shift*, was not limited to the internal politics of the Labour group. Stringer also asserted his personal (charismatic) authority over the administrative hierarchy within the council bureaucracy.

During the middle and late 1980s the politicians gained a reputation for chopping Chief Officers. [They didn't want them] to feel secure ... To some extent it was the making of Stringer in 1987 ... to get a grip. [*Q: And has he 'got a grip'?*] Oh yes! ... even to the point of him being the one person for whole periods of time who decides about filling posts. For an organisation the size of the council that is one hell of an overview to try and have ... In 1992 they [stopped making] any promises [about job security and no com-pulsory redundancies] and during that time he was the person who decided everything about every post. (Officer, MCC housing department, 1995)

The entrepreneurial strategy, which gathered momentum from 1989, was broadly similar to that which has taken root in many cities around the world (see Harvey 1989: Parkinson 1989). The new discourse of economic development is suffused with positivity and the voluntarist understanding that a city's economic fate is far from sealed, but can be swayed decisively, by the action or inaction of local elites (see Holden, this volume). But it also rests on a more implicit understanding of the limits to economic sovereignty in the era of globalisation. Thus in Manchester, 'there is a strategy that is partly informed by an under-standing of what we can't do anymore' (Officer, MCC economic initiatives group, November 1994). '*What we can't do*' is to develop integrated industrial policies, based upon indicative planning and sectoral interventions aimed at changing the underlying structure and balance of the economic base – with the support of a strongly inter-ventionist national state. *What can be done* is limited to supply-side, infra-structural initiatives, place-marketing and more or less overt competition with cities deemed to be adjacent or of comparable ranking in a putative league of European cities. These are the parameters within which the new entrepreneurialism has been developed.

In essence what happened in Manchester was that the politicians accepted these parameters and determined, on that basis, to get the best possible deal for the city in terms of attracting both inward investment and grant-aid. Setting out explicitly to garner inspiration from cities such as Baltimore and Barcelona, local policy-makers began to think in terms of a package of measures which focused in the first instance on the rehabilitation and re-imaging of Manchester as a major European city-regional capital. In so far as it entails a common language and conceptual vocabulary, one could talk about a *script* – shared and adhered to by actors involved in all aspects of urban regeneration: a script which crosses institutional and political lines. For instance city planning officers talk about doing their *spiel*: 'We are in the business of re-imaging the city. The *copy* goes something like: Manchester is a major European city, it has cosmopolitan qualities' (Officer, MCC planning department, March 1994). As actors become familiar with the script, it becomes relatively easy to juggle the various components in order to generate glossy reports and documents, tailored to the needs of specific initiatives and funding applications. A council officer described this process: 'It is more like a whirlwind, like being punch-drunk. [We produce report after report] and in the end you don't know really what you are doing. It is like a word game ... mixing all the buzz phrases up together ... and producing another piece of paper' (Member, MCC, February 1995). According to the *Manchester script*, the city has been reborn as a post-modern, post-industrial and cosmopolitan city, standing in the Europe's 'premier league'. New Manchester is a vibrant and culturally diverse place to live, and well connected to take advantage of the emerging information economy.

Continuities and caveats

Looking back on the achievements of Graham Stringer's new left administration, it is tempting to present the city's development during the 1980s into two phases: a short and rather tepid experiment in municipal socialism followed by a rather longer and more successful period of 'city chauvinism'. The watershed falls unambiguously in June 1987, with Thatcher's third victory at the general election representing the political defeat of not just the Labour party, but also the municipal left alternative within the Labour party. However, another reading of this story would emphasise the continuities (see Robson, this volume). Stringer's role is best seen as that of a *Janus* – in the sense of a bridge connecting two distinct periods of development. His leadership spanned a series of transitions in the nature of the local Labour Party, in the role of local government in local economic development and in the nature of the city; from municipal-Labourism and a traditional industrial city with a specifically working-class, northern English identity to a more hetero-geneous and less class-bound politics in a self-consciously metropolitan city with a more European perspective. Another connotation of the Janus metaphor is that of being fickle or two-faced, which perhaps fits the sense of betrayal felt by former comrades and fellow travellers on the left.

> I couldn't believe it ... I'm astounded at the political change – how far it has gone! The swing across the pendulum! It was incredible because the attack then came on us. [The Council] became anti-trade union! (Official, GMB union, 1994)

However, an interpretation which foregrounds a process of apostasy and 'sell out' not only ignores the enormity of the constraints facing local government during the 1980s, but also underplays the significant transformations which have actually taken place – not least in relation to the role of local government. Cochrane (1989a, 1995) argues that interpretations of the municipal socialist experiments of the early 1980s overemphasise the subsequent 'transition to partnership' as a political u-turn (e.g. Seyd 1990; Lawless 1990). This obscures strong continuities between the two periods. The shift towards a partnership model of development may be better understood 'as a necessary maturing and consolidation in the process of transition from theories to practices within the local government system' (Cochrane 1989b: 137). The endur-ing legacy of the socialist experiment was to legitimise and underwrite a paradigmatic expansion of the role of the local state in developing and implementing, proactive local economic strategies. The creation of the Centre for Local Economic Strategies in Manchester in 1986 came at a time when the radical councils were on the point of mounting a full-scale retreat from many of the rhetorical positions they had taken up during the early 1980s. But, at the same time, it can also be read as the culmina-tion of a process whereby the theory and practice of comprehensive local strategies started to gain broad acceptance with mainstream authorities (Eisenschitz and Gough 1993). In this light, Cochrane argues that the key break in Sheffield and elsewhere came at the start of the decade. It was a break with *municipal labourism*: 'The break needs to be defined differently, not so much in terms which stress the rise of local socialism, as in others which point to a move away from the traditional approach emphasising the delivery of services within the welfare state, towards one which more clearly and explicitly recognises the economic as a legitimate concern (even a major concern) for local government or local states' (Cochrane 1995: 20).

This interpretation certainly helps make sense of Manchester's experience, particularly in relationship to the management of a number of larger economic projects inherited by the incoming Stringer administration (i.e. the planned expansion of the airport, the Castlefield redevelopment, the Olympic bid and the Metro link). These core projects represented a continuing focus for the City throughout the 1980s. But at the same time they were always kept outside the purview and rhetorical clamour of socialist economics, and under the direct control of Stringer himself.

> The airport, the Olympic bid and so forth were always part of the Policy and Resources Committee, the chair of which was the leader. [In contrast] economic development matters … were part of the Economic Development Committee. Now it suited the leading members of the administration to retain those matters as part of the P&R Committee, because that way they retained control of the agenda … It is a common complaint among members of … other departments, that they rarely find out or get involved in matters that relate to the Airport and the Olympics. They are treated as being sufficiently important to be the personal projects of a number of leading members … and by dealing with it [like this] they avoid any kind of interference. (Officer, MCC chief executive's department, 1994)

These flagship developments relate to the 'hard city' of property-led regeneration and infrastructure. However, perhaps a more telling area of continuity relates to the 'soft city' and the way in which the hype has built on Mancunian civic pride and reinvented it to accommodate the city's iconic role as a vibrant leading centre of popular culture. Their formative experiences outside the mainstream Labour movement made the new generation of Labour councillors tuned in and sympathetic to the importance and power of cultural identity and pluralism. The most important example of this relates to the Gay Village. The early staunch defence of the gay scene around Canal Street from the incursions of prejudicial and frequently violent policing created the space for the emergence of the Gay Village. The subsequent commercialisation of the scene (though unwelcome for some within the gay community) provided a fulcrum for the enormous success of the post-Manchester club scene. It also provided an exemplar for the 'village in the city' ethos which now dominates urban residential developments in the city. Gay men, in particular, were the first to cultivate Manchester's invented city-living tradition by taking advantage of the warehouse apartments around Sackville Street.

In this and other ways Manchester has become a kind of a model for many other UK cities, and the city-centre regeneration shows little sign of slowing down. All of the principles and motifs which find expression in the new progressive urbanism of the Rogers report, are to be found in embryo at least, in the vision followed by the Stringer administration in the period after 1987.

Notes

1 This chapter is a revised version of 'Manchester first: from municipal socialism to the entrepreneurial city', *International Journal of Urban and Regional Research* (1999) 24, 3, 601–25. The author acknowledges Blackwell Publishers for granting him permission to draw upon this original piece.
2 The new corporate logo does not even contain anything that might indicate that it refers to a local authority. The dynamic entity in question is *Manchester* rather than Manchester City Council.

6

Olympic dreams:
visions of partnership

———◆◆◆———

ALLAN COCHRANE, JAMIE PECK AND ADAM TICKELL

MANCHESTER is very often held up as the very epitome of entrepreneurialism and dynamism in urban governance, as one of the proving grounds of what has been labelled the 'new urban politics'. Indeed, the city has been the site of frenzied public-private partnership formation in recent years, while, as the previous chapter demonstrated, both the character and the content of local-government strategies have in many ways been transformed since the 1980s. To be sure, this has been a complex process, and one in which there have been notable continuities as well as marked breaks with the past, but it is difficult to escape the conclusion that over the last two decades Manchester has witnessed a dramatic shift in the means and ends of urban politics. More than any single episode in this long process of transformation, perhaps, the city's bids for the Olympic Games stand out as crucial moments. The second Olympic bid in particular – the focus of this chapter – came to symbolise and to crystallise many of the new urban-political forms in an especially vivid fashion.[1] And political change was not a mere side-effect of the Olympic bidding process in the city. On the contrary, the tranformation of decision-making structures and governance systems was very much part and parcel of what key 'players' in the city would refer to as the Olympic *process*.

One of the defining features of the Olympic process was the distinctive role played by the private sector, especially the charismatic presence of Bob Scott, the bid's leader, who in the course of the city's efforts to win the Games would earn the moniker 'Mr Manchester' (*Independent on Sunday*, 3 January 1993). While at a number of levels the key innovation here was the extensive incorporation of business leaders – and the business 'agenda' more generally – into the city's governance structures, at the same time it would be quite wrong to represent this as some spontaneous manifestation of dynamic 'business leadership'. In fact, as we will show, the story is more complex than this, reflecting as it does a series of wider and more 'structural' changes in the nature of urban responses to globalisation and in the restructuring of the British state during the 1990s. But this is to run ahead of the story. Let us begin at the beginning.

> Bob Scott came to Manchester 25 years ago as a theatrical impresario. He dreamt of the curtain going up on the Manchester Olympics ... Like a good entrepreneur, he understands hype, or as he puts it, how to sit in an office with a secretary pretending to be an institution. (David Dimbleby, introducing Bob Scott on *Question Time*, BBC TV, 17 March 1994)

> The Olympic bid was a people's dream, not just a dream of the affluent, and that's what we need to hold on to. Partnership is where we started and partnership is where we'll end up. Nobody can look at Manchester and say it isn't a city on the move, as long as it holds its nerve and guards against provincial complacency. (Bob Scott, quoted in *Business Life*, February 1994: viii)

The central objective of this chapter is to explore the institutional and political preconditions of Bob Scott's fabled attempt to 'sit in an office with a secretary pretending to be an institution', to ask how he was able to do this, and why others in the local power structure were inclined to join in the pretence. But, with the help of evidence from Manchester, we also consider some of the wider claims made about the local politics of globalisation – particularly questioning the extent to which local business interests are able to take the political lead through the formation of 'growth coalitions'. The chapter starts by examining the construction of the Olympic coalition, asking which interests were – in the words of Manchester's first Olympic bid slogan – 'driving the dream', before turning to an evaluation of what such Olympic (bidding) games have meant for Manchester.

Driving the dream

In September 1993, Manchester failed in its second attempt to host the Olympic Games. The political imagery surrounding Manchester's Olympic bids involved a very clear identification with a singly dynamic personality as leader, untainted by the traditional hurly-burly of electoral and party politics. In the process, Bob Scott, the private-sector chair of Manchester 2000, the city's bid committee, in many ways became the personification of Manchester's Olympic strategy and indeed of the city itself. The nine years which Scott had spent in pursuit of the Games had seen him emerge as 'the man who gave Manchester a vision of gold' (*Business Life*, February 1994). 'There may have been many helpers', the *Daily Mail* observed, 'but Manchester's bid owed everything to Scott' (24 September 1993). The charismatic Scott undeniably played a key role in building Manchester's Olympic coalition, establishing himself as an indispensable figure in the city's partnership politics, one whose 'championing of Manchester' has been according to Law 'near inspirational' (1994: 230). In recognition of this personal contribution, Scott was knighted in the New Year's honours list of 1994.

As a schoolboy, Scott apparently described his hobby as 'being in charge' (*Daily Star*, 14 September 1993). In Manchester's Olympic bidding process, 'being in charge' meant drawing together and energising a private-sector-led coalition of the city's movers and shakers, those with interests not *only* in sport but also in urban regeneration. A principal objective of what became known as the 'Regeneration Games' was, Scott explained, 'rebuilding one of the great cities of Western Europe' (*Guardian*, 24 September 1993). This process would occur both literally and metaphorically: in bricks and mortar terms, the city secured infrastructure spending to the tune of £200 million (approaching half of which came from central government sources), while equally significant benefits were to flow from the less tangible legacy of the bidding process, measured in terms of a more positive image and heightened self-confidence. The *Daily Express* explained that there was 'a renewed sense of pride in the city' (24 September 1993), while a *Guardian* editorial reflected

> [I]t's not all about winning. Manchester lost the bid, but regained economic self-confidence in the process ... Manchester's motives were economic – the regeneration of a post-industrial city-economy. Success would have been sweet, but failure can be a catalyst for continued change ... No one knows a sure-fire formula for regenerating a city, but it has got something to do with clusters of creativity forming themselves into a critical mass to provide an infrastructure which attracts industry, services and the arts. The surge in enterprise behind Manchester's bid has already set that process into motion. In preparing its Olympic gamesmanship, Manchester has had a reflected glimpse of its nineteenth century pre-eminence. It rather likes what it sees. (24 September 1993)

This analogy with the nineteenth century may have been stretched, but it was frequently evoked by those involved to define their approach, often referring to the Victorian 'Manchester Men', those civic leaders who saw no distinction between the interests of business and those of the city (see Tickell and Peck 1996). Yet the popular emphasis on the role of Bob Scott as charismatic leader in developing and leading the bid coalition also suggested a rather more contemporary set of images, drawn from the US management literature and the search for urban 'movers and shakers' (Christie *et al.* 1991; Peck 1995). Stories of how Bob Scott first conceived of, and then constructed, Manchester's Olympic coalition reached almost apocryphal proportions. According to the version of the story told by Scott himself, the initial impetus came from a report on Radio 4's *Today* programme in February 1985 that Mrs Thatcher was in favour of bringing the Olympics to Britain. 'The assumption', Scott recalled, 'was London [but] I thought "This is ridiculous ... the one place in Britain where you can't hold the Games is London"' (*Guardian*, 6 September 1993). His mind made up, Scott contacted the editor of the *Manchester Evening News* promising that a Manchester bid, complete with bid committee, would be in place by the time of the day's first edition. Scott then 'rang six or seven of the great and good, and asked them to join the committee' (Bob Scott, quoted in *Business Life*, February 1994: viii). By that very evening, Manchester was reportedly 'going for gold'.

A second key aspect of the process was that from the outset, Manchester's bid was presented as private-sector led: in the view of the consultants to Manchester 2000, KPMG Management Consulting (1993: 1), it was 'a private sector initiative which has secured strong public sector support'. According to one (private-sector) member of the bid committee,

> [The Olympic bid was] a totally private sector-led initiative ... We've had to play a rather more sophisticated role, of combining the two sides of the public sector – a fairly strong socialist local authority with a fairly strong Conservative central government – even more reason in our situation for the private sector to lead. We've always been in the lead, I think. (1995)

The Manchester bid was soon being compared favourably with the more traditionally corporatist approach of the rival, Birmingham-based bid. While Birmingham's Olympic bid committee had been 'full of city dignitaries and councillors, ... Manchester's, as Bob Scott put it, contained "players who feel easy with million dollar games, achievers not talkers"' (Hill 1992: 106; although see Howell 1990). Indeed, after Birmingham's weak showing in the contest for the 1992 Games (in Lausanne in 1986, where it achieved fifth place in the IOC vote behind Barcelona), Manchester was to wrest the mantle of the British bid city from Birmingham. At the meeting which decided in Manchester's favour, it was claimed that Manchester's UDCs could lever £2 billion of investment during the run-up to the 1996 Games (*The Times*, 20 May 1988), and the British Olympic Association (BOA) was deeply impressed by Scott's vision of a Los Angeles-style 'private enterprise Games' (Hill 1992).

Although Manchester failed in its bid for the 1996 Games (in Tokyo in 1990, where it was placed third behind Atlanta), it retained the position of British bid city for the 2000 Games. To do so, however, it was necessary to fend off a poorly-organised counter-bid from London under the leadership of former Olympic athlete, and subsequent Conservative MP, Sebastian Coe (see Hill 1992; LOCB 1991). Now well organised, professional and highly knowledgeable, the Manchester bid committee was considered to be much better placed to pitch for the 2000 Games. Not only had the committee become acquainted with the shadowy geopolitics of the IOC, it had also established itself within Manchester at the apex of the city's new governance structure, sitting atop the hierarchy of new business and 'partnership' networks which had flourished over recent years (Peck and Tickell 1995). The core of this elite network, known locally as the 'Manchester Mafia', was strongly represented on the Olympic bid committee.

> Today, the same names crop up on virtually every committee and board, the Plowrights, Gil Thompsons, Stringers, Glesters, Scotts, etc. These men – and they are all men – are highly successful and very powerful. They know people in high places. They have clout. In the late 20th century that is how things get done. The Manchester Labour Party swims with the tide, it is part of the 'establishment' ... Local people don't have a say in Metrolink [the light rail system], the Olympics or Trafford Park [Development Corporation] – to name but a few – except through their (outvoted) councillors. (Editorial, *City Life*, 18 August 1993: 4)

> You see the links [between local business leaders]. They're on Bob's Olympic committee. Some of them are on the City of Drama committee. They're on the Hulme Regeneration committee ... You don't really know about party politics, [although] you could have a good idea ... There is a sort of collective ambition to do something for the area that is noticeable ... and generally put your shoulders back a bit, and stop walking around looking depressed. There's not much future in that ... [The Olympic bid] was a deliberate attempt to develop a chauvinist attitude. To stand up and stick your chin out and say, 'To hell with it. There is a problem, but there's no point in just going on being pessimistic about it, let's have a go'. (Olympic bid committee member, private sector, 1994)

In both the popular understanding and elite explanations, then, the Olympic bid symbolised a fundamental shift in local politics. With its new 'collective ambition', the business community had become more organised and more purposeful. The new circuits of power in the business community, however, were not linked to the traditional institutional bases of the Chamber of Commerce or the regional branch of the Confederation of British Industry, but instead were to be found within and between a range of organisations at or near the fringes of the state (such as the conurbation's six TECs, two UDCs, the East Manchester Partnership, the North West Business Leadership Team, and the Olympic bid committee). Scott's self-image was one of a trail-blazer, (honest) broker and deal-maker. To borrow a phrase later adopted by the City Council as its new slogan, the new politics he symbolised had to be about, *'Making it happen'*. This was portrayed as a commonsense and apolitical approach:

> I'm really a bit of an outsider, in a way that people who manipulate the Establishment often are. I think John Major is an outsider, and Mrs Thatcher and Edward Heath were. (Bob Scott, quoted in *Business Life*, February 1994: viii).

> Twenty years ago … we were all more public-sector minded really … we'd rather been scooped up into nanny's arms I think at that point. I think that's what's different now … We have lived through a revolution. I think Mrs Thatcher was the person who led that revolution, and I think she did free certain private sector forces, you know, to show the way and to encourage the managers to manage. (Olympic bid committee member, private sector, 1994)

This necessitated a renegotiation of the boundaries between the public and private sectors in terms of everything from committee compositions to project accounting, from discourses of development to goals of policy. It involved local actors on both sides of the public–private divide exploring what was possible in the new era of local authority marginalisation. As Scott put it, 'learning how the public and private sector work [was] like playing with Lego' (quoted in *Business Life*, February 1994: viii). As with all games, however, there had to be losers as well as winners, and in the 'power player politics' of contemporary Manchester political voice has become increasingly restricted to a narrow, male-dominated elite of '*real* people … *real* decision-makers' (Olympic bid committee member, private sector). The plethora of new 'partnership' bodies which emerged in Manchester during the last decade or so – from centrally-imposed quangos through self-selecting business lobby groups to the more nebulous 'Manchester Mafia' – have clearly exhibited a variety of institutional forms while pursuing a range of specific objectives, but in their *modus operandi* they all implied a critique of traditional local power structures. On the one hand, they have sought to embody alternatives to (or at least a reaction to) the conservative and slow-moving Establishment, instead favouring more fluid networks of brash, new-moneyed players – the 'Disestablishment' (Lloyd 1988; Paxman 1991; Jacques 1994). On the other hand, they represented a fundamental critique of (or again reaction to) traditional conceptions of bureaucracy, democracy and the local welfare state (Cochrane 1993; Peck and Tickell 1995). Bob Scott and his colleagues saw themselves breaking the (political) mould and rewriting the (bureaucratic) rules:

> One of the problems in British life is the bogus antagonism between the Labour party in local government and the Conservative party in central government. Actually an effective leader can talk to either, and be an important conduit between people who otherwise can't engage in dialogue. The most important role is that of the person who leaves the trench first and goes over the top between these great battalions. If the leadership isn't talking to each other, you have to enable them to do so. (Bob Scott, quoted in *Business Life*, February 1994: viii)

With unmistakable neo-liberal undertones, the rhetoric of freeing private-sector initiative and reclaiming the right to manage – in this case, the right to *manage the city* – is clearly central to both the self-image and the public representation of the new urban politics. The *image* is one of nimble-footed, goal-oriented business leaders coaxing and cajoling their new-found partners – the tradition-bound Establishment elites, the dogma-bound local politician, and the rule-bound bureaucrat. The movers and shakers of the business community are represented as the energisers of a tired and complacent local polity.

Making it happen

But such readings, infused as they are with business machismo, are wont to underplay the crucial *facilitative* role of the restructured public sector. Clearly, it takes two to quango (Robinson *et al.* 1994) and the factor which is persistently underemphasised in private-sector accounts of the new urban politics is the shifting orientation of local government and the wider dynamics of central–local relations (which have helped to create a political space of unelected local governance within which business can operate) (Cochrane 1993; Peck 1995). It has in fact been these developments which have been instrumental in opening up at the local level the discursive and institutional spaces into which business elites have stepped. It is significant, for example, that despite the presentation of the Manchester Olympic bid as unequivocally business-led (or even Scott-led), it was in fact predicated upon a fragile alliance of local institutional interests underpinning the City Council.

To highlight the emergence of self-confident and self-conscious businessmen and business organisations, significant though these may be, underestimates the degree to which they have had to act in partner-ship and alongside existing public-sector institutions. The groundswell of political consciousness and activity which became evident in the business community after the late 1980s was a product of the ways in which the private sector organised to take advantage both of its new-found leverage over local authority priorities and of the newly available positions of influence on TECs, UDCs and other 'partnership' bodies. Even two of the private-sector members of the bid committee, Peter Hadfield and James Grigor, who so impressed the BOA were there by virtue of their respective positions as chairs of the Trafford and Central Manchester Development Corporations. The structuring precondition in Manchester's new urban politics was not Bob Scott's shaving mirror revelation but the changing stance of the City Council, particularly after 1987 (see Quilley, this volume). The 1987 General Election was the crucial tipping point for the City Council that until that time had been pursuing a municipal socialist strategy (see Robson 1988; Beynon *et al.* 1993). In comparison to its neighbours in Sheffield and Liverpool, however, Manchester's strategy was at this time rather more rhetorical than concrete. While Manchester used the *language* of municipal social-ism, and like other cities did heavily rely upon a Labour victory in the 1987 General Election, the City Council had been more cautious in terms of resource commitments and organisational changes. Accord-ingly, Manchester was able to respond to the return of the Conser-vatives through a rapid political reorientation – with the help of leading officers as well as senior councillors – which (perhaps grudgingly) espoused the local boosterism promulgated by the third Thatcher government.

After 1987, the City quietly dropped its slogan that made a rhetorical commitment to 'Defending jobs, improving services' and somewhat reluctantly embraced the politics of trickle-down by 'Making it happen'. As a senior councillor explained, the Olympics were, within the Council at least, seen within this context:

The City Council is very clear about its aims for the welfare of the people of Manchester. We would like to have better education, better social services, better welfare services, altogether. Unfortunately, the government have taken a great deal of grant away from Manchester, so that means we can't provide as high a level of service as we once did. On the other side, we have a responsibility for the economic welfare of the city and the people of Manchester. What we are trying to do is create a city where less people are dependent welfare, whether it's the government's welfare by the social security system, or whether it's the City Council's welfare services. So we're trying to create an economically viable city ... The Olympic Games and the various other initiatives that we're taking are trying to relate directly not just to jobs for anybody but jobs for people in Manchester, who if they don't get those jobs actually need the welfare services provided by the City and government. (Councillor, Manchester City Council, 1994)

This new pragmatism on the part of the City Council was inevitably seen in some quarters as a process of 'selling out' to central government. The Council's justification for its Olympic strategy – one which might be summarised as 'investment, growth and jobs first, (residual) welfare services later' – is clearly one which chimes very strongly with the government's approach. This apparent volte-face entailed a wholesale discursive repackaging of the Council's development strategy. Whereas before 1987 political principle and the objective of job creation were tightly bound together in the language of municipal welfarism and *in opposition to* 'Tory cuts and the recession' (see MCC 1984c), after 1987 both political principle and job creation were increasingly redefined through a civic boosterism which allowed them to be *complementary to* the government's national strategy of service cuts and competitive financing. Following the logic of place-marketing, welfare was reinterpreted in ways which emphasised potential gains from boosterism, rather than the effective delivery of welfare services (see Cochrane 1994).

We're fundamentally opposed to the direction the Conservative government is taking this country and the damage that they've done to local democracy and local services. However, it would be pretty churlish wouldn't it, if when you've got a government – albeit of a different political persuasion – prepared to put money into the city ... that will be good for jobs, will be good for the city's image ... if we said, no, we don't want to sit down and co-operate with you? So I wouldn't see that as support for the Conservative government. (Councillor, Manchester City Council, 1994)

The financial and political costs of this pragmatist turn were minimised by the city's relative success in playing the partnership game, though there is always the risk – even the likelihood – that this success will be short-lived.

It is important to be clear about the extent to which agency is being exercised locally. While an experienced political leadership and a cadre of entrepreneurial officers may have enabled Manchester to exploit its new possibilities to the full, the parameters of the city's strategy were externally (and quite tightly) drawn. As the following comments from Council leader Graham Stringer illustrate, while the Olympics was seen to represent an unparalleled development opportunity for the city, there was also an important sense in which the Olympic bid was a game Manchester felt it *had* to play. Manchester may have opted for an Olympics-based development strategy, but this was a choice made from a menu with few alternatives:

> Cities, like sprinters, can't stand still. They have to make progress or go into decline. The great days of heavy industry won't return. We have to find new ways forward. And that's where the Olympic Games come in. Our bid for the 2000 Games is no town hall fantasy. It's a calculated move capable of transforming Manchester. (Graham Stringer, *Manchester Evening News*, 17 February 1993)

> [A]bout of dozen of [Europe's 40 or 50 second-tier cities] will become the cities where decisions are made ... We have to try and get there, because the alternative is to gradually decline. It would be reprehensible and irresponsible for any politician to let that happen. It's happening at the other end of the Ship Canal [in Liverpool]. We're not letting it happen here. (Graham Stringer, *Manchester Evening News*, 1 October 1993)

There is an important sense in which Manchester's strategy – like those of Europe's other 'second-tier' cities – was prescribed, at least in its general form if not its specifics. Playing the regeneration game meant adhering to a set of (globally defined) competitive rules. What should be emphasised, however, is that in learning to play this game, the City Council's senior officers and political leaders were in effect transforming the *modus operandi* of local economic development. The new approach would be based on elite networking, opportunism and a more entrepreneurial approach both on the part of officers and the organisation as a whole.

> We set up a committee of the great and the good ... and the rich and the powerful, who went about raising money to fund the bid ... What we found was that structure was much looser [and had] freedom in a way that a large bureaucracy doesn't ... It's not just become the model for the Olympic

Games, but it's been a model for a number of other things that we've done. What we have found in Manchester is a way of co-existing with the private sector, where we use many of the strengths of the public sector and the private sector, not in competition, but by setting up bodies where we can use [those] strengths ... rather than being in a sense confronting each other or separate from each other all the time. (Councillor, Manchester City Council, 1994)

[The Olympic bid] was the catalyst. It is only really since that that you can see how important it has been. Because what it did, what it achieved in the city ... was everyone working towards one ultimate goal. And it wasn't there before. The atmosphere was what really amazed me. People sat there and said, 'We can't stop. We just cannot stop' ... The private sector was saying, 'We'll put money in. We have just got to keep this going'. And I think without that catalyst to actually pull people together, you know, things like City Pride would just never have happened ... [Other initiatives would not have happened] if it was not for the fact that those people trusted each other and were used to getting on and doing things ... We have suddenly learned how to work together. A part of the trick is to let the private sector think they are running the show. That is very important. They have got to feel they have ownership and can make a difference ... not just the council. (Officer, Manchester City Council, 1994)

Notwithstanding this extension of elite networking and the new spirit of partnership, council officers and members tended, not surprisingly, to underline the fact that control over the new strategy remained with the local authority. While this may have acted as a useful corrective to those accounts which presented the Council as one 'captured' by private-sector interests, it is in many ways an equally unsatisfactory explanation of the city's new politics.

In fact there is a sense in which *both* partners – public and private – have limited control over the development process. While at its most benign, this might result in a mutually beneficial local pooling of resources and influence, it may just as often create a situation in which the goals of both parties are undermined (whether being subordinated to the centre or being defined by the wider – global – rules by which the place-marketing game is being played). Focusing obsessively on the ways in which power and control are being redistributed *locally* may mask the extent to which the locus of power has already shifted away from these local actors, be they in business or local government. Despite this, in the new language of partnership, it must be presented as a process of local negotiation.

> It's very difficult, in some of the partnerships that we have, to say that the control is absolutely here [with the City Council]. You can say, if it comes to some of the schemes, that the control is with the Council, ... you can say that control is with central government, ... you can say it's with the people who are actually running the bid ... [In reality] they're partnerships where people have vetoes. (Councillor, Manchester City Council, 1994)

Few in the city were inclined (or indeed sufficiently knowledgeable) to question this informally-regulated system of local checks and balances while the prospect of winning the Games nomination remained. Eyes were being firmly fixed on the big picture – the possibility of winning the Games and the imperative of retaining a unified voice during the bidding period – it being deemed counter-productive and even treacherous to question the politics or finances of the bidding process during this time of maximum global sensitivity. Any bid for the Olympics must, above all, be about 'feel-good politics' (see Hill 1992). The Olympic bidding process consequently exerts a kind of local hegemonic discipline on urban political actors: it was taken as axiomatic in Manchester that the city's ability to 'deliver' the Games was predicated on the continued strength of its new 'partnership'. If there were skeletons in cupboards, they would have to stay there for the time being.

Politics of spectacle

> The impact of holding the Games is far greater than simply the 17 days of the Games themselves. You get an incredible amount of work done in your city ... you get a world focus on you for a number of years – which are very helpful for the local economy ... and you really become the centre of the earth for a time in a funny sort of way. (Olympic bid committee member, private sector, 1995)

It has become a cliché that the modern Olympics is no longer simply about two and a half weeks of sport but instead has become a geopolitical spectacle of power, money and corruption (Simson and Jennings 1992). The stakes are high, but so is the cost of playing the game. Bidding for the Olympics means submitting to the competitive rules laid down by the IOC: 'Manchester naturally could not afford to behave differently from its competitors' (Hill 1994: 347). Cities are consequently induced to engage in Olympic boosterism, to pledge higher and higher levels of local financial support, servicing and infrastructure provision, to trade concessions with the IOC (for example, concerning TV rights, merchandising or promises of subsidised places to athletes and officials from poorer countries), and to lavish more and more generous gifts on junketing IOC delegates, simply in order to stay in the Olympic competition (Simson and Jennings 1992). In so doing, of course, bid cities are through their own actions reproducing the very competitive structures from which they hope that success will allow them to escape. Significantly, the only recent exception was Los Angeles, which was the only bidder for the 1984 Games and as a result was in a position to exercise an unusual degree of bargaining leverage with the IOC. In the mythology of the Olympic bidding process, however, the success of the LA Games (measured of course in terms of profitability) has since been attributed to the agency of its energetic private-sector leadership, not the structural condition of the absence of competition for the Games (Reich 1986; Hill 1992). Heightened recognition of the value of the Olympic franchise subsequently led the IOC to take steps to ensure that a vigorous – and ever more elaborate – competition is fostered amongst the bidding cities. Correspondingly, the cachet of even bidding for the Games means for participating cities that – in the words of the Olympic adage – taking part really *does* count.

Competitive localism within nation-states is, of course, part of a wider process of seeking to ensure sites as attractive for mobile investment. Beneath the accentuation of the positive which is the hallmark of such urban boosterism – free and fair competition being of course another of the Olympian ideals – is the ruthless process of competition for global investment. Here, as in sport, the stakes are sufficiently high often to bring out the worst, as well as the best, in the competitors. The bidding process creates an opportunity to parade a city's strengths, but at the same time creates an imperative to deny its weaknesses, even if this comes to trading relative murder rates:

> A lot of people who are investing, whether it's pension funds or international finance, take people at the way they value themselves. And if a city has the confidence to go out and bid for the Olympic Games, then we will be of more interest to Japanese companies or North American companies who are likely to invest … I think bidding for the Olympic Games will have enabled us to show all those strengths that there are in the Manchester economy to those people who can locate their newer industries anywhere they want. (Councillor, Manchester City Council, 1994)

> People say, we've got riots in Moss Side [an inner city district of Manchester], and this is bad for our bid; and we've seen seven murders in the last few months, and it is dreadful. But if you actually think seriously that the Moss Side troubles are the equivalent of Tiananmen Square, I mean,

it's a joke. You know, we are an incredibly peaceful society. Moss Side you can drive through easily and regularly. You can't drive through whole areas of Atlanta, and they were awarded the Games. (Olympic bid committee member, private sector, 1995)

Scott insisted that as 'an Olympic city the old image of Manchester would simply evaporate' (quoted in Hill 1994: 343), an oblique reference perhaps to the city's long-edured image as a 'damp post-industrial city where it rains much of the time and there is a lot of crime' (Lynch 1993: 9). Drawing on rainfall data for July/August, the Olympic bid committee sought to contest this prevailing image, emphasising that these (presumably highly-oxygenated) conditions were ideal for record-breaking.

Manchester's bid committee claimed that the Games would provide an opportunity not only to draw new money into the city, but would also have the effect of shunting Manchester up the urban hierarchy. The Olympics has become the ultimate expression of 'place-marketing' (Kearns and Philo 1993), allowing cities to join that small global elite whose names are recognised world-wide.

> If Manchester gets the Games, Manchester will be Britain's front door in the year 2000. Now, we're used to London having been Britain's front door for hundreds of years ... I think something as massive as the Olympic Games will actually shift the axis of the country slightly. (Olympic bid committee member, private sector)

> A targeted and managed economic and social programme of urban regeneration linked to Olympic sporting and multi-cultural investment could bring Manchester and the region a handsome and irrevocable dividend in the next century. Indeed by 2001, Manchester has the opportunity to emerge and remain unchallenged as:
> • Britain's second city – the capital of the Northern region;
> • a European regional capital – a centre of investment growth not regional aid;
> • an international city of outstanding commercial, cultural and creative potential.
> Therefore, the Games should not be regarded as an end in themselves but rather as a vehicle by which Manchester can achieve its vision. (KPMG Management Consulting, 1993: 2)

The Games were, therefore, always understood by the bidders as a means of driving change in – and improving the image of – Manchester, and most certainly not as 'an end in themselves'. The image-building was oriented internally as much as externally. Local politics was redefined in terms which made opposition difficult. They stressed the overarching

Plate 7 The *Daily Mirror* comes down on the side of Manchester as the city's 'movers and shakers' go for gold

notion of 'Manchester' as a place with an uncontested identity and shared goals through a powerful expression of urban entrepreneurialism (Harvey 1989). Journalist Dennis Johnson described a visit to Manchester in September 1993 as 'an eerie sensation. All but the most case-hardened cynics in the city seem stunned and tongue tied' (*Guardian*, 8 September 1993). Every one of the city's major civic institutions signed up to the Games bid. In 1991, a local poll revealed that three-quarters of local residents were in favour of the Manchester Olympic bid (cited in Hill 1994).

> [Opposition to the bid] is fantastically small. You actually have to search for opposition to Manchester's bid in Manchester. You may find scepticism, because we are a very sceptical race ... But actually, the consensus is very positive. (Olympic bid committee member, private sector, 1994)

This high level of support certainly reflects the attractiveness of the Games themselves and the region's deep-seated enthusiasm for sport, but it also reflects the successful campaign waged in the (supportive) local media and the fact that the bid was represented locally as an *addition to*, not an option in, the region's development agenda. There was, however, the odd dissenting opinion voice nationally.

The goal of getting the Olympics meant that the bidding process was systematically insulated from politics-as-usual, while crucial long-term commitments that were being made at the time were effectively concealed from public scrutiny. A feel-good discourse was adopted (the Olympic bid slogan was *We can win!*), which literally marginalised any dissent. At the same time there was a sharp focus on the issue of 'new money' for Manchester. Olympic cash, the argument went, was new cash. As Hill (1994: 345) put it, 'No poll tax money was to be spent ... for it was important that no section of the local population be alienated'. The Olympic bid was never subject to the kind of political forces that would have been released had it been seen to be draining revenue from elsewhere in the city, for example from the education budget. The discourse of 'new money' (in essence, *extra-local* money) effectively wrong-footed local opposition to the bid by (mis)representing the bidding process as one with no local redistributional consequences.

> What it did was absolutely secured the private sector leadership; it secured [our] independence. We were able to say, listen, if we have a meeting at the town hall, we'll pay for the coffee and biscuits. This bid will cost the rate payers of Manchester not one penny ... and that has always been the case. And so there's never been the political dimension of can we afford this, is this a right way of spending of public money. That came later with a debate through central government. (Olympic bid committee member, private sector, 1994)

> Although we could see enormous benefits in marketing Manchester around the work in the bidding process, and immediate economic benefits, it would be very difficult [to direct local authority funds into the bid] when we've been going through a period of cuts, caused by the government removing grant ... When situations in our schools and elderly people's homes are getting worse ... it would have been terribly divisive, and actually would have damaged the bid process itself, because it would have given us an in-built opposition to the bid. (Councillor, Manchester City Council, 1995)

This was not, of course, entirely true. The City Council did incur costs in a range of 'less noticeable ways, for a good deal of officials' time would necessarily be committed, and municipal land would be made available' (Hill 1994: 345). Crucially, the City Council also took on liability for any losses incurred by the Olympic bid company.[2]

The representation of the funding for the bid as 'new money', and the associated insistence that the benefits both of bidding and of winning would be *additional to* those which could otherwise have been expected, secured the Olympic bid a privileged position ostensibly above, or more accurately outside, the local political process. The bidding team stressed that the Olympics would secure new money, foreign direct investment, additional visitors and extra business for Manchester and the North West region. In this process, rhetorics of regeneration were of vital importance but were, in themselves, insufficient. The bidders needed to provide 'concrete estimates' in order both to convince central government that the bid was viable (and consequently that the Games would not become a drain on public funds) and to underwrite local support. The bid committee commissioned the international management consultants KPMG to produce estimates of the costs and benefits of the Games. KPMG's estimates, which assumed great importance in the Olympic bidding process, suggested that the Games would cost £973 million, of which £360 million (37 per cent) would come from central government while the remainder would be raised from other (mainly private) sources (*Financial Times*, 4 March 1992; KPMG Management Consulting, 1993). A surplus of £92 million was projected, though this was conceded to have 'as much to do with politics as the IOC's decision in September' (*Financial Times*, 23 June 1993).

Yet a significant paradox lay at the heart of the whole *entrepreneurial* imagery of the Games. Although presented as a private sector initiative, it was fundamentally oriented towards the generation of grants from the government. It was an attempt to redirect public funding towards Manchester, and, in particular, towards the reimaging of Manchester. The 'new money' was not private-sector money but central government money, as members of the bid committee explained:

> Although you hear a lot about spending cuts, the Government is absolutely stuffed full of spending programmes and if you come up with an idea, you've got to shape it to fit their programmes. For instance in the Olympic bid I never used the word 'sport' because you were then told to talk to the Sports Council. But we needed more money than the Sports Council spent in a year, and therefore we talked about urban regeneration, employment opportunities and reclaiming land. (Bob Scott, quoted in *Business Life*, February 1994: viii)

> Michael Heseltine ... was an absolutely key supporter, but I have to tell you, with great respect, Michael Heseltine doesn't really know the difference between a bat and a ball, and he was not an enthusiast for sport. What he was an enthusiast for was the regeneration of a part of Manchester which had been wholly resistant to quite big sums of public money being showered upon it over the years. Suddenly he saw in Manchester's Olympic proposals ... the solution to one of the great urban problems of the north of England. I have to tell you, we're on the way to solving it, even before we know if we've got the Games. (Olympic bid committee member, private sector, 1995)

If the aspect of the Olympic bid which attracted the greatest publicity was the one associated with spectacle and promotional activities, the practical orientation was targeted rather more modestly towards the attraction of grants from a range of state agencies. In other words, the bid committee looks more like a locally-based *grant coalition* than a US-style growth coalition (Logan and Molotch 1987; Cox and Mair 1988; Jessop *et al.* 1999). The approach was not one which aimed towards freeing up areas for private-sector development, nor was it directed towards developing a strategy aimed at sustaining the position of existing local businesses. On the contrary, the aim was to use public expenditure on a massive scale to construct new 'partnerships' between developers and 'sport' (i.e. generally state-subsidised sport). In a neat inversion of mainstream discussions of 'leverage' in local economic development (which stress the extent to which public spending can draw out private-sector investment), in this case – with the help of seedcorn funding from local firms and infrastructural support from the local authority – the aim was to lever money raised by the public sector into the private sector. As the consultants to the bid committee put it, 'Alongside the partnership between the public and private sector in the Bid itself, many other partnerships are emerging on elements of the city's preparation for the Games. Such partnerships and future opportunities arising from the Bid offer an unparalleled chance to marry the provision of sporting facilities with urban regeneration' (KPMG Management Consulting 1993: 1).

One consequence of this shift in emphasis was that, despite the emergence of what looked like a more vibrant local politics, Manchester's Olympic project was heavily dependent on the decisions of national political actors. Manchester's 'new money' was, of course, anything but, since it was top-sliced from urban spending programmes (Dalby 1993) and Manchester achieved the unique position of having its own expenditure line in the Department of the Environment's published spending plans (DoE 1993). Manchester's Olympic bid consequently needs to be seen as part of a wider reorganisation in the funding and delivery of urban aid, as part of what Stewart (1994: 143) sees as a competitively- (and centrally) orchestrated 'new localism [based on the] decentralisation of administration as opposed to the devolution of power and influence'.

Playing Olympic games

Many of the arguments around the Olympic bid built on appeals to Manchester's nineteenth-century glories, heavy with the symbolism of that era in which local economic power coincided with local political power, one in which the merchants and manufacturers of Manchester worshipped at the alter of (their version of) Free Trade (Redford 1934; Briggs 1963; Lloyd-Jones and Lewis 1988). Yet while there may be superficial similarities between the 'Manchester Men' of the nineteenth century and the new elite of the late twentieth century, it is the differences that really tell the story. Rather than helping to write the rulebook for global capitalist competition, the birthplace of the factory system and 'Manchester School' economics is now on its receiving end: Manchester has gone from global*iser* to global*ised* (see Dicken, this volume). The politics of the Olympic bid (and its associated business elite) reflect not so much this nineteenth-century heyday, but rather the structural conditions facing such semiperipheral cities in the late twentieth century: continuing economic decline coupled with the effects of the ongoing crisis of the British welfare state.

While individual business leaders such as Bob Scott have come to epitomise, both in popular discourse and in neo-liberal rhetoric, the supposed re-emergence of a maverick urban business elite, their actions are better understood as part and parcel of a much wider process of institutional and political restructuring (Peck 1995). The new mode of urban politics that propelled the likes of Bob Scott to the fore cannot be reduced to stories about charismatic leadership nor to some grass-roots revival in corporate responsibility, even if they are often presented in this way. Rather, they are part of a contested political project, in the context of the twin imperatives of globalisation on the one hand and state restructuring on the other. The new urban politics should be understood as a dual process of 'elite localism' and 'local elitism' (Peck and Tickell 1995), in which Bob Scott and friends occupied a discursive and institutional space opened up through struggles over the future shape and purpose of the state against the backdrop of powerful globalising and neo-liberalising tendencies. As we have seen, while local coalitions led by the likes of Bob Scott, may talk about growth and regeneration, they are typically involved in claims-making against the state.

More often than not, the business elite is spending (or seeking to spend) public money not private money, bidding for grants rather than boosting for growth. In British policy discourse, however, it has become necessary to talk about growth to get grants. It is this that makes it more appropriate in the UK context to think of grant coalitions than growth coalitions (Jones and Ward 1998). Such coalitions also help to redefine popular understandings of welfare in ways that stress the importance of competitive success rather than service delivery, the possibility of getting bread through the effective promotion of circuses. Since the old arrangements of municipal labourism are no longer able to deliver the welfare goods, the new politics of 'business' appear to offer a way forward, precisely because of their promise to deliver 'additionality' – extra resources and the vision of dynamic entrepreneurial growth (Cochrane 1994; Jessop 1994).

The politics of elite localism in Manchester can be seen, then, as a response to globalisation that involve struggles over the role, and meaning and structure of the state, as well as straightforward attempts to appropriate more public cash. But they are also a relatively unstable and fragile politics that rely on an extensive insulation from processes of public accountability and even from political debate. The bidding strategy was also about constructing a consensus around the high politics of 'the good of Manchester', rather than the low politics of cash and cuts that had come to dominate the terrain of local government. It remains to be seen for how long this apparent 'transformation' in local politics can be sustained, or even if it is – in principle – sustain*able*. The experience of other entrepreneurial cities would suggest that 'successes' are often fleeting and that long-run trends toward economic decline are exceptionally difficult to turn around. Although Manchester hosted the Commonwealth Games in 2002, this must be seen as no more than a consolation prize. Absent the stimulus of continuing competitive successes, the city's elite politics will no doubt lose their dynamism, even their legitimacy. Redistributional issues seem destined to reappear on the local political agenda, and in such a context the actions of local political actors will increasingly be brought into question, a harsh environment indeed for the unstable politics of elite partnership. As Harvey (1989: 273) notes, the politics of the spectacle 'is a fragile and uncertain tool of unification', not only because the illusion is often difficult to sustain, but also because it may help to generate its own problems: 'to the degree that it forces the consumer to become a "consumer of illusions" [it] contains its own specific alienations'.

It is important to be clear about the results of the bidding process. Manchester *did* achieve some of the short-term objectives of its political leaders – in the shape of extra public sector funding, partnership building and local state entrepreneurialism – but this has meant accepting the logic of neo-liberal competition. Manchester may have benefited from taking part in the Olympic bidding process, but this was at the expense of other British cities in the short term and at the expense of the Council's effective control over its development agenda in the long term. The partnership process that the Olympics so clearly symbolised has led to a major reimagining of local governance. As subsequent experience has confirmed, this new approach to entrepreneurial urban governance has effectively been normalised in Manchester. If the effect on local state functionaries and politicians, that they are both more prepared to accommodate with business and act in a less bureaucratic fashion, has been foregrounded in this chapter, the effect on local elites has been no less profound. Although local businessmen were sponsored as an apolitical (read Conservative) alternative to the socialist local state, their experience of working with Labour politicians such as Graham Stringer has gone some way to reducing the vigour of attacks on the left as being fundamentally anti-business. Accordingly, it may have contributed to the rehabilitation of Labour as a party of government in the mid-1990s. In this sense, Manchester's Olympic bidding process may also have played a part in creating a form of protoBlairite politics at the local level – pragmatic, goal-oriented, and business-friendly. And in a final irony, which only serves to underline the interconnectedness of national and local political circuits and the fragility of local entrepreneurialism, even 'Mr Manchester' was to leave town in the wake of the failure of the city's Olympic bid. But old habits die hard, and after relocating to London, Sir Bob Scott subsequently became a central player in another local boosterist project, this time based – of all places – in Greenwich.

Notes

1 This is a revised version of the paper 'Manchester plays games: exploring the local politics of globalisation', *Urban Studies*, 33, 8 (1996), 1319–36. The authors acknowledge Carfax Publishing for granting them permission to draw upon this original piece.
2 In the previous bid, losses were underwritten by the trustees. The 2000 bid was legally constituted as a company, wholly owned by the City Council, but controlled by a triumvirate of the bid committee, the British Olympic Association and the City Council (Hill 1994).

7

Metropolitan manoeuvres:
making Greater Manchester

———————

IAIN DEAS AND KEVIN WARD

THE structure of the contemporary Manchester conurbation reflects its roots at the vanguard of nineteenth-century industrial capitalism. The advent of mechanised cotton spinning and textile weaving was the principal stimulant for unprecedented urban growth, prompting an intricate metropolitan economic geography in which Manchester acted as a focal point for an array of manufacturing towns in the Pennine foothills. The towns of Bolton, Bury, Rochdale, Oldham, Ashton, Stockport and Salford grew as distinct nodes within this broader integrated 'industrial region', each supported by separate pools of labour and natural resources. The modern structure of the Greater Manchester conurbation reflects the development of Manchester as a central place encircled by these linked but separate towns (Rogers 1986):

> Manchester was the capital of cotton, and as the industry grew so did 'cottonopolis'. The open space which lay between Manchester and its surrounding towns was shrinking rapidly and, by the middle of the [nineteenth] century, these towns were so close together and had so much in common that we can consider each of them part of a single entity – a giant Manchester with a population of a million people. This was Britain's largest urban region by far, excluding London, and it was the largest manufacturing centre in the world. (Bee 1984 quoted in Taylor *et al.* 1996: 51)

The economic geography of the metropolis was eventually reflected in the structures through which the conurbation was governed. As the ultimate 'unregulated' factory city, Manchester and its political establishment had little time for those who pushed for the state to get involved in the business of governance. As befits the home of liberal free trade, Manchester was keen for its economic development to go unchecked. During the nineteenth and for most of the twentieth century Manchester

Figure 7.1 Greater Manchester local government boundaries

successfully avoided any top-down state reform of its position at the hub of the metropolitan and regional economies. Only in 1972 with the Local Government Act did Manchester eventually buckle. This reform saw an attempt to delimit the functional reach of the metropolitan area through the creation of an overarching Greater Manchester Council (GMC), covering an area of 1,300 square kilometres and providing territorial unity for the core city and its satellites. At the same time, it also meant rationalising complex intra-metropolitan local government boundaries, replacing an administrative geography that embraced an intricate array of seventy-two units at different spatial scales with one consisting of ten modernised local governments. The city of Manchester, at the heart of the metropolitan area, is the largest of these and, together with its metropolitan twin, Salford, and parts of neighbouring Trafford and Tameside, forms the core of the conurbation (see Figure 7.1). Beyond this, a ring of free-standing industrial towns – Wigan, Bolton, Bury, Oldham and Rochdale – and the suburban commuter belt of southern Trafford and Stockport comprise the remainder of Greater Manchester.

The advent of metropolitan government for Greater Manchester did not extinguish some of the long-standing fissures that underlay the conurbation. Most strikingly, GMC boundaries failed to embrace the conurbation's affluent Cheshire commuter belt, which, while integral to the metropolitan economy, remained resolutely resistant to Greater Manchester's expansionist overtures (Rodgers 1986; Wannop 1995). The boundaries of GMC, in common with the other metropolitan counties, remained 'singularly narrow' when measured against the functional extent of the conurbation (Lefevre 1998: 13).

Other factors also served to limit the viability and effectiveness of metropolitan governance. The complex, and often fraught, relationship between the core city and the other nine districts within the GMC area meant that metropolitan loyalties were always divided. With only one fifth of the 2.4 million population of the conurbation, the city of Manchester never enjoyed the ascendancy of more generously drawn core cities such as Leeds or Birmingham within their respective metropolitan areas (Hebbert and Deas 2000). And there is also evidence to suggest that social and economic disparities within the Greater Manchester conurbation – and, in particular, between the impoverished core city and its relatively affluent surrounds – are more acutely drawn than elsewhere in England, lending a further piquancy to these territorial rivalries (Turok and Edge 1999).

These were fractures that, reflecting the fundamentally fragmented structure of the conurbation, were to undermine GMC throughout its existence. Although it was able to make some headway – notably in adopting a metropolitan structure plan, in agreeing initial arrangements for public transport and developing the roads infrastructure, in supporting a series of landmark property developments such as the G-MEX exhibition centre, and in laying the foundations for local regeneration strategies upon which later bodies were able to capitalise (Law 1988, 1992) – GMC failed to suppress some of the territorial hostilities which underlay the governance of the metropolitan area.

These tensions were exacerbated in the 1980s by a national political climate unsympathetic to metropolitan government. Compounding the local difficulties faced by GMC, the view from central government at the time was that metropolitan authorities such as GMC exemplified outmoded approaches to governance. Prompted by more general unease about the growth of big government, concerned about the confrontational stances adopted by political leaders in some metropolitan authorities, and worried about its lack of electoral representation in Britain's major cities, the Conservative Governments of the period cited metropolitan authorities such as GMC as typifying the anti-entrepreneurial, bureaucratic and profligate tendencies characteristic of Labour-led local administrations.

This combination of a national political climate inimical to metropolitan government (and big city local government more generally), and the particular local difficulties presented by Greater Manchester's fragmented economic and political geography, might have been expected to preclude the creation of new metropolitan institutions. And of the plethora of short-life specialist agencies established under the Conservative governments of 1979–97 to replace functions previously executed by local authorities, most operated at sub-metropolitan level. As a result, the 1980s was a decade in which there was little momentum underlying efforts to construct a metropolitan tier of governance. Rather, it was a decade of *metropolitan deconstruction*, leaving in its place a tangled web of task-specific, locally-focused and loosely co-ordinated agencies. The few metropolitan scale bodies established during the 1980s were tasked with replacing routine service delivery responsibilities formerly the preserve of the metropolitan county, and their struggle to do so in a broader context of local authority fiscal retrenchment meant that most were marginalised from key axes of strategic decision-making within the conurbation (Hebbert and Deas 2000).

This began to alter in the 1990s as a number of developments imbued Mancunian metropolitanism with a renewed impetus. The advent of regionally-based economic development structures prompted unease on the part of some local policy-makers about the prospects for government regeneration resources remaining channelled to locally based partnerships (Deas and Ward 2000). At the same time, proposals for a new tier of government for London accorded renewed momentum to arguments that provincial metropolitan areas should also be granted parallel conurbation-wide structures of government (DETR 1998; Hebbert and Deas 2000). And at a local level, in part spurred by these national changes, policy-makers in Manchester continued to advocate the expansion of Manchester's boundaries to allow it to compete effectively against other larger, better-resourced cities, and to obviate the long-standing difficulties stemming from its low tax base (City Pride Strategic Planning Group 1998a). Such expansionist arguments were further fuelled by the exemplar provided by Manchester Airport: one of the fastest growing in Europe and, significantly, one of the few remaining enterprises in the hands of the ten unitary authorities that formerly comprised the component parts of the GMC.

In combination, these pressures have facilitated a discernible axis – the metropolitan region – around which some of the recent efforts to create new institutional structures have focused. This chapter explores the dynamics of these efforts in Greater Manchester. Through three case studies of 'multi-scalar' initiatives – city, metropolitan, regional, national

Table 7.1 Metropolitan and city governance

Institutional form	City Pride Partnership	MIDAS	Marketing Manchester
Context for formation	Central government initiative initially limited to Birmingham, London and Manchester to produce city-wide prospectuses that set out frameworks for development for the forthcoming decade	Frustration amongst city-based elites with the ineffective performance and anti-urban bias of regionally-based inward investment efforts; concern to maintain the viability of Trafford Park industrial estate	One of the policy outcomes of the first City Pride document, reflecting local unease about the marketing of Manchester to potential investors and visitors
Geographical remit	Manchester, Salford and Trafford	Manchester, Salford, Tameside and Trafford	Manchester and the surrounding nine boroughs: Bolton, Bury, Oldham, Rochdale, Salford, Stockport, Tameside, Trafford, Wigan
Policy area	Extensive. Covered economic and social policy and produced 42 policy objectives as part of a wider development plan for the city	Attempt to attract 'high quality' inward investment to the four metropolitan boroughs. Provides a database on local area 'assets' to potential investors and other economic development agencies, and engages in more general marketing efforts	Co-ordination of existing marketing strategies and the branding of the 'city-region' through the 'We're Up and Going' and 'Great Britain. Greater Manchester' slogans
Political issues	Attempt to broaden policy-making to include voluntary and community groups and balance economic competitiveness and social cohesion objectives	Conflicts with remaining regional-orientation of inward investment promotion. Uncertainty over the extent to which its remit includes generic place marketing, and related concern regarding duplication of effort with Marketing Manchester.	Prompted the mobilisation of youthful entrepreneurial elites (the McEnroe Group) in reaction to the perceived inadequacy of the agency's marketing campaign

and global – it considers the viability of new institutional forms of and for metropolitan governance (Table 7.1). The first example is that of City Pride, a central government initiative announced in 1993 and launched in 1994 to encourage policy-makers in three English cities – Birmingham, London and Manchester – to produce ten-year prospectuses to shape future policy agendas (Randall 1995; Williams 1995a, 1998). The chapter also considers two related initiatives, both of which have their roots in City Pride: MIDAS, an agency established in 1997 to promote Manchester to prospective inward investors; and Marketing Manchester, an agency formed in 1996 to market the city and surrounding boroughs to outside investors and tourists.

Through the three examples, the chapter explores the implications of these developments in light of corresponding institutional innovations at the regional and sub-metropolitan scales. Utilising material gleaned from a series of semi-structured interviews with key economic and political actors, it situates the 'local' analysis against a conceptual backdrop provided by academic and political debates over the changing role of the nation-state in struggles over metropolitan governance. Specifically the chapter interprets the attempts to re-scale the city of Manchester and re-place Greater Manchester in light of three inter-related political processes: the re-designing of governance, the rescaling of the city as an economic and political entity and the re-imaging of the city-metropolis-region axis. At the core is an on-going political battle over how different economic development possibilities are 'imagined' at different scales. In this chapter, we examine how the 'imagined economy' is constructed and controlled through different political representations.

Regeneration unbound

The advent of City Pride in 1994 was triggered in part by perennial concern about the difficulties in co-ordinating different regeneration initiatives within cities, and in part by a concern to bolster urban competitiveness and thereby contribute to national economic well-being (Williams 1998). City Pride responded to these concerns by providing another exhortation for the formation of public–private partnership, but more significantly by encouraging the disparate network of actors involved in developing and implementing urban regeneration initiatives to agree a *longer-term* strategy within which to frame their efforts. There was no substantive budget from central government associated with City Pride, and it was not to represent a formal plan; rather, the resultant prospectus would simply set out a broad vision and a series of aims, objectives and targets to guide future regeneration efforts.

The City Pride initiative was initially restricted to three pilot cities – Birmingham, London and Manchester – and later to an additional seven provincial cities. Unlike Birmingham or London, however, the process of developing a City Pride prospectus for Manchester was to involve agencies beyond the formal city boundaries. Although the invitation from central government to prepare a City Pride prospectus was directed to Manchester City Council, it was decided from the outset that this should be extended to involve the councils of Salford and Trafford, and the development corporations of Trafford Park and Central Manchester. The management team was made up of representatives from each of the five organisations, supported by an advisory panel comprising ninety members from agencies across the three areas, chaired by the leader of Manchester City Council. The resultant City Pride prospectuses (City Pride Strategic Planning Group 1994, 1998a) carried the imprimatur of some 160 public, private and voluntary agencies.

City Pride was significant in terms of its role in reinforcing inter-institutional relations, and conjoining public, private and voluntary sector agendas. It was intended explicitly to support further the ongoing reorientation of political relations in Manchester, and to help cement links between the leaders of bodies such as Manchester City Council and the Training and Enterprise Council (TEC), which had been character-ised by mutual unease. Equally significant, but less frequently acknow-ledged, however, was its parallel role in wider attempts to redefine Manchester's geographical extent. By persuading the leaders of Salford and Trafford Councils to commit to a Manchester-centric view of local urban development, City Pride represented one of the earliest of recent attempts by the metropolis-builders to create new institutional entities whose coverage extended beyond the core city. But unlike earlier waves of metropolitanism, the impetus for this came from within Greater Manchester, in contrast to the top-down *dirigiste* solution of local government reorganisation. Hence, while the origins of City Pride came from central government, the reaction of Manchester City Council drew upon its existing and previous methods of institution building.

In terms of regeneration, the particular form of development pursued in Manchester continued largely unchallenged, if anything encouraged by the consensus that emerged around the production of Manchester's document. One of the significant shifts around City Pride was that a number of one-off or smaller projects were reinterpreted as component parts of Manchester's overall City Pride strategy. This served to give what in reality was an incremental series of developments a greater sense of coherence. In this sense, City Pride might be interpreted as a forerunner of (retrospective) 'joined-up-thinking' of the sort encouraged under the Blair Government through programmes such as the New Deal for Communities. As a local political actor commented: 'City Pride has helped tremendously to co-ordinate a lot of [regeneration initiatives] and the City Pride committee structure is the way in which the whole thing comes together' (Senior executive, business sector institution, 1997).

The momentum underlying the City Pride process began to dissipate with the change of national government in 1997. At the local level, too, there was an expanding critique of Manchester's 'entrepreneurial turn': the city evidently has an aptitude for 'grant grabbing', but much greater difficulty in allocating resource judiciously, implementing objectives effectively and securing outcomes in the form of improved socio-economic fortunes for its residents (Griffiths 1998; Herd and Patterson, this volume; Jones and Ward 1998). At the same time, even the extent to which the private sector has genuinely been involved in the formulation and delivery of policy – something for which the city has been widely extolled – has been questioned. As one senior actor commented:

> [There is a] need to integrate [the private sector] into strategic development ... The City Pride process has stuttered over the last couple of years ... [Strategic policy-making is] better than it was eight years ago, but it's not as integrated as it could be ... [it] could even be on a Great Manchester basis. (Senior officer, local government, 1998)

There is also a perception that regardless of the ostensible coherence of institutional structures and formal initiatives arising from City Pride, the city's economic fortunes depend upon a more subtle personal chemistry among senior decision-makers and, more specifically, the presence of a shared agenda amongst them. Developing a clear agenda rather than building new structures is now seen as the key to economic development:

> [T]he City's done City Pride documents, [but] that's not the real message about what the City's about – there's something missing ... if it was there, then we'd be more successful ... It's not about structures ... and formal processes ... it's as much about networking, relationships ... it's about personalities ... A lot of the reality of what happened in Manchester is the coincidence of Graham Stringer, Bob Scott, Alan Cockshaw ... Heseltine .. and their adeptness at using structures ... They'd agreed ... what they were trying to achieve, and once you get that there's an aura and a buzz and people want to join in ... It's like Canal Street: you've got Carol Ainscow

[director of Artisan Holdings which own a number of the bars and properties in and around the city centre of Manchester] and Tom Bloxham [director of Urban Splash which owns properties in central Liverpool and Manchester] and then later you've got the Whitbreads and £50 million of investment ... [T]he bulk of new economic activity has not come through a standard inward investment approach ... China Town and the Gay Quarter ... – none of this has happened because of inward investment ... it's because people are passionate about the city, they've stayed after graduation, they've invested in the city and made a buck there ... All that's as significant as standard investment ... [but] it's happened because of the way people have come together, not institutionally, but by having a shared goal. (Senior officer, inward investment agency, 1998)

As this senior officer argues, it is undeniably important to have the 'right' people in the 'right' place at the 'right' time. It is also necessary not to lose sight of the wider political–economic logic that lies behind the creation of the parameters in which local agents manoeuvre. While Manchester was without question good at persuading local business elites to get involved in decision-making networks, these alone could not arrest the city's economic decline.

MIDAS touch?

One result of policy-maker deliberations under the auspices of City Pride was an overhaul of structures dedicated to inward investment promotion. In part, this was informed by a shared perception that long-standing regionally-based inward investment efforts had proved insensitive to the distinctive needs of sub-regional areas generally, and to Manchester in particular. This view was reinforced by arguments citing the ineffectiveness (and sometimes ineptitude) of the regional inward investment promotion agency, Inward. The regional body, it was argued, had benefited from fewer government resources than its counterparts in the North East and Yorkshire & Humberside (Dicken and Tickell 1992) and, even more markedly, in comparison to the well-funded development agencies in Scotland and Wales. Partly as a result of this, the North West had historically failed to benefit from substantial flows of inward investment, or to secure high-profile foreign direct investors (Dicken and Tickell 1992).

Dissatisfaction with regionally-based inward investment was reinforced by a perception that corresponding city-based initiatives had been markedly more effective. Trafford Park Development Corporation (TPDC), in particular, was cited as exemplifying the benefits resulting from coherent city-focused promotional efforts. Its perceived success in reinvigorating the conurbation's oldest and most significant industrial estate – an area of 'global significance' (MIDAS 1998) – and in attracting precisely the sorts of economic activity in both manufacturing and service industries which were held to have bypassed Greater Manchester under the direction of Inward, was highlighted as justification for an exclusively conurbation-based inward investment strategy. But with TPDC due to end its limited-life tenure in 1998, the City Pride team feared the core city's marginalisation if Inward was to resume sole responsibility for inward investment promotion. In response, it was decided that a new agency, MIDAS – Manchester Investment and Development Agency Service – should succeed TPDC and extend its pioneering approach by providing a dedicated inward investment function across the entire conurbation core.

MIDAS was established in 1997. Initially it had fourteen staff and a modest working budget of £1m, of which £600,000 constituted core funds, and the remainder top-up monies from other regeneration programmes. Public and private inputs were deliberately balanced to avoid conflicts over the benefits accruing from MIDAS activities. Likewise, local authority financial inputs were identical. However, board membership was restricted to the public sector – the four core local authorities plus a representative of the *de facto* public-sector TEC and (during 1997/98) TPDC – until the new body had a chance to 'bed-in', after which time the twelve-strong board was to include private-sector representatives. Unlike Inward, it was decided that MIDAS would not be a membership/subscription body, thereby helping to avoid the conflicts between constituent districts that so undermined Inward.

The work of MIDAS involves business development, employment and training and marketing. Much of this is deliberately reactive, through a site and property database for the MIDAS area, and through an on-line enquiry service that provides intelligence to potential advisers on land supply, labour force attributes, grant incentives, communications and other urban 'assets'. MIDAS does not intervene directly in land and property markets; its role is to encourage other public-sector agencies and the private sector to ensure an appropriate supply of sites and premises. The thrust of MIDAS's efforts has tended to be on commercial, rather than industrial, development, reflecting a desire to diversify from the traditional industrial focus of Inward, and to attract what is deemed more appropriate investment to Manchester city centre and its surrounds.

On first inspection, MIDAS represents merely another agency in a succession of economic development bodies established during the

1990s, reflecting the City Council's recently discovered predilection for dedicated economic development agencies. But what distinguished MIDAS from most of its counterparts was not its professed entrepreneurial bent or its supposed embodiment of private-sector values, but the geographical ambit of its responsibilities, straddling the neighbouring City Pride authorities as well as the core city. In an attempt to wrestle primary responsibility away from regionally-based bodies and to focus on sub-regional areas, the definition of 'Manchester' extended beyond the narrowly-drawn local authority jurisdiction and reiterated the city's long-standing desire to embrace its neighbours more formally.

But attempts to redefine the city as a metropolitan entity, rather than a narrowly conceived administrative one, and to articulate the perception that the interests of the metropolitan area are tied umbilically to that of the core city, did not go unchallenged. Although the MIDAS articles of association allow for it to extend beyond the current core by invitation, coverage of all ten Greater Manchester districts was resisted by senior staff and politicians on the grounds that Mancunian domination was more likely amongst ten uneven authorities than four comparable core ones. It was also resisted on the grounds that it would be too time-consuming formally to absorb each district. That said, there are some links beyond the four, notably with authorities like Wigan, where discussions have centred on potential areas for collaboration, and on the implications of the North West Development Agency.

Intra-metropolitan tensions are illustrative of the uncertainties arising from the emergence of new forms of governance. When added to the set of conflicts arising with regional bodies – and most notably the Regional Development Agencies created in 1999, part of whose remit involves inward investment (Jones and MacLeod, this volume) – it is clear that the advent of metropolitan scale institutions, and the related reconstruction and redefinition of metropolitan identities, has not gone uncontested, either within Greater Manchester itself, or in the surrounding North West region (Deas and Ward 2000).

Marketing Manchester

The third issue with which local agencies have recently grappled is how best to project a coherent and single image of the 'city-region', and who should control this image. In line with other cities' efforts, contemporary political and economic elites have turned to ever-more sophisticated strategies of place promotion. In this case, and like the MIDAS example, the roots of Marketing Manchester stem from discussions under City Pride:

A co-ordinated marketing strategy will be developed which determines a positioning statement and brand image for the area within its designed target markets and provides a framework within which both public and private sector can participate. It will provide a strategic base on which all future marketing activity can stand, and will provide a promotional backdrop against which individual agencies can market their own products. Such a framework will reduce overlaps between agencies and will identify gaps within the marketing programme. (City Pride Strategic Planning Group 1994: 52)

Again, policy-maker deliberations were informed by the apparent success of the conurbation's second UDC, Central Manchester Development Corporation (CMDC). Just as TPDC was considered to represent a model of what could be done in terms of luring incoming companies to a suitable location at the heart of the conurbation, CMDC was perceived as similarly dextrous in fulfilling its role of marketing and manipulating the image of the city centre – and of (Greater) Manchester in a broader sense – and attracting new economic activity to the city centre peripheries as a result (Deas *et al.* 1999). Manchester's positive experience in bidding (unsuccessfully) to host the 1996 and 2000 Olympic games – which was held to have raised the city's profile, to have facilitated the development of new institutional alliances and to have reinforced the boosterist orientation of economic development policy (Cochrane *et al.*, this volume) – was cited as particular justification for the establishment of an agency with specific responsibility for place promotion. What the city and surrounding area lacked was a single body that could co-ordinate existing efforts and design and launch its own marketing campaigns.

As a result, it was decided that a strategic marketing agency would be created. Initially, it was proposed that it include only the three City Pride authorities, but this was later revised to cover all ten Greater Manchester districts: the first institutional entity formally to do so since the immediate aftermath of GMC. Unlike the former County Council, however, the impetus for the formation of Marketing Manchester came from local policy-makers and not through the top-down redrawing of government boundaries. The decision to give the agency a Greater Manchester brief was justified on the grounds that the constituent districts continued to own Manchester Airport, the new body's principal sponsor. The Visitor and Convention Bureau of GMC was expanded, refocused and re-branded, and given responsibility to market Greater Manchester (Marketing Manchester 1997b). With its wider geographical coverage and broader strategic remit, the expectation was that Marketing Manchester would complement the efforts of MIDAS in attracting investment in specific sectors to sub-units within the conurbation.

Marketing Manchester was formed as a limited company in 1996 with a first-year budget of £2.5 million. The most significant financial contribution came from Manchester Airport, which donated £1 million in each of the first three years of the new agency's tenure. The size of this financial involvement was mirrored by the organisation's wider support for the initiative. In part, this stemmed from Graham Stringer's position as chair of Manchester Airport. Stringer's involvement ensured his continued role in the city's elite-based politics and reaffirmed the appearance that, by design at least, Marketing Manchester was a Manchester-first agency. This sense was further reinforced when Sir David Trippier was appointed as the first chair of the agency – a former Conservative minister and local MP who had been pivotal during the late 1980s and early 1990s in mediating between Manchester City Council and the national Conservative government (Ward 2000a), and who had played a significant role in the city's two Olympic bids.

The initial political skirmishes around the re-presentation and re-branding of the city were protracted (Ward 2000a, 2000b). After a period of informal negotiations with existing institutions about what was and was not possible (or preferable), the agency launched a high-profile campaign to raise the international standing of Manchester. Consultation took place across public and private sectors, with the thrust of the campaign being that Manchester's economic and physical transformation should act as a leitmotif for the successes across the wider conurbation. A series of focus groups and consultancy exercises culminated in the launch at the steps of the recently opened Bridgewater Hall, in May 1997, of the *We're Up and Going* and *Great Britain, Greater Manchester* slogans. The selection of the launch site was deliberate. The Hall has played host to a series of international musical events and, as one of the city's most striking buildings, was seen as emblematic of Marketing Manchester's vision of an entrepreneurial, competitive, cosmo-politan city: 'The world needs to know all about these developments if Manchester is to take its rightful place on the world centre stage and command its share of global investment' (Sir David Trippier, quoted in *Manchester Evening News*, 15 May 1997: 1).

One of the first brochures produced by the agency again stressed the need to bridge the gap between the changes that had taken in place in Manchester (although interestingly not Greater Manchester) and more widely held negative perceptions of the city:

Manchester is surging ahead on a floodtide of economic and cultural innovations. But the world needs to know this if Manchester is to continue to attract its share of global investment, of sporting and other events, and of business and leisure events. (Marketing Manchester 1997a: 1)

Despite the apparent disjuncture between the agency's Greater Manchester remit and its narrower focus on Manchester, it was the *We're Up and Going* strand of the campaign that first received widespread local media attention. A group of local property developers formed the McEnroe Group – as a 'you cannot be serious' commentary on the agency's efforts – and set about designing their own set of slogans. At stake in the debate was a desire to maintain the recent vibrancy of property market fortunes in the city centre by influencing how it was represented (Ward 2000b). Eventually the political pressure was such that a number of key actors left the agency, including the inaugural chief executive, Elizabeth Jeffreys, and the McEnroe Group disbanded, believing that in questioning the agency's campaign it had done its job.

Claims and counter-claims over whose interests were represented through the *We're Up and Going* campaign served to suppress any discussion over the ways in which Greater Manchester was inscribed into the campaign. Specifically, one of the central goals of the campaigns of Marketing Manchester appears to have been to activate a sense of metropolitan identity. This is not rooted at any one territorial scale but rather simultaneously at a number of scales, taking a more nebulous 'imaginative' form. As the following quotes make clear, Marketing Manchester was seeking to move beyond existing political boundaries and to adopt a variable geography dependent upon the precise aspect of the city to be marketed:

Manchester is more than a geographical location or a political entity: it is a state of mind. It is Manchester United [*Trafford*] ... and the friendliest international airport in the world [*Cheshire/Manchester boundaries*]. The Manchester city region is the economic and cultural focus of the North West [*the region*], ... [and] England's North Country [*cross-region*]. (Marketing Manchester 1997a: 1)

The perception of city regions and the mental image we have of them are crucial to their economic success or failure. (Marketing Manchester 1997b: 2)

This attempt to conflate Manchester with Greater Manchester, the North West and the North of England, could be conceived as part of the agency's wider strategy to construct a 'new economic space'. This did not adhere to existing political and institutional geographies as it cross-cut and overlapped various administrative territories: the new 'Manchester' was to transcend existing formal boundaries. Rather, its constituent parts were discursively mapped and in the process were imbued with a sense of place. Through this process Marketing Manchester sought to invoke a Greater Manchester identity across its constituent villages, towns and cities and construct a positive geography that would draw selectively on major economic and political sub-areas of the metropolitan area and which could be represented across scales. For example, inward investment might have a different imagined geography than that of tourism. The point is that Greater Manchester was taken as synonymous with Manchester, while areas beyond the city's boundaries – organisations and tourist landmarks – were co-opted as Mancunian in essence and spirit, if not in physical location. This process of reimagining was outlined in explicit terms in Marketing Manchester's briefing to advertising firms bidding to work with the agency in designing the campaign:

> The whole 'city region' will be referred to as Manchester … This will necessitate a short-term communications campaign to inspire the 'locals', as well as detailed work through newly created 'sector partnerships' in order to share understanding and inspire support for a potentially difficult concept e.g. for a lifelong resident of a town such as Oldham to be proudly projecting the area as part of Manchester. This geographical hurdle is an important one. (Marketing Manchester 1996: 2)

This third example of the politics around re-placing Greater Manchester has focused on the creation of Marketing Manchester. It has dwelt on the agency's attempts to increase economic investment in Manchester and the surrounding area through a process of reimagining. If we leave to one side for a moment issues around identity and representation, this strategy is a politically complex one, as a leading local political actor involved in the marketing process acknowledged:

> I am not a Mancunian, I am a Rochdalian, and I regard Rochdale as part of the city region. And Rochdale is very different from Tameside, and is very different from Stockport. All of that [the agency is] supposed to market … If you said to a Rochdalian that the city centre of Manchester dominated their lives they'd slit your throat. So you must be careful. I spend a lot of my time actually pacifying everybody and saying '[We are] representing all of you'. (Senior executive, local institution, 1998)[1]

Highlighting the difficulties bound up in manufacturing a single identity for a diverse and politically vocal group of local property entrepreneurs, Marketing Manchester reveals how important Manchester City Council remains in local political circles. Its decision slowly to withdraw support from the agency not long after its high-profile launch could have undermined all the good partnership work done in Manchester over the last one and half decades. Instead, the flexing by the Council of its political muscles met with approval from local land developers and bar owners: the sort of elites the Council was keen to curry favour with.

Remaking metropolitan governance

After nearly a decade of city-centric governance in and of Manchester, the late 1990s saw the beginnings of a growth in metropolitan, regional and city-region institutional innovations. In part, this has been triggered by Labour's redrawing of state boundaries through such initiatives as the move to the mayor-led governance of London and the creation of Regional Development Agencies; in part, it has also stemmed from attempts within Manchester to consolidate and extend its political and economic space. What might be characterised as the City of Manchester's imperialist tendencies – which remained dormant for much of the period after the abolition of the County Council – were resurrected as the city's political actors responded to altered national political stimuli. As this chapter has outlined, this took three different but interrelated forms.

The first manifestation of a process of 're-scaling' of governance was the City Pride initiative, the geographical coverage of which was widened beyond the confines of the city of Manchester and included neighbouring Salford and Tameside. Second, a new inward investment body – MIDAS – was created to cover these three core authorities, plus adjacent Tameside. Again, tensions around the process of re-scaling of governance were evident in terms of the conflict with regionally-based mobilisations of political actors, and in terms of the debates concerning the precise configuration of the new body. And third, the advent of Marketing Manchester was significant not only in that it represented one of the few initiatives formally to cover the entire territory of the old County Council, but also in its attempts to articulate the singularity of the interests of the core city and its satellites.

The case studies of City Pride, MIDAS and Marketing Manchester illustrate the uncertainties and tensions that have underlain contemporary efforts organically to re-create metropolitan institutions and, in so doing, to create a Mancunian consciousness that extends beyond the city's artificial administrative boundaries. What these efforts reflect is the continuing frustration on the part of Manchester's policy-makers over the parsimony of these boundaries, and the continuing relevance of the metropolitan scale of governance. While the strains prompted by these metropolitan-oriented efforts are exemplified by the experience of Manchester's attempts formally to enlarge its boundaries, its regulation by unpredictable political processes (as opposed to formal institutions such as the GMC) allows it a great deal more political flexibility.

The long-standing aspiration of policy elites in Manchester to extend the city's boundaries were reinforced by the broad geographical coverage of City Pride, MIDAS and Marketing Manchester. Entrepreneurial functions are now leading the institution-building process, rather than being grafted on to existing agencies. Their ascendance represents the temporary victory of (often undemocratic) voluntaristic networks over formal structures. However, the rapidity and certitude with which these efforts were rebuffed by the surrounding boroughs is illustrative of the continuing potency of intra-metropolitan rivalries (Hebbert and Deas 2000). At one level, the peripheral boroughs appeared to be prepared to accept that their economic fortunes were bound up with those of Manchester, and they were even prepared to concede some of their political power to the new metropolitan agencies. But while many of the surrounding boroughs viewed this pragmatically as reflecting functional economic linkages, there was also a corresponding and powerful desire to remain politically independent. There is, then, a palpable tension between Manchester's attempt both to construct and own some form of new 'state space' (Brenner 1999), and the reluctance of many of the core city's neighbours to accede to this. Contemporary (Greater) Manchester, it seems, can be characterised by an economic and political geography that is as elaborate today as it was at the birth of this prototypical 'industrial region'.

Notes

The authors would like to acknowledge the compliance of economic and political actors in the North West region who gave their time during the many projects from which this chapter draws. The authors would like to thank Graham Bowden for preparing Figure 7.1. Iain Deas would like to acknowledge the assistance of the Economic and Social Research Council (award L130251032) in supporting part of the research on which this chapter is based.

1 This quote comes from an interview carried out by Adam Holden, School of Geography at the University of Manchester. Thanks to him for letting us use it here.

8

Bomb sites:
the politics of opportunity

————◆◆◆————

ADAM HOLDEN

Architecture or revolution? (Le Corbusier, 1927)

O N 15 June 1996 at 11:15am a massive explosion ripped through the heart of Manchester city centre. The 3,300lb IRA bomb, situated in a white van at the junction of Cross Street and Corporation Street and Market Street, brought devastation to people, businesses and the built environment.[1] An initial survey showed that some 1,200 buildings had been damaged, over an area over 1.2 million m². Some 49,000 m² of retail space and 57,000 m² of office space had been taken out of use and would have to be rebuilt. Despite an initial loss in city-centre retail capacity of nearly 70 per cent, only a handful of buildings were structurally damaged (Gordon 1997). The Marks & Spencer store, the Royal Insurance building (Lonridge House) and the environs of St Mary's Gate bore the brunt of the blast and were condemned to demolition. The Arndale shopping centre and tower, which dominates a whole block of the city centre, was also badly damaged. The Royal Exchange Theatre and the Corn Exchange (both Grade 2 listed buildings) were left in need of major renovation. Altogether 674 businesses were displaced by the bomb. Many people who owned or were employed by city-centre businesses faced the consequences of loss of stock and income. The vulnerability of small-scale traders was exacerbated by a high level of under-insurance (Gordon 1997). After an initial survey, the total bill for rebuilding the city centre was estimated at £500 million, excluding loss of income. While it was expected that much of this could be met by insurance companies and private developers, there was understandable concern in the city about the need to find an estimated £100 million of public funding.

In the days following the explosion local media and city leaders tended to stress the scale and economic costs of the damage, but also the

THEY WENT FOR THE HEART OF MANCHESTER. BUT MISSED THE SOUL.

TOGETHER WE CAN REBUILD OUR CITY.

Manchester Evening News

Plate 8 Manchester fights back ...

resilient spirit of the city and its people (Plate 8). Within a few weeks, however, the tendency to emphasise the negative social and economic consequences of the bomb had been replaced, or at least complemented, by a tendency to 'talk up' the opportunities it presented for urban regeneration (Plate 9). At a local and national level this politics of opportunity came to characterise the dominant response to rebuilding. In light of these opportunities, and the discourses and resources mobilised around them, the Manchester bomb has become understood as a pivotal moment in the city's *revolution* of partnership and revitalisation.

Managing crisis as opportunity

The first few days after the bombing of Manchester city centre were dominated by feelings of shock and anger, and a palpable sense of communal loss. The commercial, geographical and symbolic heart of this distinctive regional capital had been badly bruised. Nevertheless, the rapid response of the city, co-ordinated through the existing partnership networks, helped to minimise the damage and get the centre up and running quickly.[2] As well as co-ordinating the practical response city leaders began to assess the situation – in both public and private – and articulate how the rebuilding should proceed. A basic discursive tension emerged between (a) the opportunity for genuine improvements and (b) the negative economic consequences of the bomb. The 'threat' to the city centre was constructed in terms of both the issue of losing trade to other economic spaces (such as out-of-town shopping centres) and in terms of uncertainty surrounding the flow of financial support from

AFTER THE BLAST, THE REPERCUSSIONS.

JOIN THE DEBATE ABOUT MANCHESTER'S FUTURE.

Manchester **Evening News**

OPENING UP THE ISSUES

Plate 9 After the bomb, let the regeneration begin ...

central government and the private sector (including insurance). This discursive construction of the common interest of 'the city centre' against 'external threat' has been fundamental to the evolution of the rebuilding process at every stage. It is the various manifestations of this tension – at several political scales – that the city partnership has attempted to manage, both practically and discursively.

The politics of opportunity emerged through three interrelated domains. First, the formal and informal meetings between key representatives of public- and private-sector interests, including the city-centre landowners. Second, the support and interest from central government, primarily through visits and meetings with Michael Heseltine and John Gummer. Third, a wider public discourse of opportunity in the city, focused around the media and a series of public debates.

Although the cost of funding the rebuilding remained a worry for the city council, the dominant concern was to mobilise the opportunity in terms of Manchester's entrepreneurial strategy. At first there was an opportunity to demonstrate Manchester's dynamism and spirit: 'Manchester is famous for self-help, getting on with the job. It is not a city which quits and runs. We are used to winning on all fronts, including economic fronts. I know some of my friends already see in as an opportunity to rebuild. (Terry Thomas, Co-operative Bank, *Manchester Evening News*, 17 June 1996). This was further rooted in a unique opportunity to improve the quality of the built environment and the retail centre. The city centre had long been considered as an important but highly problematic site for redevelopment (MCC 1984a). Through the selective development work of the Central Manchester Development Corporation

(CMDC) and the analysis of City Pride, the city partnership had established a commonly accepted understanding of the weaknesses of the city, in terms of the design and planning legacy of the 1960s and 1970s (Deas *et al.* 1999). Equally, just prior to the bomb, Manchester City Council (MCC) had been preparing to update the city-centre local plan drawing on the urban design and development framework established through Hulme City Challenge (HRL 1994). In this sense the city was, in development terms, perfectly poised to respond to a wholly unexpected contingency. Moreover, the opportunity to redevelop totally a large part of the retail core had resonance with the desire to establish Manchester as a quality European city. The opportunity to enhance the symbolic and functional value of the city centre promised to give greater credence to the wider regeneration of the city-region. The sheer scope of the opportunity to manage and co-ordinate development was, however, totally outside the experience of MCC's leadership. While the bulldozer-led 'regeneration' of the Hulme estate had provided something akin to a *tabula rasa*, the city centre presented a planning and implementation scenario that was both highly time-critical and characterised by a complex pattern of built form and ownership.

The institutional response to the bomb was both rapid and multi-faceted. Within MCC an emergency committee (Manchester City Centre Task Force) was set up and a team of planning and regeneration specialists was established: As one officer explained 'The bomb went off on the Saturday, I was seconded at 8:30 on the Sunday morning' (Officer, Manchester Millennium, June 1998). Characteristically, however, MCC resisted any temptation to impose itself or its solutions too forcefully on the crisis. Instead, MCC acted to extend its hegemony over Manchester city politics. As we shall see, the rebuilding process gradually enabled MCC leaders to occupy a central and highly visible role in managing the whole project and making explicit demands on private-sector partners and central government. In a rare reversal of the usual 'enabling' attitude, the statutory responsibility of MCC to secure satisfactory development actually became understood as a strength. It gave the leadership a mandate to make demands on others in the name of the good of the city and was 'a fabulous opportunity to be dominant' (Senior business leader, November 1996). Particularly in the initial stages, however, the MCC leadership did what came most naturally: they worked on the 'inside' within the wider city partnership and with central government.

The first days after the bomb saw a great deal of 'behind the scenes' work between the key players in the public and private sector. In an initial meeting in the former Bank of England building a meeting took place with 'a number of worthies around the table' (Officer, Manchester Millennium, November 1996).[3] The discussion was contextualised by strong and suggestive support from Central Government, in the familiar figure of Michael Heseltine:

> At the time the bomb went off there was a very strong Government view from the deputy Prime Minister, Mr. Heseltine ... that the way forward in terms of turning a disaster into an opportunity ... was some form of joint public-sector/private-sector arrangement. (Officer, Manchester Millennium, 1998)

While it was clear that Heseltine was particularly keen on instigating some form of competition to maximise the input of design and planning from the private sector, the specific institutional solution was worked out by the local public-private partners. A private-sector officer recalled how this discussion was couched in terms of a collective opportunity:

> This is a one-off opportunity to radically treat an area of the city that may have developed over time. There has never been ... an opportunity to look at a big [central] chunk of a city and impose some real quality on it. It is normally a piecemeal process which is full of compromises because you put up a certain building in a certain place because it fits ... This time we've looked at the whole transportation links into the city ... It's given us the chance to take an overview ... to really redesign the city centre as we think it should be. We in the widest sense. (Officer, Manchester Millennium, 1996)

With verbal guarantees of financial and political support from Central Government, the city partners began to establish a group of public and private sector secondees under the joint leadership of Sir Alan Cockshaw (AMEC) and Howard Bernstein (Deputy Chief Executive of MCC).[4] On 1 July 1996, the Task Force officially became 'Manchester Millennium Limited' (MM), a public-private partnership dedicated to overseeing the rebuilding process. Heseltine's rhetorical support for the local politics of opportunity was rapidly backed up by material and institutional concessions, in some ways confirming Manchester's status as a 'favoured' city. On 3 July 1996, Heseltine announced a two-pronged support package that would become the focus for MM. First, came the provision of £20 million as the initial instalment of an aid package. In fact this was not 'new' money, but involved the reallocation of European Regional Aid (ERDF) for 1997–99.[5] Second, an International Urban Design Competition was to be launched, and run by MM to help formulate a new vision of the city for the twenty-first century. The costs of design competition were to be covered through £1 million from the ERDF and matched by £1 million from MCC.

Only two weeks after the bomb had exploded, therefore, the basic institutional and policy mechanisms for the rebuilding programme had been established. Despite the reallocation of £20 million of European regional aid to MM, actual financial support from Central Government was extremely weak. They contributed only £150,000 as part of a wait-and-see policy which allowed Manchester to compete for additional public-sector funding once the basis for the rebuilding programme had been established. While this (public) funding 'gap' was an ongoing source of tension between local and central government, it did not interfere with the work of MM. Indeed, the institutional space created by MM enabled MCC to act as both an entrepreneurial agent within the local partnership process and as a statutory body 'fighting' for Manchester's allocation of public resources. Nevertheless, officers in MM and MCC worked rapidly over the following week to create a documentary basis for the competition.

At the same time as the Government's announcement, the notion of rebuilding as an opportunity (for redesign and regeneration) gathered popular support in the city. This culminated, at least symbolically, in a televised public debate in early July 1996. In the immediate aftermath of the bomb the *Manchester Evening News* (the regional newspaper with the largest circulation outside London) had begun a poster campaign which supported the notion of a rebuilding opportunity. The second poster announced and helped to popularise the idea of a city-wide debate about Manchester's future. This 'Rebuilding Manchester Debate' was organised by the *Manchester Evening News*, Manchester Civic Society and Marketing Manchester in an attempt to provide a forum for public debate about the future of the city. There were a significant number of angry and discontented voices – notably those concerned with the treatment of employees and retailers in the Corn Exchange and Royal Exchange. The basic tone and thematic content of the debate, however, was framed by the axioms of realising opportunity through partnership, in order to secure economic regeneration through redevelopment (Box 8.1).

The scope of the debate was effectively limited to a form of consultation about redesign. As such the hegemony of the entrepreneurial mode of development was never really challenged. This did not, however, detract from the importance of *talking about debate* as a way of promoting the public ownership of the rebuilding process. The debate was an important event, however, not least because it publicly set out the parameters and tensions of the opportunity. Moreover a number of the themes emerged which complemented and fed into the principles of the design competition, particularly through a taken-for-granted assessment

Box 8.1 Content analysis of the first rebuilding debate

Pretext and context. A video made by BBC North was screened in order to prime the debate. This set a discursive context that emphasised the opportunity for redesign. Rebuilding, with a more flexible approach to planning was seen as a way to revitalise and diversify the city centre, and thereby stimulate the economy.

Introductions. The panel and key experts were introduced. They tended to stress the opportunity to rethink the layout of the centre, but outlined the general conflict between radical change and continuity of trade.

Local conflict. A series of conflicts emerged over the plight of businesses. For example, staff in the Royal Exchange who had lost their jobs and Corn Exchange traders who could not access their stock. The issue of insurance and compensation from central government caused considerable anger. This led to suggestions that more resources should be provided for the city in both the short and long term.

The Arndale shopping centre. It became the focus for a debate about the redesign of the look and plan of the built environment. The imposing size and 1960s-style of the Arndale was attacked by almost everyone. There was also a rejection of earlier planning practices.

Improving the city centre as a place for living, working, and playing. There was a particular focus on improving the diversity and accessibility of the shopping areas. In general, however, there was a concern to attract people back to a more 'pleasant' centre, and thereby stimulate the economy. For example, improving the urban environment, tackling crime, and opening up certain 'dead' spaces, were all seen as ways to revitalise the centre.

Transport. This was seen as fundamental to sustained redevelopment. Pedestrianisation and investment in public transport were identified as important ways to attract people back to the city centre. This renewed vitality would then bring prosperity and regeneration back to the core.

The need for a strategic vision. This would co-ordinate the wide range of ideas and inputs, and ensure the city could 'get it right'.

of the positive and negative effects of the 'opportunity'.[6] The real decision-making, however, had already been undertaken by the city elite. On 17 July 1996, the discursive fluidity produced by the moment of crisis came to an end. The politics of opportunity was given an official concrete-institutional form just one month after the bomb as the design competition was launched in Manchester.

Designs on Manchester

The Task Force's stage one document (MCCTF 1996a) demonstrated the manner in which the hegemonic assumptions and practices of the entrepreneurial city underpinned the vision of the rebuilding process. The text is worth quoting in full:

> A recovery plan is now underway to support businesses and people affected as they now rebuild their livelihoods. The City, already noted for its resilience and dynamism, has drawn upon the strengths of its existing partnerships, and, working with Government, has committed itself to ensuring that out of adversity, a stronger, more vibrant City for the 21st Century will emerge over the next 2/3 years, to rival anywhere in Europe. What we rebuild will be better than that which was damaged. In order to make this happen the City Pride Partnership is now launching a major international urban design competition, so that the world's best talents can contribute to the achievement of this vision. We believe that this is a unique opportunity to play a role in the re-planning of the World's first industrial city, so that it becomes a model for other cities approaching the next Millennium. The Government and the City Council have established a Task Force to oversee and champion the regeneration programme, and to work closely with the private sector and the wider community, to ensure successful delivery. We look forward to the submission of imaginative and realistic ideas to complement the needs and aspirations of a great Regional Capital City. (MCCTF 1996a: 1)

A number of important discursive practices can be identified which embed the general vocabulary of 'rebuilding Manchester' in the hegemonic discourses of the entrepreneurial city. Two examples of this strategy are: (a) the linking of public-private partnership to a pluralistic mode of consultation which can ensure 'successful delivery'; and (b) linking the rebuilding aims to an ideologically invested vision of Manchester as a vibrant, futuristic, and European city.

The launch of the competition gave the first public insight into the city-wide negotiations which had enabled the partnership to build a consensus. The role of MCC in co-ordinating all the city-centre interests was emphasised:

> The City Council really took a pre-emptive strike. Obviously they had emergency procedures already set up, but they took a very strong lead and people looked to them for guidance ... It's amazing how in the face of adversity so many people can work together. (Senior business leader, 1996)

It was also made clear that the talks which occurred before and after the announcement of the competition had greatly benefited from the relationships and forms of decision-making which had emerged in the city over the past decade or so. This slim-line and flexible group of public- and private-sector partners, with its high level of inter-connectivity, was seen to hold the key to the process of consensus building:

> That [city partnership] started in the late 80s, early 90s. And so people already start off on the basis of knowing each other. It's a big city, but it's a very small world. There is a hundred or so people, and we meet here, there, everywhere. … If the bomb had gone off ten years ago, then we'd have had total anarchy. (Senior business leader, 1996)

The launch of the design competition also introduced the public–private partnership to the city. On 29 July 1996, Millennium Manchester was launched as a limited company, empowered to co-ordinate and implement the rebuilding strategy. Headed by Sir Alan Cockshaw (chairman of the building firm AMEC), MM gave further institutional legitimacy to an already powerful elite of 'movers and shakers' in local governance (Peck 1995). It also, however, developed a powerful role for MCC's chief regeneration officer, Howard Bernstein (then Deputy Chief Executive). Setting up offices in the prestigious 81 Fountain Street Development, the basic structure of the MM Task Force was established by the time the first round of the design competition closed on 23 August 1996. The MM board of directors was composed of a variety of public- and private-sector agents, with central government represented through Marianne Neville-Rolfe, the then Regional Director of the Government Office for the North West (and later to become the first chief executive of New East Manchester Ltd). Although MM was designed to operate as an independent body, it reported ultimately to MCC's City Pride Emergency Committee, chaired by City Council Leader, Richard Leese.

The remit of the MM Task Force was three-fold: first, to co-ordinate the logistics of the initial rebuilding and assistance; second, to manage, judge and implement the vision provided through the design competition; and third, to lever funding from central government and private investors. In an important sense the Task Force was an attempt to institutionalise the tension between fully and efficiently realising the opportunity, and the desire to mitigate the negative economic consequences of rebuilding. A member of the team commented: 'That's the Task Force's role … To balance urgency with quality' (Senior business leader, 1996).

A number of informants stressed the leading role played by the Town Hall. Nevertheless, the Task Force was seen to be the best solution in terms of managing future consensus and delivering the final master plan.

This structure was seen as flexible, politically neutral and at arm's length from MCC (who have extensive interest in the competition area as land-owners):

> It was felt that this [Task Force] was the best solution, in terms of: Let's set up a brand new public-private partnership, give it a glossy name, and a front door. And then people know exactly, it's the shop window, really, for all the other activities that happen in the town hall and the land owners and for everybody else. So everybody would know exactly where to come to for help, assistance. So we are the sort of glue that holds things together. The idea was that it was always going to be a small tight team bringing in legal resources from the City Council and property resources from the City Council ... Nobody has had their nose put out of joint and I think a large part of that is to do with Howard (Bernstein) still having his feet in both camps in certain respects ... Howard's a very innovative person, and he's always looking for the next challenge and this is one hell of a challenge. (Officer, MM, 1996)

The role played by Howard Bernstein, on behalf of the City Council, was clearly a pivotal one and it will be discussed in more detail at the end of the chapter. At this stage, however, it is clear that MM afforded MCC a considerable degree of control over the whole process, while ensuring the creative, legal and financial inputs of the private sector landowners. Once again, however, those involved strongly emphasised the importance of building on an existing vision of the city's development and delivering growth through partnership.

The first phase of the design competition closed on 23 August 1996 with a total of twenty-seven entries. The entries were evaluated by the MM Task Force, in consultation with the landowners. Just eight key landowners controlled the majority of the competition area, and were crucial to the overall shaping of the second stage.[7] The concentration of these direct interests in relatively few hands, and the fact that there was a degree of overlapping ownership, greatly facilitated the co-ordination process at every stage:

> We couldn't have gone through this process if there had been a hundred [land] owners. There are half a dozen people or companies that are either going to make or break this whole initiative. And I should add the City Council in with that, because they are a major land-holder. In terms of levers that is a key level – the City Council as freeholder. And it's also got some fairly substantial leasehold interests in the area. (Senior business leader, 1996)

This did not prevent conflict emerging between some interest groups (Holden 1999), but it did simplify the basis for consultation and negotiation. Indeed, because of the privacy rules exerted by both the competition and MM's status as a private company, the whole process was managed internally within the Task Force executive. In the initial stages, however, there was a progressive formation and consolidation of the group of people and organisations who would co-ordinate the second round. This was clearly rooted in the perception of trust and shared objectives which characterise the city's governance and self-image.

On 4 September 1996, the five short-listed designs were announced, along with a document outlining the objectives for the second round (MCCTF 1996b).[8] The second round signalled a considerable advance in the rebuilding consensus, both in terms of the vision of regeneration through 'quality design', and through the formalisation and intensi-fication of the negotiations between the interest groups and competitors. The document also outlined the structure of the jury, the detailed requirements for each of the building sites, and the overall aims of the evaluation. During this stage of the process, MM sought to manage and guide the formulation of the second-round bids without inhibiting the range or creativity of the designs. Following the submission of the five final designs on 18 October 1996, the evaluation process involved the preparation of a series of reports by the MM Task Force (and others in Town Hall) for the jury. To this end MM's staff were divided into a series of evaluation groups dedicated to considering commercial, technical, transport and architectural-design issues. Each drew on a range of experts, although it is notable that Bernstein played a direct role in the commercial evaluation group (the most sensitive aspect of the negotiation process). The jury was composed of a number of MM board members along with some independent advisers, most notably Joe Berridge, the Canadian urban design specialist whom Cockshaw had first brought in as a consultant on Hulme City Challenge.[9] Following Stringer's example, the MCC leadership blended their own interests with the expertise and legitimacy of independent and private-sector advisers.

Manchester City Council also took a strong role in the various forms of public consultation and civil debate that emerged in parallel to the MM negotiations. These included the results of a MORI poll, and a number of focus groups with local adults, children and organisations. The five competing designs were also put on display at Manchester Town Hall, with about one-third of the 3,000 visitors completing the evaluation sheet. Prior to this on 21 September 1996, a group of environ-mental campaign groups, headed by Manchester Friends of the Earth, held a public consultation exercise in Shambles Square. The findings of this unofficial exercise, entitled 'Planning for Real' (Manchester Friends of the Earth 1996), were also incorporated into the judges' evaluation. Once again the *Manchester Evening News* played an important role in supporting the public ownership of both the rebuilding process and the notion of a vision for the millennium. It announced: 'your chance to shape the Manchester of the twenty-first century' (*Manchester Evening News*, 18 October 1996).

It would be misleading, however, to suggest that the consultation was particularly important to the overall decision-making process. The MM Task Force sought the widest possible range of opinion, but the choice of detailed design remained with the key landowners. Instead, the major features of public concern (pedestrianisation, green spaces, safety, and public transport) were integrated into the delivery of specific improvements to public spaces and infrastructure, and in terms of overall 'quality'. Indeed the whole evaluation process was predicated on the need to secure broad consensus about the nature of the framework. The selection and evaluation of the second-round bids only consolidated that process. The designs were judged in terms of design quality, deliverability and the overall *creativity* needed to 'bring it all together'. Five criteria were emphasised (MCCTF 1996b: 25): (a) the creation of a compelling urban design vision; (b) the imaginative interpretation of the design and development aspirations; (c) the demonstration of a clear, workable approach to phasing and implementation; (d) the encouragement of private-sector investment; (e) the economy of and justification for public expenditure.

The judging took place behind closed doors, and the true nature of what might be called the 'rebuilding settlement' was not made clear until the winner was announced. In the meantime all but seventy of the displaced businesses had been successfully relocated, and much of the city centre had been reopened. Despite the high cost to individuals, businesses and the city as a whole, the first four or five months after the bomb were characterised by a remarkably dynamic and (in some ways) high-profile political and institutional effort to make the very most of Heseltine's international design competition. To an important degree, however, this period was characterised by a suspension of the real forces of competition between interests, and – most crucially – the uncertain nature of the public and private funding regime. These pressures were limited by a basic trust among the city partners and the belief that the scope of the opportunity would sow its own success. Nevertheless, with the final stage of the design competition immanent, the honeymoon period of the politics of opportunity would shortly come to an end.

The winning design was announced on 5 November 1996, with EDAW[10] as the judges choice:

EDAW, together with six consulting partners, for the international, national and local team of architects and consultants whose new urban framework has been chosen by the competition jury from five finalists. This scheme will form the basis of an urban design and planning framework for the reconstruction of a city centre which will carry Manchester proudly into the 21st Century. The jury also recommended to Manchester Millennium Limited … that Building Design Partnership be retained to refine, within EDAW's framework, their imaginative proposals for the River Irwell and Cathedral/Cheethams area. (Task Force, press release, 5 November 1996)

The details and vision of this nascent master plan received a great deal of press coverage. While some in the national press were disappointed by the conservative and pragmatic solution – 'City prefers commerce to vision' (*The Times*, 6 November 1996) – the regional daily led with an understandably more positive and boosterist message: 'Welcome to 21st century: Square with a view and a wintergarden' (*Manchester Evening News*, 5 November 1996). A more complete review of the EDAW plan is given below (Box 8.2).

In many ways the EDAW bid was the more conservative and cautious choice. The judges noted that Manchester First had provided the most imaginative, locally sensitive and radical design, including the popular idea of a large public park. Clearly, the issue of deliverability and commercial viability had ruled this out in favour of EDAW. In a manner that echoes the tensions discussed at the public debate, Jonathan Glancey observed: 'The judges' choice has made it clear that what was wanted was a team and a design that could give birth to a new centre on a tight budget and in the shortest possible time' (*Independent*, 6 November 1996). This does not, however, deny the overall excellence of the EDAW design. The simple, but sophisticated, pedestrian spine running from St Ann's Square to the cathedral, for example, was seen as a crucial concession to non-commercial needs (Owen Luder, Task Force press release, 5 November 1996). In the end, however, the success of the EDAW scheme was rooted in the ability of the Task Force to represent the common interest of the city in terms of an overall increase in quality, at both the commercial and public level. In short, it was felt that the EDAW plan (and the Task Force) had struck the right balance between the need to pull in the private sector, and the need to secure additional benefits for the overall quality of the environment:

EDAW went through a very thoughtful process about how to make a quality city … We want a much bigger and better city centre but in order to get the land owners to do this we need to add value. So there was quite a

Box 8.2 Summary of the EDAW master plan

A new, bigger Marks & Spencer to be rebuilt on its old site. A walkway through the centre of the M&S store will link the Arndale to Shambles Square.

The Arndale centre will remain largely untouched, but the Arndale Tower will be re-clad and sections of the roof and walls will be replaced with glass to allow more natural light into the shopping centre.

A pedestrianised route will run from St Ann's Square to the Cathedral, incorporating a new public square and a park around the historic place of worship. The Sinclair's pub in Shambles Square will be moved to allow for this new walkway, and residential buildings will be constructed at the rear of Shambles Square.

Cannon Street will be turned into a covered Winter Garden creating a new shopping street to replace the bus station.

A new Arndale Food court will be created at the Withy Grove side of the shopping complex with an expanded market behind it.

Corporation Street will be reserved for pedestrians and buses only, and a special 'bus loop' will be created around the centre.

A Trocadero is planned for Maxwell House, with a cinema and games complex. EDAW will also construct a cultural centre on the site of the existing NCP car park with a library and theatre.

Source: EDAW 1996

strong theme of commerciality running through this. And fortunately, when it came to making the decision the urban design and vision and quality – what EDAW was trying to create – ... worked commercially as well. (Senior officer, MM, 1998)

Richard Leese summarised the result in a manner that implies a remarkable success for MCC and the people of Manchester:

Just days after the IRA bomb we promised to rebuild the city centre in a way that befits the 21st century. We wanted a centre with more shops, more leisure activity, more housing and more jobs. One that is greener and friendlier to pedestrians but with first class transport access. EDAW's winning submission gives us a superb basis for doing just that. (Leader of MCC, press release, 5 November 1996)

In one sense Leese's analysis of the moment is correct. The design competition and the EDAW plan set out a framework to deliver a bigger, better and higher-quality city centre. It also lent material credence to the boosterist efforts of the wider partnership and the entrepreneurial city strategy. Nevertheless, at a practical level the period that followed the announcement of the EDAW masterplan saw a significant change in the mood and vibrancy of the rebuilding process. The period from November 1996 to April 1997 was characterised by considerable uncertainty and difficulty as MM and MCC struggled to secure the financial, planning and technical conditions from the implementation of the EDAW masterplan. Equally, after a long period dominated by the dynamics of the rebuilding process, 1997 saw the re-emergence of the wider projects and processes associated with the legacy of Stringer's entrepreneurial phase (Quilley, this volume).

With the design competition over, the rebuilding process largely receded from the public gaze. Subsequently, EDAW and the MM Task Force worked to refine the details of the plan. This was described as negotiating 'with the gloves off': according to an officer at MM, 'There's been a strong consensus to date, and now people are actually getting down to the hard realities of negotiating position' (November 1996). Behind closed doors, a series of tensions surfaced in terms of a large area of the Arndale Shopping Centre. Mostly owned by P&O, but with some parts controlled by MCC and the Prudential, the Arndale dominated much of the redevelopment site. While parts of the facade had been damaged, the majority of the structure remained in place. Contrary to the aspirations of MCC, the other landowners and popular opinion, P&O wanted to keep the Arndale largely as it was. The site was particularly significant for the commercial redevelopment because it was adjacent to the prospective site for the replacement Marks and Spencer's store. In public these conflicts went largely unnoticed, with emphasis being given to MCC's desire to 'fast-track' the integration of the EDAW masterplan with its City Centre Plan, producing a Supplementary Strategic Planning Guidance. Within MM, however, both 'carrots and sticks' were deployed in negotiations with the land owners and MCC in attempts to overcome these problems. As one MCC officer explained: 'It's all about rounding them up and pointing them up in the right direction' (Officer, MM, 1998). With this process dominating the energies of MM, the rest of the city adjusted to the life after the design competition.

Heart of the city

Within the city at large, the issue of funding remained a crucial, but sore, point. While the private sector insisted that they would provide the real source of money, MCC came increasingly to call on central government to guarantee and deliver public money. This central–local tension became even more apparent after Manchester's Local Government Financial Settlement left the City facing a £14 million shortfall, prompting a potential 15 per cent rise in council tax. Throughout the general uncertainty surrounding the funding of Manchester's nascent 'growth (or grant) regime' (Jones and Ward 1998), a pervasive image of the city as both a victim (of terrorism) and a site of dynamic and innovative partnership was articulated to construct a city-centred form of solidarity. Bitterness over the 'unfair' treatment of Manchester did not, however, detract from claims that the rebuilding process had instilled the partnership with renewed dynamism and vision. Within the city the rebuilding process began to enter the ongoing (re) narration of the decade of radical change: 'making it happen'. One member of the Task Force commented:

> There's a certain arrogance in the nicest sense about Manchester. It feels it deserves the best, and I think this is an attempt to give the best within the framework of the city that's already there. Yeah it's about creating a regional centre – which the city was anyway – but, really building on that and increasing its value. (Senior business leader, 1996)

This re-valuing of the heart of the city centre has been, and always was, linked into a distinctive, yet contradictory, hegemonic project to restructure and reimagine Manchester's political economy (Holden 1999). The politics of local opportunity both demonstrated, and reinforced, the hegemony of the entrepreneurial city as a vision of place and a mode of economic strategy. The design competition and Task Force gave a new focus and lease of life to the wider narrative of Manchester as a 'happening' and successful place. In many ways the experience of the bomb was remarkable and unique. But the long-term contradictions concealed by this pragmatic and opportunistic mode of politics were not seriously addressed. Equally, the wider 'entrepreneurial' economic strategy, which was reasserted and re-inscribed through the rebuilding process, remained dependent on a post-Labourist form of intervention. In particular, the post-bomb period saw MCC's most innovative, dynamic and high-profile energies spent on 'making it happen'. The need to present a positive image of the city to prospective retail capital led to a continuation of the hegemonic representational regime that had emerged through the Olympic bidding process.

The post-Labourist nature of the politics of opportunity also impacted on the selective nature of the city-wide 'collective interest'. In a manner that was as much neo-corporatist as it was entrepreneurial, MCC's desire and ability to champion popular interests within the city was firmly limited by their partnership with the big land and property owners. An interesting example of this emerged in the context of the first and second public debates on the rebuilding process. In the second public debate (28 November 1996) the issue of the exclusion and mistreatment of some of the small-scale traders in the city centre emerged again. A particularly aggrieved group of about one hundred traders were displaced from their tenancy in the Corn Exchange. Initially, their complaints focused around the fact that safety experts in MCC would not allow them to enter the damaged structure to recover an estimated £500,000 in stock. In December 1996, however, the source of the antagonism became clearer. Before the bomb, the owners of the Corn Exchange, the London-based Frogmore Investments Limited, had been the archetypal absentee landlord. With little interest in investing in either the stimulation of business activity or the Corn Exchange building itself, Frogmore's investment had become characterised by inertia and neglect. The only income came from the 'under-valued' rents provided by the hundred or so businesses that sub-let space through long-term and legally cast-iron leases. To the great surprise of the traders in December 1996 Frogmore terminated all the existing leases and announced its intention to refurbish the Corn Exchange in order to attract higher-quality retail units. In a bid to popularise and legitimate this, the idea of a Manchester-based Harvey Nichols department store was circulated. This resonated with the dominant entrepreneurial city principle of inter-urban-competition, by arguing that such a development would put Manchester on equal terms with Leeds city centre which had recently opened the first Harvey Nichols store outside London. Despite the protests and legal action taken by the Corn Exchange traders, Frogmore's plan was wholly legal, utilising an obscure sub-clause in the leasing arrangements which asserted the right of the landowner to renege on all existing contracts in the event that the property should require 'major structural redevelopment'. The Manchester bomb, that mother of all contingencies, provided just this circumstance. MCC and MM made provision for the surviving small traders, providing financial assistance through the Lord Mayor's charitable fund and assisting relocation to the Oldham Street and Northern Quarter areas of the city. Nevertheless, MCC clearly sided with big business in an attempt to reshape the retail geography of the city centre. The strategic 'solidarities' of the entrepreneurial city demanded that MCC take the opportunity to enhance the quality and value of the previously run-down part of the city centre. On the one hand, this was a perfectly common-sense response to the maximisation of opportunity in the interests of the city. On the other hand, it reveals the way in which the opportunity to regenerate the city centre of Manchester must be understood within the broader context of urban renaissance and the urbanisation of capital (Holden 1999; cf. Deben *et al*. 1994; Harvey 1985).

Explosive entrepreneurialism

The institutional and political processes that accompanied the rebuilding of Manchester city centre precipitated three forms of opportunity. First, the bomb literally cleared a space for the physical redesign of the existing commercial core and allowed an influx of private and state capital to fund redevelopment in line with the City Pride vision of Manchester as a quality European City. Second, the rebuilding project re-energised the much-vaunted public-private partnership and gave further legitimacy to the vision of Manchester as a vibrant entrepreneurial city. Third, it enabled MCC to move centre stage within the partnership in a way that affirmed its strategic project for a more entrepreneurial and innovative role within local governance.

At a broader level the period from 1996 to 1999 saw the emergence of complex and contradictory tendencies in Manchester city politics. Within this the role of MCC, and its ongoing attempt to develop and influence a locally-networked hegemonic project, was altered in a significant way. The establishment of MM provided MCC with influence through a distinct institutional and discursive space, that was somewhat removed from the constraints and responsibilities of the town hall. Although MM has a specific remit and a limited life-span, it helped to establish a leading role for Howard Bernstein and thereby secured an explicitly entrepreneurial view of urban regeneration at the heart of MCC. Bernstein's role as a mover and shaker – 'with his feet in both camps' – was very important in terms of the ability of the Task Force to deliver (and guarantee) the synergies offered by co-ordination and partnership. It is worth noting the enabling and entrepreneurial role that Bernstein played. A Task Force member saw Bernstein as an exemplar of success in Manchester's local governance:

The more innovative and dynamic local authorities are actually becoming more like the private-sector players than the private sector. ... I mean Howard [Bernstein] bends the rules, does deals and then works backwards in terms of ... do the deal and then work backwards, and intuitively knows that it's the right thing to do. And then we'll sort out all of the paper-work afterwards. (1996)

It is this ability to manage the wider vision, while delivering specific benefits to the landowners in a flexible manner, which has ensured the pivotal position of the City Council in the rebuilding process. In one sense the particular conditions of the bomb has enabled the City Council to take up a dominant, yet enabling, position at the heart of the current partnership.

The kind of role for MCC that Bernstein has developed is simul-taneously assertive about the capacity of local government's ability to 'make it happen' and realistic about the way this capacity is strongly prescribed by MCC's relation to other partners. Consider these two contrasting statements:

The City Council is without doubt the most effective local authority in pioneering economic change and economic development, investment and all the rest of it. Yet in those terms [of electoral democracy] it is largely invisible, because *it's* the power structure. But it is the way the *Council* decides to share power with other structures to deliver change on the ground. I think in those terms the City Council is probably the most sophis-ticated structure of government anywhere to be found anywhere in the country. (Senior officer, MM, 1998)

What you have to recognise is that the key agencies which have the most powerful influence of all where social regeneration is concerned are all agencies that are not under the control of local government ... (for example) you know transport is deregulated. We can't even oppose a bloody bus stop for God's sake, well not effectively! Employment policies have been placed in the hands of unaccountable TECs and you know the list is endless. And therefore when authorities like Manchester say 'the great cities of the next Millennium will be the ones which marry more effectively greater competitiveness internationally with local benefits'; we have to recognise that our capacity to deliver that by ourselves is pretty limited, because we haven't got control over the apparatus which secures local benefit. (Senior officer, MM, 1998)

This position is fundamental to the ambiguity at the heart of both Stringer's project and the sometimes uneasy post-Stringer consensus. The basic attempt to depoliticise local government should not simply be understood as the prerogative of the right. In Manchester the new urban left has developed a contradictory but powerful project to break with the limitations of the Keynesian welfare state (see Quilley, this volume). By accepting the fundamental weakness of its position, MCC has pursued a high-risk strategy. But by reimagining a future polity and economy that are united in the prospects of the entrepreneurial city, the leadership has at least attempted to transcend its historical position. During the Stringer period, however, there was little evidence of the city's ability to secure a hard economic core for hegemony. With the exception of the airport, the majority of 'economic' projects were fundamentally limited by the scope of the funding and the weaknesses of 'supply-side socialism' (Thomas 1996).

What has changed in the post-Stringer period is the conspicuous division of labour between two strands of MCC strategy. The first, represented by MM and personified by Bernstein, attempts to match the movers and shakers at their own game. The second element, reflected in Leese's leadership of the social agenda, is attempting to develop alternatives alongside this 'fire-fighting role'. Important though this reassertion of the politics of need is, in the light of New Labour's apparent inability to move beyond the crisis of the Keynesian welfare state, the *combination* of urban entrepreneurialism and local corporatism is seen to be the best way to exploit those few opportunities to 'make it happen' that arise.

Three elements of 'entrepreneurial' practice can be tentatively identified. First, MCC operates through elite-based practice based around the development of 'a highly focused, skilled, but informal series of relationships' (Officer, MM, 1996). Second, its management of opportunity is holistic and responsive. Third, it develops the potential of institutions that are at some distance from the town hall in order to allow a dedicated elite to operate around and within certain existing structures. This issue is particularly pronounced in terms of MCC's statutory powers. A significant part of the rebuilding process involved MCC in a fairly managerialist and corporatist role, using its statutory responsibilities to co-ordinate the process and legitimise demands made on other partners. Through MM, and Howard Bernstein in particular, however, MCC was able to tap directly into an alternative way of 'making it happen'. Commenting on the way of working in MM, one MCC officer argued, 'Because we haven't got statutory powers it is actually possible to become a much more potent and radical force' (Senior officer, MCC and MM, 1998).

Although this entrepreneurialism has compounded an absence of direct democratic involvement and subordinated decentralisation to relevancy, it has succeeded where more managerialist practices have often conspicuously failed. In the post-bomb phase, MCC's overall project is therefore rooted in the selective articulation of entrepreneurial and corporatist-managerialism strategies to gain influence, develop a city-wide agenda and – above all – grab grants (Jones and Ward 1998).

In a manner that resonates with much of its history, the contemporary attempts to reconstruct Manchester politics and rebuild the city have been wrought from a combination of pragmatism, opportunism and localist individualism (Holden 1999). The politics of the post-bomb rebuilding process, however, are far removed from any real sense of revolutionary change in the foundation of economy and society. Equally, far from the involvement of a mass of people in this process, the politics of opportunity has been characterised by an elite-based strategy. Consent has only been sought in so much as it provides the semblance of consensus. Moreover, the consent on which Manchester's hegemony is founded is a fundamentally passive one, rooted in the continuing crisis of the passive revolution of the Keynesian welfare state. Finally, in terms of its view of the economy, and practical intervention in the creation of opportunity, Manchester's political 'revolution' has almost exclusively relied on the hope that a new 'architecture' – a new form of governance, a new quality in the built form, and a newly restructured image – will of itself provide the seeds for radical and progressive change.

Notes

1 Given the great size of the blast, and the presence of some 80,000 people in the city centre just an hour before, it was incredible that no one was killed. Despite the efforts of the emergency services, however, at least ten people were seriously injured, and several hundred more were hurt by flying glass.

2 For example, a business help-line was set up the next day drawing on a range of local partners to provide advice and information about possible relocation (*Manchester Evening News*, 17 June 1996). A few days later the Lord Mayor's emergency fund was launched in order to provide grants and loans to businesses facing hardship.

3 This included key members of the 'Manchester Mafia', representatives of key land-owners and developers, as well as MCC officers headed by Howard Bernstein (Peck and Tickell 1995).

4 With the establishment of the Task Force, the role of Hulme Regeneration Limited as a leading aspect of the City Development Guide Advisory Panel was wound down. This enabled Howard Bernstein to dedicate his time as chief executive of the Task Force.

5 This was the second time that Manchester had been provided with its own column in the Treasury accounts (the first time being the Olympics, see Cochrane *et al.*, this volume). The distributional implications of this top slicing, perhaps understandably, raised less than a murmur of disapproval. It was, however, further evidence of Manchester's exceptional ability to procure additional funding.

6 On the positive side was the opportunity to tackle the downtrodden, dysfunctional and disliked features of the city centre. A key example of this was the negative impact that the widely-disliked Arndale shopping centre was perceived to have had on the city. At a broader level the debate linked a rejection of the post-war form of the city (and particularly the grand municipal mode of planning), to the opportunity for economic regeneration through quality design and built environment improvements. On the negative side of the equation was the real and potential damage to the city's economy. In this sense there was an emphasis on the need to act with urgency to protect the medium-term competitivity of the city as a regional centre.

7 The major landowners were: Manchester City Council (who owned leases on much of the land, as well as having statutory responsibility for the public realm); P&O (who owned the Arndale shopping centre, along with interests in the Ramada Hotel and Shambles Square); Marks & Spencer (whose largest store outside London was destroyed by the blast); Frogmore Investments Limited (who owned the Corn Exchange, leased out to small traders); Co-operative Insurance Society (who owned the damaged CIS tower); Prudential (who owned the Royal Exchange Theatre, along with significant interests in Shambles Square and the Arndale); Sun Alliance and Royal Insurance (who owned a building damaged in the blast); National Car Parking, which owned two multi-storey car parks and land.

8 The five shortlisted bids were from: Halliday Meecham, EDAW, Building Design Partnership, Manchester First and Llewelyn-Davies. Each received expenses up to a limit of £20,000, with the possibility of future design work from their involvement in the scheme.

9 The IUDC jury was composed of the following: Sir Alan Cockshaw (MM), Howard Berstein (MM and MCC), Councillor Richard Leese (MM and MCC), Marianne Neville-Rolfe (MM and GONW), Councillor Pat Karney (MCC Chair of city centre sub-committee), Owen Luder (President of the Royal Institute of British Architects), David Gane (transport adviser), Joe Berridge (master planner adviser).

10 EDAW consists of a diverse team: Urban Design and Economic Development (London), Simpson Associates: Architecture (Manchester), Alan Baxter (Transportation and Engineering), Benay (Retail Development), and Hillier Parker (Property Consultants).

9

City building:
developing Manchester's core

GWYNDAF WILLIAMS

THIS chapter considers the contribution of spatial frameworks and strategies in supporting the physical redevelopment of Manchester's core over the past decade. An initial concern with the wider metropolitan context involves a review of both statutory development plans and informal strategies. It then proceeds to focus on the implementation of strategic frameworks for the conurbation core, and teases out the tensions implicit in balancing the requirements of a city centre with that of a regional capital. Looking at both statutory and non-statutory frameworks, it considers a variety of institutional settings that have facilitated a partnership approach, and discusses the consequences of implementation experience in supporting the emergence of a model of urban entrepreneurialism. The city provides an excellent example of the impact of buoyant property markets on the vitality of the metropolitan core, and the contribution of multi-agency partnerships and networks in repositioning the central area both nationally and internationally.

The land use planning system has experienced a series of challenges over the past few decades as the *negotiative pluralism* of the 1970s gave way to the *neo-liberal* perspectives of the 1980s. This envisaged the promotion of a more deregulated environment to encourage market responsiveness, with spatial planning being only *a* material consideration in development deliberation, expected to provide an enabling context for property-led regeneration (Thornley 1993). Negative market and community based reaction to the unco-ordinated nature of such responsiveness, however, led to an increasing acceptance of the need for establishing strategic spatial frameworks. This resulted, in the early 1990s, in the emergence of *collaborative consensus building agendas*, with the plan led system as *the* material consideration in determining development proposals. Additionally, with cities thrust into new competitive relationships the 'partnership' implicit in such an approach has stressed the shift to a more interactive planning practice capable of accommodating the key values of public- and private-sector stakeholders (Bailey 1995; Healey 1997). Thus over the past decade partnership and networking arrangements have become central to the realisation of urban revitalisation and development strategies, with this collaborative thrust undoubtedly influencing the implementation of land use policies (Hall and Hubbard 1998). Nowhere has this shift become more evident than in relation to city centres, increasingly the focus of new action plans and management frameworks (Evans 1997).

Building metropolitan cohesion

Growing awareness during the early twentieth century of the human costs of explosive urban growth and the environmental degradation and infrastructural deficiencies implicit in such an unregulated policy sphere led to ambitious attempts by civic leaders in Manchester to produce plans for the city region that could influence and shape future processes of urban change. A 'nested trilogy' of urban land-use frameworks were produced in the immediate post-war period – City of Manchester Plan, Manchester and District Regional Planning Proposals, South Lancashire and North Cheshire Advisory Plan – in an attempt to influence urban form (Rodgers 1986; Williams 1996). However, the first metropolitan-level plan to be produced on a statutory footing had to await local government reorganisation and the establishment of a metropolitan authority in 1974. The Greater Manchester Structure Plan (1981) focused on urban concentration and the efficient use of existing urban infrastructure, and attempted to promote the redirection of development towards the metropolitan core as a means of countering the conurbation's emerging duality. It stressed the importance of maintaining the regional centre and the protection and enhancement of established town centres, and promoted resource conservation and amenity and the enhancement of environmental quality (Fenton 1983). In sharp contrast to the emergence of a strong conurbation-wide land use and infrastructural strategy that focused on core areas of the conurbation, this period was also marked by the appearance of an overly-static and fragmented patchwork of statutory Local Plans that did little to reinforce the metropolitan framework or to meet the challenges of urban social and economic processes.

The policy vacuum arising from the abolition of Greater Manchester Council (GMC) in 1986 was filled by voluntary structures, expected to prepare an overarching planning framework for the conurbation –

Strategic Planning Guidance (SPG) – that would guide the preparation of district level development plans (Hebbert and Deas 2000). Statutory development planning was transferred in its entirety to the ten lower tier unitary authorities making up the conurbation, these being mandated to produce a new set of district-wide plans – Unitary Development Plans (UDPs). The transition to this new system was undoubtedly aided by the establishment of a number of inter-district officer working groups aiming in a collaborative manner to provide a metropolitan-wide basis for co-ordination and co-operation. However, this institutional restructuring also reflected the neo-liberal orthodoxy of the day, which was highly critical of the need for strategic planning frameworks that would in any way attempt to regulate development.

The preparation of continuing conurbation-wide development guidance was to prove generally consensual. Subtle differences and tensions did, however, emerge, exemplified by variations in arguments concerning town-centre strategies and out of centre developments, the identification of strategic employment sites, and the scope for review of green belt boundaries. Inevitably, for some districts and political leaders on the periphery of the conurbation, the disappearance of a metropolitan authority gave them the opportunity to escape from what they perceived to be the straitjacket of policy orthodoxy. Manchester lay at the heart of such discourse, with its politicians less parochial and not constrained by the limitations of the city's boundaries, and possessing both strong views and a capacity for strategic thinking. The resulting published guidance based on mediating such tensions was brief and generalised, representing the 'lowest common denominator' in policy formulation implicit in such voluntary co-operation. While it represented a downgrading of the significance of city region concerns as an entity, it nevertheless retained a focus on urban concentration and regeneration; a recognition of the key role of Manchester as a regional centre; an acceptance of the strategic targeting of industrial, commercial and infrastructural investment; and the promotion of environmental enhancement and restraint policies (DoE 1989).

The new generation of district-wide plans were expected to be fully in place by the mid-1990s. In reality the process was attenuated, as authorities struggled to translate the generality of SPG statements to the specificity of policy expression in emerging plans (Williams 1999). Many of the early stages of UDP preparation, particularly away from the core, were to prove an educating process for local members unaccustomed to debating strategic concerns. Additionally, given the added significance afforded to adopted plans, formal objections were extensive at draft plan stage, with tensions often inherent in the relationship between central government and local authorities on the scope of issues that the plans might address. This was particularly the case in Manchester, as the City Council searched for flexibility in the provision of implementation frameworks given its new-found commitment to public-private partnership working (Kitchen 1996). Overall, however, the process was well regarded, due to the extent of already established policy networks and the profile this provided for forward planning activity, even if this was somewhat detached from emerging urban regeneration instruments, programmes and working relationships.

The recent restatement of the conurbation's strategic planning framework continues the established focus on urban concentration and regeneration (Association of Greater Manchester Authorities 1997), but introduces urban sustainability and capacity themes, the focus of significant current policy debate (Ravetz 2000). Inevitably, however, present preoccupations with an emerging regional focus in setting development frameworks raises concerns over the role of sub-regional agendas in general, and city region aspirations in particular (Deas and Ward 2000; Jones and MacLeod, this volume).

Planning the core

Reviewing the experience of development planning within the city, Kitchen (1996) notes that over the past half century Manchester has experienced three intensive periods of statutory plan making, with significantly longer informal interludes in-between dominated by the generation of a series of non-statutory documents. Whilst the output of the formal phases have proved valuable at the level of broad strategy, the predictive capacity of such documents has proved particularly weak in anticipating issues of economic restructuring and change, and to complementing the increasing diversity of regeneration initiatives.

Arising from the process of handling inner city redevelopment, officers have long recognised the limitations of the statutory plan system and have valued the flexibility inherent in the development of informal strategies. This confidence is based on the extent of the authority's land holdings and powers as landlord; doubts on the efficiency of the time spent on the statutory planning process when compared with the speed and flexibility of the non-statutory process; and a desire to see the planning process respond positively to community and political aspirations. Thus during the 1970s and 1980s the main components of the city's approach to development planning involved:

- a willingness to allow the established statutory plan to fade into obscurity, and not to be seen as a constraint on positive action;
- active participation in conurbation-wide strategic planning processes so as to ensure that its policy framework did not introduce constraints to decision-making at the local level;
- a limited role for statutory local plans where justified by specific circumstances, these being restricted to the city centre and the airport that were both the subject of major concerns relating to economic capacity, competitiveness and change;
- an informal and pragmatic approach being increasingly promoted at neighbourhood level to reinforce local aspirations and concerns (Kitchen 1997).

The UDP process that emerged in the early 1990s, with its requirements for a district-wide plan, saw the city build upon such established planning perspectives and development networks, and took the form of a 'structured debate' amongst key stakeholders around particular themes. The final plan aimed to improve the city's 'liveability' and to revitalise the local economy, reinforced by the goal of enhancing the city's role as a regional capital (MCC 1995). From the outset, however, there were concerns that the plan would rapidly date due to the extent of physical and socio-economic transformation that was taking place in and around the city centre. Within this area the increasing fragmentation of decision-making had necessitated the establishment of a City Centre Sub-Committee to provide political leadership and co-ordinated action within the core. At this stage it was clear that established development plan frameworks and the handling of major regeneration initiatives must be integrated, and that a variety of mechanisms might be needed to ensure that this was achieved.

Framing city centre development

The zeal of the *Nicholson Plan* (1945) set out fundamentally to redesign the core, stressing civic pride and achievement, with this being reinforced by the much delayed *Development Plan* (1961) which aimed centrally to erase war damage. Such proposals were only partially implemented, however, due to the massive costs involved in comprehensive clearance and redevelopment. The subsequent *City Centre Map* (1967) focused on extensive transport proposals and the promotion of commercial activity, giving little weight to the economic and cultural benefits of retaining the Victorian core. It signalled instead the build-up of land holdings to facilitate the creation of a Comprehensive Development Area within the commercial core, the culmination of two decades of earnest activity.

A growing realisation of the size and complexity of the centre and the limited role of local authority landownership in influencing change, led the city to seek a more formal set of statutory powers for the area. The *City Centre Local Plan* (1984) was thus produced to provide a framework supporting the regeneration of the core, and it has provided a central backcloth for the launch of a range of recent flagship developments and major physical changes. In land-use planning terms it was ahead of its time, stressing the improvement of accessibility and the need for integrated public transport, the promotion of mixed land uses and commercial balance, the encouragement of residential development and active street frontages, the value of existing waterways and the role of gateway sites in structuring development opportunities. The subsequent launch of the Central Manchester Development Corporation (CMDC 1988–96) did not result in any significant change to this strategic thrust, with the established framework offering sufficient flexibility for the development corporation's mandate and activities. It did, however, introduce a new 'style' of working within the city that heralded further collaborative initiative in the 1990s.

Manchester's *Unitary Development Plan* (1995) set a context for the role of the regional centre – as an employment, commercial and administrative centre; as a regional shopping and financial services centre; as a focus for city-centre living, and as a concentrated location for health and higher education facilities – with its overall vitality perceived to be critical to the conurbation's broader regeneration concerns. It notes that the established planning framework had served the city well, and argued that a full review of city-centre policies should be 'put on hold' during the operational life of CMDC. Thus its central area strategy reiterates established policies, albeit for a slightly enlarged area, with consideration of how a changing core might require a different policy mix only now beginning to be addressed as the UDP as a whole is reviewed (Box 9.1).

While statutory planning has so far targeted Manchester's city centre, the issue of the boundaries (and meanings) of the 'regional centre' has risen in prominence. Thus the emerging concept covers areas currently administered by three local planning authorities (Manchester, Salford, Trafford), and for most of the 1990s by two development corporations (Figure 9.1). While it has been impractical to achieve a detailed planning framework for this area as a whole, it has proved important in planning terms not to feel constrained by such administrative complexities.

Box 9.1 Manchester's established city-centre policies

- A positive commitment to mixed-uses, ensuring active ground floor frontages, together with the encouragement of residential development.
- The improvement of the city centre environment for shopping, the upgrading of open spaces and improvements to waterways.
- The promotion of city-centre tourism, and the strengthening of Manchester's role as an international and regional centre for arts and culture.
- The enhancing of the city's environmental and historic assets, and the promotion of its main gateways.
- Improvements of accessibility to the city centre, enhancing of pedestrian priority and the creation of new and improved public squares.
- Introduction of positive traffic management policies that remove extraneous through traffic from the city centre, discourage long stay parking, provide better access for buses, and improve conditions for pedestrians and cyclists.

Informal agreements between the three authorities and development corporations provided an input to early stages of UDP preparation, this being subsequently mirrored in the approach to the City Pride prospectus. Here, the strength of the regional centre was not limited by administrative boundaries, and the management of its policy framework came of age as a high-profile and distinctive activity.

While the established statutory framework has clearly been central for the achievement of development realisation, the city centre has remained a focus for a host of non-statutory strategies that have stressed collaboration with key private-sector interests. Key amongst these in setting the parameters for promoting the emergent 'entrepreneurial city' has been the launch of City Pride, with its prospectus setting agenda aiming to enhance the city's role as a European regional capital, and a centre for investment and growth; maintain its outstanding commercial, cultural and creative potential; and has sought to ensure the sustenance of its community structures and enhance local quality of life (City Pride Strategic Planning Group 1994). In reality, however, this latter element requires further application and focus, which the emergent local governance agenda is presently attempting to reflect upon.

While its mandate extended beyond the boundaries of the conurbation's core, City Pride identified a series of key themes forming a core strategy for regeneration and image construction. Central to the progress of such strategic developments were the establishment of new

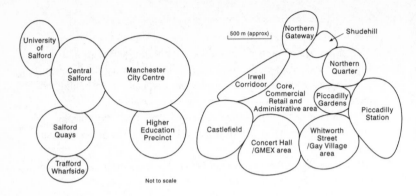

Figure 9.1 Manchester's city and regional centre

operational partnerships, and a clearer focus for the delivery of public- and private-sector investment, with wider community interests being subsumed. Priorities highlighted were the repopulation of the city centre, a reduction of physical dereliction, and the broadening of the city's economic base, and achieving the development of an integrated transport strategy. The crucial need to provide an internationally acceptable infrastructural context and to attract key decision-makers, would, it was argued, enable the city to compete effectively with other European regional capitals both for global investment and as an international play maker (Williams 1998).

With specific reference to the regional centre, the prospectus sought to enhance the city's role – involving the expansion of the city's core; greater integration of land uses and regeneration of the city's main gateways; the development of central area retailing of an international standard; and the attraction of a major international political institution to the city. Thus the regional centre, with its facilities and services, and its strategic regeneration projects, was seen as the focus and barometer of the strength and competitiveness of the wider sub-regional economy. Subsequent monitoring of City Pride's strategic objectives noted, however, that ranking of the city on the basis of investor perceptions was significantly poorer than that based on factual indicators relating to both infrastructural quality and business-related services. This has reinforced concerns relating to the effectiveness of its marketing and success of its re-imaging strategies in 'modernising' perceptions of its urban qualities and opportunities.

Central to the rapidly changing conurbation core have been the host of strategic regeneration initiatives that have come to fruition over the

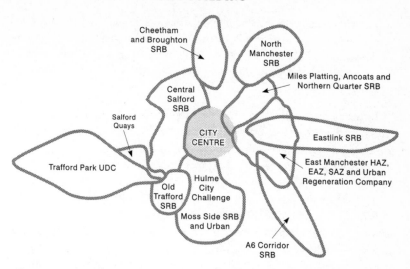

Figure 9.2 The city centre's regeneration necklace

past decade, seen to represent a necklace of development activity around the city centre (Figure 9.2). They signify the city's broadening experience with partnership working, with high-profile political leadership, a strong commitment to networking with government and commerce, and the leveraging of private-sector investment. Facilitating such growth coalitions has increasingly made Manchester the national model in transforming the physical character and market potential of urban core areas. Examples have included Hulme City Challenge and the Moss Side URBAN initiative; Salford Quays and Trafford Park Development Corporation; a host of SRB Challenge Fund programmes and projects; the Commonwealth Games and the variety of emerging initiatives being co-ordinated by the East Manchester Urban Regeneration Company. They have provided the backdrop for a host of flagship developments that have been spawned in the city centre and its environs (Loftman and Nevin 1996). Evaluating the significance of such high-profile regeneration activities for the long-term health of the city centre is premature, but they will undoubtedly contribute to its changing form, function and vitality. Concerns are emerging, however, at the core's increasing detachment from its wider area, and the effective creation of a 'dual speed' city in terms of investment priorities. The consequence for economic opportunity, social inclusiveness and urban development quality all impact on surrounding inner city communities, and provide a real challenge for the city's political leadership within the context of the current modernising agenda for local government.

Notwithstanding the propinquity of the city centre and inner city areas that surround it ... interactions between the two are nothing like as strong as they ought to be ... in many ways the city centre is an oasis ... on the whole the problems of deprivation in the inner city are getting worse. (Kitchen 1997: 142)

In terms of development planning two informal strategies currently structure the debate on strategic planning within the city centre, namely the City's *Development Guide* (1996), and the *Planning Guidance for the Bomb Damaged Area* (1996). The *City Development Guide* argues that the interplay between the range of factors that create the built environment – sense of place, high quality design, density and mixed use considerations, successful streets and sustainable transport policies, stewardship and security concerns – are all at a premium in considering development activity within the city centre (Box 9.2). Concerns by external investors at the specificity of the guide's intent with regard to their commercial interests led to a loss of political will by the City Council's leadership, and a significant diluting of the range of technical standards originally included in the draft (Flage 1998). Whilst the guide has undoubtedly proved useful in informing area specific regeneration activity within the core, the City Council was forced to accept arguments by the business community that exemptions would be inevitable where the provisions of the guide were contrary to site-based development concerns; over urban conservation issues in conflict with business practices; and where change of use rather than development was being considered.

As a result of such experience, specific contextually based guidance was to rapidly emerge within the city centre in relation to the redevelopment of the city's bomb damaged area. This recognised that the purpose of city-centre redevelopment was to provide a strengthened and forward-looking city able to compete on the international stage, and which was attractive to live in, work and visit (Holden, this volume). It thus set out a set of strategic aims for rebuilding, the need to enhance linkages between the rebuilt core and the rest of the regional centre, surrounding regeneration areas and gateway locations. It divided the overall area into a series of smaller parcels, and provided detailed guidance principles for new development, paying particular regard to the quality of the public realm.

More generally, a number of other informal city-wide development strategies have undoubtedly had major consequences for the operation and realisation of city-centre objectives, and in providing a climate for

Box 9.2 Established guidance on built environment quality in Manchester

- The careful design of buildings and streets and the spaces between should help to achieve a strong sense of place (building lines; landmarks; vistas; corner buildings and street junctions; public open space; art and street furniture).
- Promotion of high quality environment that combines contemporary design with the city's best architectural traditions (integration, order and unity, plan and section, expression, integrity and detail).
- Development density and mixed uses promoted as factors that enhance the sense of safety and well-being and encourage a diversity of activity in a '24 hour city', integrating housing, business and retail users.
- The promotion of successful streets providing both urban patterning and rich infrastructure for both meeting and trading.
- Promotion of adaptability and flexibility of development, and reinforcing public transport priorities.
- The promotion of safety and security, with one of the most effective measures for community safety and crime prevention being the creation of lively, lived in urban areas and public spaces that are easy to overlook and oversee.

investment activity. In particular, the *City Centre Environmental Improvement Strategy* (1994) aimed to improve the qualities of the commercial core, to contribute to the development of new activity in city-centre fringe areas, and to improve accessibility and linkages both within and between the core and the rest of the city. This has been reinforced by the recent implementation of a central area CCTV strategy that has attempted to strengthen aspects of community safety and of emerging public concerns. As part of its *Arts and Culture Strategy* (1994) the City Council recognised the potential for expanding economic activity within the core, through the extension of activity hours. The opportunities afforded to enrich and enliven conventional commercial areas, both in terms of urban art and the provision of leisure-oriented commercial activities, underpinned the city's intention to review the regulatory environment constraining the promotion of the '24 hour city', and to attempt to create a more distinctive identity and sense of place for Manchester. All these informal strategies prepared by a variety of local authority departments but centrally co-ordinated and with clear political direction have had as their objective a commitment to ensure the retention and enhancement of commercial opportunities.

The rapidly expanding range of residential developments within the city centre has made Manchester a national leader in such provision, and contributed significantly to the economic fortunes and lifestyle characteristics of the core (Fitzsimmons 1998). Such developments are intended to create a sustainable massing of residential use to help support and to expand the provision of local services. Finally, the city's transport strategy aims to improve accessibility both to and within the city centre, and to promote further integration of a multi-modal public transport system (bus quality partnership, Metrolink expansion, enhanced commuter rail investment, inner relief route). Within this context the emergence of a more proactive traffic management system has seen commitments to upgrade short-term parking facilities, improved pedestrian linkages within and between specific areas, and with measures to restrict private transport increasing in policy priority.

The prioritising of investment and job growth has ensured that local politics has lost the community dimension of the 1980s, and has become increasingly centralised. This has placed a premium on co-operation between local political and business elites, the achievement of a limited number of concrete goals based on flagship developments and supply-side infrastructural initiatives, with these being largely insulated from wider processes relating to community aspirations and accountability.

Delivering a strategic focus

Dramatic changes experienced by the conurbation's core over the past decade have pressurised the main stakeholders and locally established partnerships to consider the need for a new management framework for the city centre as a whole, with this currently being translated into the establishment of a free-standing city-centre management company. The time has additionally come to reflect on the consequence for the regional centre of an expanded political, cultural and functional role, and it is thus useful at this stage to consider the lessons to be learned from the key instruments that have been utilised. Central Manchester Development Corporation's activities (1988–96) clearly introduced the city's officers and senior politicians to a new approach to urban management that facilitated public-private collaboration, whilst Manchester Millennium Task Force's (1996–2000) masterplanning framework reflected the maturity of such an approach, delivering major and complex regeneration initiatives to an impossibly tight time-scale.

CMDC was established by Central Government as a short life body, aiming to tackle the challenge provided by the structural decline of

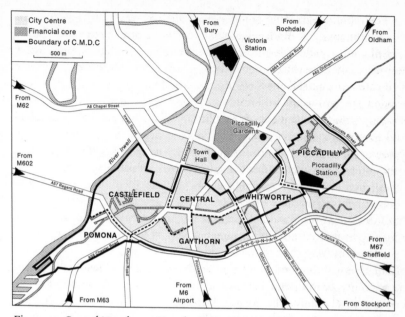

Figure 9.3 Central Manchester Development Corporation's geographical remit

traditional industry, commercial blight, environmental degradation and weak property demand. The local authority's political leadership was initially lukewarm to the need for such a body, seen to cut across established processes of local accountability and responsibility. Such concerns were mediated, however, by the prospect of major resource inputs, and the emerging political awareness of the benefits of partnership working: 'if this was going to happen it was better for the council to be attempting to shape this in ways that it saw as being in the long term interests of the city, than to stand off from the process' (Kitchen 1997: 38). Principles of the established *City Centre Local Plan* were accepted by the CMDC Board as their agreed local planning framework, with its development control responsibilities being undertaken on an agency basis by the local planning authority, and the two bodies began what was to become an increasingly interactive working relationship that was to substantially influence the process of regeneration within the city centre for the following decade (Figure 9.3).

In complementing the established statutory planning framework, the agency immediately moved to launch a *Development Strategy* (1990), that targeted its work on major development parcels, with the strategic intent of extending the city centre functionally and geographically, and of promoting its economic diversity. It aimed to promote Manchester as a major international city; reinforce the qualities of its built environment and capitalise on the unique assets of the central area's waterways; facilitate the enhancement of the public realm; and encourage further mixed uses within the centre. To reinforce such objectives it additionally aimed to extend the range and choice of housing and to ensure high environmental standards; and to extend the range of office types, promote the development of speciality retailing, and pursue the development of tourism and leisure opportunities. Finally, the strategy aimed to focus on integrated management of transport facilities into and within the central area and to improve city-centre accessibility. This strategy, perceived to build upon established local authority policies and private-sector investment experience, set out a framework for development acceptable to both the city's business and political leadership, and set the local authority on a steep learning curve relating to working styles and methods.

It is not the intention here to evaluate CMDC's detailed achievements, outputs and outcomes, since the area was partly delimited at the outset to maximise the potential for success. Suffice to say that it undoubtedly played a valuable role in helping to initiate a series of flagship developments that fuelled the economic health of the city-centre, reinforced by a continuous programme of environmental improvements. It additionally provided the impetus for the rapid expansion of city-centre housing, the resources and quality of marketing and promotion that benefited the city centre as a whole, and as a consequence of the process extended it geographically. All these were enduring legacies, and benefited from the cultural appreciation by both officers and members of the City Council and the Corporation's Board of what might be achievable through partnership, tangible evidence of which would have been considerably less without CMDC (Deas *et al.* 1999).

More negatively, however, arising from CMDC's initial view that its key role was to promote development, during its early years an accumulation of office consents resurrected 'hope' value that the established local plan had attempted to dampen. Additionally, it failed to be very active on the outer edges of its territory that offered opportunities beyond the trajectory allowed for in an avowedly short life organisation, and such areas are only now being regenerated. Its conservation remit was also open to criticism, and it failed to deliver a broader vision on the enhancement of townscape, with a stance probably too focused on economic regeneration. Finally, its development strategy was not linked to the employment and training needs of areas and communities beyond the city centre, where regeneration initiatives took place almost in isolation from CMDC's shadow. The demise of the agency left a number of challenges for the city centre and its key stakeholders, particularly with regard to how they might address the problems of promoting the city in the absence of CMDC's significant marketing budget; how to maintain the momentum and expectations within the area, complete unfinished projects and to develop further the relationship with established partners; and how to sustain revenue budgets needed to take care of areas subject to CMDC's substantial environmental improvement programme.

Manchester Millennium Task Force was established following the bombing of Manchester city centre in June 1996 as a public-private sector partnership body, felt best able to respond in a focused way to the scale of development required, and its exacting time-scale. Its remit was to bring forward a strategy for rebuilding the city centre, to oversee its effective delivery, and to secure the necessary public- and private-sector resources. The final masterplan was expected to create a compelling urban design vision; an imaginative interpretation of the design and development aspirations of the city; clear demonstration of its implementability and deliverability; and as a focus for private investment and justification for public expenditure:

> a development and investment framework which creates an architecturally distinctive core ... is responsive to access needs ... Physically and socially integrated with the rest of the city ... maximises private investment and stimulates economic activity ... promotes the widest possible range of opportunities ... minimises the risk and fear of crime ... and where activity can take place at most times of day and night. (Urban design brief, 1996)

Since a small number of commercial interests held the key land assets, their commitment to the development of the masterplan and investment programme was critical for ensuring the delivery of this vision. Out of the complex evaluation process associated with the launch of an urban design competition, the winning team's solution was publicly perceived as being realistic if somewhat conservative in its response to the challenge. As an actor involved outlined:

> the very process of the competition, with each of the design firms being given separate working sessions with the landowners and City groups, ensured that development and community realism informed the plan. These were tough sessions, with the owners shooting down anything that stepped off the straight and narrow. (Masterplan adviser, 1998)

Key elements of the winning design were defined as respecting the visual structure of the city; creating a new city-centre focus whilst reconnecting

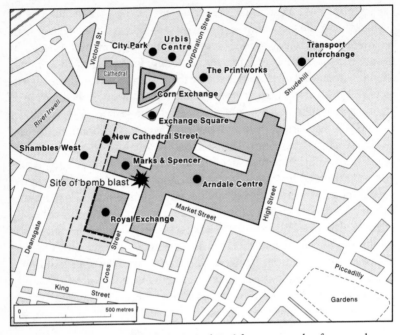

Figure 9.4 Manchester Millennium Limited Taskforce masterplan framework

key elements to the core, linking key streets and squares along a clear pedestrian route; and establishing proposals for an integrated transport system. It was seen to best meet the key objectives of the rebuilding programme in both introducing new uses and enhancing quality, and to enable investment to expand the city centre rather than merely redistribute existing activity (Figure 9.4).

The consultants were retained to develop their winning scheme further into an initial masterplan, gaining feedback from the main parties involved in refining the framework, and in preparing site-specific design guidelines capable of acting as development briefs for individual owners. Alongside the emerging urban design solution, a wider strategic planning framework was provided by the local authority's *Supplementary Planning Guidance for the Bomb Damaged Area*, and by the Task Force's provision of a *Programme Management Strategy* framework, to accommodate the amalgam of individual projects arising from the refurbishment, reconstruction and new build to be initiated in the core.

From the outset it was clear that the plan had to be clearly set within the parameters of sound commercial criteria and realism with regard to the availability of public-sector resources, with four-fifths of the total

Box 9.3 Key strategic objectives of the masterplan delivery

- Restoration and enhancement of retail core.
- Stimulation and diversification of the city's economic base.
- Development of an integrated transport strategy.
- Creation of a quality city core fit for the twenty-first century.
- Creation of a living city by increasing residential population.
- Creation of a distinctive Millennium Quarter.

cost of delivering the rebuilding programme to be financed by the private sector. Thus public funds were largely aimed at helping to fund infrastructure and public realm improvements linking the commercial development parcels, and giving the private sector the confidence to invest in the key commercial components. With the masterplan in place and a broad funding package agreed, a detailed implementation process was initiated, involving the production by the Task Force of annually updated *Implementation Plans,* to manage the delivery of the programme and to provide a framework for project realisation that has helped to replan and rebuild the city's heart on an unprecedented scale (Box 9.3).

The final masterplan was intended to provide a flexible framework to inform and guide development, and in execution it has been continually refined, updated and developed as detailed land requirements, design issues and investment plans have been firmed up. The broader goals of masterplan realisation were implemented through a series of key strategic objectives, within which around fifty interlinked projects were delivered over a five-year period. Given the complexity of the pro-gramme, the implementation strategy was developed both to maximise opportunities and to address and accommodate the potential risks to delivery. Indeed a balance had to be struck between prescription and the flexibility to adapt to market opportunities; the changing priorities of the key landowners; the availability and phasing of public-sector support; and delivering the most complex regeneration initiative ever undertaken in Britain (Williams 2000). An overarching commitment to keep private-sector stakeholders on board meant, however, that the transparency of Task Force activities and its broader public accountability were inevitably compromised.

While the majority of the programme's main physical outputs were expected during the latter years of the core's recovery, the completion of a number of flagship elements were realised by the millennium, helping to launch a forward-looking perspective on prospects for the 'new' city centre. Indeed, the expectation of substantial spin-off investment beyond the masterplan area is already being realised as the city centre delivers a greater variety of market opportunities in a buoyant commercial setting. The Task Force was formally wound up as a company in spring 2000, with its outstanding commitments transferred to a Special Projects Team within the City Council, and with the final elements of the masterplan to be delivered by 2002. As a mechanism for delivering effective strategic regeneration, the Task Force instrument has been widely applauded for establishing a benchmark for urban quality, programme and project deliverability, and as a model of multi-agency working. Indeed, the City Council's approach was widely lauded by the Rogers (1999) report, with the model currently being applied elsewhere through the establishment of urban regeneration companies in targeted locations (Robson, this volume; Peck and Ward, this volume).

Flagship development

Central to the programmed regeneration of Manchester's core has been the parallel promotion of prestige projects, both as a means of securing physical regeneration of strategic locations and of ensuring the city's high-profile place-marketing ambitions (Ward 2000b). Existing litera-ture on such flagships argue that they signal the intention to regenerate sites with development potential, act as magnets for further initiative, and are symbolic of a city's capacity to restructure. They undoubtedly form a cornerstone of a city's place-marketing strategy, boosting civic pride and business confidence, play a catalytic role in reinforcing established facilities, and by concentrating resources enable a flotilla of such developments to be paced so as to retain both profile and invest-ment interest (Loftman and Nevin 1996; Smythe 1994).

Critics of such projects note that they encourage the fragmentation of cities by targeting on specific zones and sites, have huge financial costs generally underwritten by the public sector and often involve 'reverse leveraging' as a result of the private sector's strong bargaining position, are susceptible to instability within property markets, often being over-ambitious and involving high financial risk. Politically, they may curtail and undermine public debate and accountability and change local policy priorities, with the gains often being ephemeral as innovative flagships are followed by a whole series of serial imitators (Imrie and Thomas 1993).

Within Manchester such prestige projects have a long tradition in relation to city-centre modernisation, with the current phase being launched by the G-MEX Exhibition Centre (1986), and with the past decade seeing the Metrolink light rapid transit (1992), the MEN Arena (1995) and the Bridgewater Hall (1996), and with the Lowry Arts Project (2000) and the 'Sportcity' initiative (2002) continuing this tradition. Here we briefly consider the impact of the Arena leisure and sports facility, and the Bridgewater concert hall initiatives as exemplars of the centre's continuing concern with flagship projects as a focus for retaining competitiveness.

As noted elsewhere, the City Council's Olympic aspirations during the early 1990s provided the focus for subsequent pro-growth strategies and civic boosterist activities, with developments associated with the proposed games being seen as a catalyst for wider urban regeneration initiatives, and for binding public/private-sector partnerships and networks (Cochrane *et al.*, this volume). A tangible early outcome of such enterprise was the Arena facility, situated at the northern gateway to the city centre. Originally conceived as part of a phased package of leisure and commercial development, the property market collapse of the early 1990s ensured that it has remained the only element to be completed. As part of a special central government package in support of sports initiatives for the Olympic bid, the Arena provided the focus for the largest single funding opportunity. Over three-quarters of its cost was met by central government, European and local government resources, with the remainder the focus of private sector investment. The outcome of the project has been the provision of a 20,000 seat facility, the largest indoor arena in Europe, at negligible capital cost to the Council.

Since its launch, its utilisation has been considerably in excess of its initial business plan, in that it has introduced a new leisure development into the city centre, enlarging the city's critical mass of facilities, and has led the way for further leisure and consumption-oriented activities (Printworks, Great Northern). Whilst it has made use of a site in a part of the core exhibiting weak market demand, and has helped rebuild Victoria rail station, it has failed until recently, however, to unlock the potential of this gateway location. It is only now with Railtrack investment commitment, and delivery of the Task Force's masterplan, that there is some positive evidence of the cumulative benefit of this project in helping to regenerate the northern gateway. In urban design terms, its bland treatment in relation to the listed station, and its lack of architectural distinction and visual appeal has meant that criticism has remained of its negligible built form contribution to its surrounding area.

The increasing inadequacy of the Free Trade Hall as a home for the city's Hallé Orchestra, and as a venue for promoting the city's international credentials, led to the search for a new site for an international concert hall. The 'driver' for this was provided by CMDC, who envisaged a 'central zone' for international business and leisure tourism, and with the area already accommodating an exhibition and convention area (G-MEX), an international business hotel (Midland) and proposals for a major commercial and leisure facility (Great Northern). Property market instability in the early 1990s led to the recommissioning of initial proposals, with the 'Great Bridgewater Initiative' intended to provide both a new concert hall and a new commercial district within the core. The outcome was a 2,400-seat concert hall, 220,000 sq. ft. of offices, a new canal basin, hotel and residential development.

Unlike the Arena, which required only nominal local authority resources, the Bridgewater Hall has received substantial public support for its construction, this being offset by the sale of the Free Trade Hall for hotel development, the sale of land surrounding the concert hall for commercial development, and the provision of European funding matching capital funds provided by the City Council and CMDC. Launched with no capital debt, the hall has been in operating profit since the outset, effectively doubling attendance as compared to the old venue, thereby increasing its national and international prominence. In addition, the City Council has been successful in relation to both the Arena and the Bridgewater Hall, in passing the operating risk entirely to the private sector, with the designated facility manager operating both facilities on a twenty-year lease without public subsidy.

The Bridgewater Hall has undoubtedly acted as an impetus for wider restructuring and regeneration, in the process creating a vibrant new office area within the city, together with hotel and residential developments, and within the wider development area stimulating the construction of a new international convention centre, the Great Northern leisure and commercial initiative, and the creation of new public spaces and environmental improvements. Doubts remain, however, that one of the most important civic buildings to be completed this century has not significantly enhanced the area's established urban form and structure. While the Hall is regarded as reflecting individual identity, the commercial elements of the initiative are expected to date quickly. In the medium term, however, the area may reflect well on both the leadership of the CMDC and the initiative of the City Council in delivering creative urban regeneration whilst enhancing the city's competitiveness.

New urban landmarks

Over the past decade there has been a series of transformations in Manchester. These have had major economic, socio-cultural and physical consequences, and include changing land-use relationships and the evolving character and vitality of the city centre. Economically, such changes have seen the increasing impact of the globalised economy on local commercial prospects, a greater competitive environment between the city and other urban cores, and an increasing governance culture that facilitates business (Peck and Tickell 1995). Tendencies for spatial stratification and social polarisation have been reinforced, particularly between the central area and inner city communities, transforming the debate concerning urban development goals. The city is only now beginning to grapple with such issues of inclusiveness as part of the 'modernising' governance agenda which is focusing on local community strategies and local strategic partnerships. Politically, the concern has been to build up a capacity for governance that facilitates a wider range of arenas for informed policy debate, and that has facilitated the development of a coherent local view on the qualities of Manchester as a place. Physically, and in land-use terms, the challenge has been to achieve change on the ground that balances the need for a collective agenda whilst accommodating institutional and individual perspectives. This has necessitated the promotion of variety and flexibility within the core, greater ingenuity in exploiting the central area's indigenous assets, and a commitment to enhance the core's accessibility, permeability and sense of collective ownership.

The new millennium sees Manchester city centre as the crucible of a major redrawing of urban relationships that has transformed the core's prospects, and that has given local political leaders and officers a growing national reputation for successful pro-growth strategies and active public-private partnership working. The fundamental question remains, however, as to the extent to which this undoubted success has in a significant way impacted on the prospects of the conurbation's inner areas more widely, where it is clear that despite extensive physical change over the past decade the social and economic challenges remain. Property- and investor-led approaches to regeneration, although an essential component of urban revitalisation, are on their own clearly an inadequate response to the multiple task environment inherent in revitalising cities, particularly those associated with community building and a socially inclusive urban development agenda.

I O

Regional tensions:
constructing institutional cohesion?

MARTIN JONES AND GORDON MACLEOD

THE conspicuous economic achievements of regional 'success stories' like Silicon Valley, Baden-Wurttemberg and the Italian industrial districts have put regions back on the agenda, both for policy-makers and for theorists of economic development. In a parallel fashion, devolution and local autonomy are also back on the agenda for politicians, both on the right and on the left. Why this widespread appeal to regions? On the one hand, the region is increasingly seen as a necessary element in the 'supply architecture' for learning and inno-vation and in helping to establish economic competitiveness (Florida 1995; Storper 1997). In substantive terms, this means that regional prosperity is partly harnessed through an 'institutionally thick' network of support structures in business development and training, helping to diffuse entrepreneurship and technological spillovers and to collectivise economic interests (Amin and Thrift 1994; Cooke and Morgan 1998). On the other hand, there are those who see the regional scale as offering prospects for healthier and more participatory channels of democracy (Hirst 1997; Keating 1998; *New Statesman* 1998). The corollary of all this is that the nation-state is in some sense to be afforded a lesser role in the regulation of economy and society (though see Peck and Tickell 1995; MacLeod and Goodwin 1999). Spurred on by this exciting new agenda of territorial restructuring, a growing number of academics have sought to explore the interactions between economic development, social capital and political institutions in order to cast some added light on how to revive old industrial regions. It should be of little surprise too that representatives from such older, lagging regions are increasingly glancing with envious eyes to winners like Silicon Valley, in the hope of developing strategies to bring about economic success (Murphy and Caborn 1996; Hudson *et al.* 1997; MacLeod 2000).

It is with this purported academic and political sea change in mind that we view the recent attempts to refurbish economic governance in the North West region of England. Alongside elected Assemblies for Wales, Northern Ireland and London, and a Parliament for Scotland, the Blair Government has established eight English Regional Development Agencies (RDAs). These are heralded to provide 'new structures and new opportunities in the English regions to enable them to punch their weight in the global market place' (DETR 1997a). In step with the New Regionalist orthodoxy, then, England's regions are being roused to learn and to innovate in the hope of establishing competitive advantage in the global economic sphere. Thus, along with associated 'partners' in other regions, the North West Development Agency,[1] established in April 1999, has been charged with the highly complex task of raising regional competitiveness (DETR 1997b). Expectations are high and there is little doubt that this institution will have an important bearing on the future governance of the region:

> The creation of the North West RDA is a significant and long overdue initiative designed to rationalize and co-ordinate economic development and business support and provide a more focused delivery of services to the region. The vacuum created by the absence of this type of statutory structure has cost the North West dearly over the past decade ... It is a belated cause for celebration that the overwhelming logic for a single unifying organisation has eventually prevailed at Westminster ... *The RDA movement represents the best chance that the North West has of recovering from its past mistakes* and levelling the playing field sufficiently to make substantive progress in the early years of the new millennium. (Alan Benzie, KPMG, quoted in Newsco 1997: 4, emphasis added)

This chapter focuses on the institutional processes that saw the introduction of the North West Development Agency (NWDA). It is not explicitly concerned with sub-regional tensions emerging as a consequence of NWDA (on which see Deas and Ward 2000), although brief attention is given to rivalries over inward investment. Instead, we examine a series of strategically significant efforts that emerged throughout the early 1990s to harness a robust institutional framework and regional vision within the North West region (NWRA and NWBLT 1993). Anecdotal evidence points to the North West as representing a 'leading-edge region' in the implementation of RDAs. It has a staff of 180 and the largest budget of the eight RDAs with gross expenditure for 1999/2000 at £176 million (see Pike 1997; Robson et al. 2000).

What our study exposes, however, is the extent to which the impetus generated through the earlier 1990s endeavours to collectivise economic interests and enable entrepreneurship are being frustrated. This frustration is not least down to the extent to which England's own brand of regional renewal appears to be driven by political fiat and central government diktat (Jones and MacLeod 1999; Deas and Ward 2000). This centralist orchestration is, of course, in stark contrast to the organic form of economic governance that prevails in the more successful regions of North America and Western Europe. We conclude that some meaningful lessons can be gleaned from this and that these should help inform a genuine national debate on RDAs. For not to take cognisance of these lessons may mean that this latest experiment in England's economic development may only serve to *re-scale* rather than *resolve* Britain's long-standing regional economic problem.

Mapping Regional Development Agencies

English regionalism has a long and somewhat chequered history. Some of the key moments have included: the introduction, in 1958, of a network of regional offices to oversee regional planning and population overspill; the creation in 1964 of the Department of Economic Affairs (DEA), itself subsequently to be disbanded; the perseverance with Economic Planning Committees and Regional Forums between the early 1960s and the late 1970s; the rise of Scottish and Welsh nationalism in the 1970s; and the introduction of the Integrated Regional Offices (later Government Offices for the Regions) in 1993. The extent to which these institutional innovations have provided the basis for effective economic development has often been questioned (Parsons 1988). It is in this context that the post-1995 regionalist proclamations of the Labour Party are of key significance.

The election of New Labour in May 1997 and the implementation of the influential recommendations of the Regional Policy Commission (established by John Prescott early in 1996) promised an ambitious programme of regional reform. This has served to re-ignite the regional debate in England at a time of renewed interest amongst academic and policy-maker interest in regional dimensions of economic development. The New Labour approach is that the English regions should become 'divorced from Whitehall' and, in the process, that regional development should become 'people-led' (Mandelson and Liddle 1996). The recent legislation appears unequivocal:

We do not want to impose a blueprint from Whitehall. It is well understood that the English Regions are very different from one another. The *Regional Development Agencies Bill* will not specify a single prescriptive model for agencies. We want to allow each region to have arrangements which fits its own circumstances, building on the work that many different bodies are currently doing. (DoE 1997: 1)

There are clear resonances between this statement and the new regionalist language proclaiming a need for bottom-up institutionalisation and inter-agency synergies. A more historical line has been expressed by the Deputy Prime Minister, John Prescott MP, when launching the Government's RDA White Paper *Building Partnerships for Prosperity*:

For far too long, the English regions have been disadvantaged by the denial of development agencies which helps to explain why English regions have lagged behind other regions in Europe. ... Since 1945, successive Governments have introduced many programmes aimed at achieving economic and social objectives, but those have often lacked coherence, particularly at the English regional level. Now, more than ever, the English regions are demanding a strategic lead – for greater focus on wealth creation and jobs, for effective policy integration, and for co-ordination and local effort. (*Hansard Debates*, 3 December 1997, col. 357)

These statements are also indicative of a growing consciousness that the plethora of agencies established over a period of fifty years to tackle urban and regional socio-economic disadvantage have failed to provide the basis for economic success. Accordingly, the White Paper called for the need to re-establish an 'entrepreneurial spirit' to help 'regions fulfil their economic and social potential' (DETR 1997b: 8). To enable this, RDAs have been given varying degrees of flexibility in order to influence several spheres of policy including: economic development and social and physical regeneration, business support, investment and competitiveness, enhancing skills, promoting employment, and sustainable development. It is also worth mentioning that while representing a new institutional form, RDAs do actually bring together the staff and the functions of English Partnerships, the Rural Development Commission and sections of the Government Regional Offices. A sub-regional balance of interests and constituencies is to be ensured through the formation and composition of RDA boards. According to the Government:

The success of RDAs will largely depend on their boards ... The Government intend that boards should be business led, but they will also need an effective presence from the public sector ... We propose that chairpersons should have private sector background. (DETR 1997b: 48–9).

Since April 1999, the RDA boards and their officers have been busy constructing regional economic strategies as their first role in shaping the landscape of economic development. These are important long-term statements aimed to 'improve economic performance and enhance the region's competitiveness, addressing the removal of market failure which prevent sustainable economic development, regeneration and business growth in the regions' (DETR 1998: 6).

Following the academic arguments presented briefly in the introduction, it would appear that, at least from the vantage point of central government, English regions can become active ingredients in the 'supply architecture' (Storper 1997) for economic development in the search to reconvert Britain's deindustrialised wastelands. Indeed, when presented with data showing widening gaps between the rich and poor regions in Britain, Richard Caborn (then Minister of Regions in waiting) argued: 'I am absolutely convinced that we must tackle this problem at the regional level' (quoted in Wagstyl 1996: 23). As with previous experiments in economic development, however, there is always a gap between the rhetoric of national policy and the experience of local implementation. The chapter now considers this disparity in the North West of England.

New regionalism, North West style

With its robust economic base in cotton and coal, the North West region has a claim to be the first in the United Kingdom to experience significant industrialisation (DETR 1997b: 59). However, throughout the twentieth century the region's economy was never to repeat those early distinctions, and continual decline prevailed. To be sure, throughout the post-war period, Britain's national programme of regional policy was partially successful in ameliorating the worst effects of dereliction and decline, but the newer Fordist industries were really to take off in the South and Midlands (Massey 1984). Thus with a weak infrastructure and no substantive transformation in social and political relations, the North West failed to rekindle the fire of earlier eras (DEA 1965).

Yet worse was to come. Between 1979 and 1993 manufacturing employment in the North West fell by 47 per cent, although over 500,000 still reside in the blue-collar sector. This was not to be replaced by a wholesale post-industrial or informational revolution as service sector employment growth, at 10 per cent, lagged behind the British average of 16 per cent. Per capita regional GDP fell from 94 per cent of the British average to 90 per cent between 1980 and 1990 and the latest data put this measure at 91 per cent (DETR 1997b). New firm formation rates are the lowest in mainland Britain (DTI 1998) and only 2 per cent of regional GDP is spent on research and development activities. This compares with a figure of nearly 4 per cent for the Eastern region.

To date, the political responses to this economic dereliction have been largely premised on the imposition of private-sector-led agencies and non-elected arms of the local state (Peck and Tickell 1995). On the one hand, there has been a movement within the public sector to 'go private' via urban regeneration partnerships. And on the other, the private sector has 'gone public', largely through the formation of centrally orchestrated representational agencies such as the Business Leadership Teams (BLTs), Training and Enterprise Councils (TECs), and Urban Development Corporations (UDCs). For instance, the North West Business Leadership Team (NWBLT) – although drawing its support from the leading thirty private-sector companies in the region – has procured limited financial power with which to implement a proper business agenda. The effect of this is that collective representation and any claims towards regional institutional thickness have only really been exercised through fragile institutional fixes established by external forces such as central government and the European Commission.

It was within this context of centrally-orchestrated localism that the North West Regional Association (NWRA) emerged. The NWRA represented a local authority consortium, which was formed in 1992 out of a growing acknowledgement of the need for more effective and integrative tiers of regional economic governance. NWRA was also keen to form an alliance with the region's Business Leadership Team, a process which ultimately saw the two bodies mutate into the North West Partnership. One important outcome of this process was the establishment of the 'Regional Economic Strategy for North West England' (NWRA and NWBLT 1993). This has been identified as part of 'the most significant attempt to overcome perceived deficiencies in the UK's territorial distribution of power' (Burch and Holliday 1993: 29). Others, though, view it to have been a shallow institutionally thin framework (Peck and Tickell 1995). These latter sentiments would appear to concur with the view of one influential regional politician:

> [At a conference of] the movers and shakers of the North West ... Graham Meadows of the European Commission's DGXVI ... said that not only are you [the North West] an important region, but the European Union is important and you can expect help from Europe to get yourselves back on your feet ... He told us that the first thing we had to do was to write the regional economic strategy and form a partnership ... I said that if we didn't

act on Meadow's words then we would be whistling for our money from Brussels ... The Regional Economic Strategy was a concept that most people were estranged to. *This was the first attempt to do anything at a North West region level, characterized by Marianne Neville Rolfe [the then regional director of the Government Office for the North West], sometime later, as being the apple pie and mother earth statement, you know, saying all the right things in the covers of one document.* ... The thing has gone on from the early days to something well established – a firm institution with a secretariat. (Senior councillor, local government, 1998)

This quotation underlines the imperative to form a coalition whose instrumental objective was to obtain additional financial support from Europe. This exercise in short-term 'grant grabbing' (Jones and Ward 1998) also leads one to raise serious questions about the extent to which the North West region can boast of building an institutional ensemble to provide regional stakeholders with a genuine ownership of the emergent regional agenda. All this has major implications for the emerging RDA experience and of the region's future economic governance. One interviewee has expanded on this point:

The North West has had an extremely difficult evolutionary history. ... much shorter than say the North East. ... *Regionalisation has a shorter tap root.* This makes a difference for a number of reasons. One is that the North West didn't start to gel, in a sense that the major stakeholders didn't start to see the point of developing a regional level of activity until very late in the day. *Essentially region building didn't occur until the 1990s.* Because they came to it late, they actually came to it without presuppositions and institutional structures, unlike the North East with its strong institutional structures. The North West came to the 1990s with a *tabula rasa* in a sense that the local authorities had the most appallingly weak regional organisation – it hardly existed. (Higher education sector representative, 1998)

The first Regional Economic Strategy emphasised three objectives to turn round the fortunes of the North West (NWRA and NWBLT 1993) – fostering the region's production and export base, environment and image, and internal and external links (see also NWP 1996). These themes have recently been carried forward into the NWDA's regional economic strategy – *England's North West: A Strategy Towards 2020* (NWDA 2000a). This has an obligatory marketing slogan – 'the right angle on the region' – and proffers four key themes designed to ensure economic success over the next twenty years:

- *Investing in business and ideas*: develop world-class clusters to maximise employment and growth potential; accelerate new business development; and encourage excellence in existing business.
- *Investing in people and communities*: develop skills for all; deliver urban renaissance; tackle social exclusion.
- *Investing in infrastructure*: secure clear physical plans, strengthen strategic communications; support regional culture and sports infrastructure.
- *Investing in image and environment*: project a positive image; restore the environmental deficit; promote quality design and energy conversation.

At the launch of this important document, NWDA Chair, Lord Thomas, spoke of a consensus existing around this form of economic development:

> It is important that a more integrated approach [to economic development] is adopted between all those concerned with the region. I am convinced there is nothing we cannot achieve together ... A hallmark of the strategy is the unity of purpose in both its conception and its implementation. The strategy and priorities for action have been identified by the region, for the region, and responsibility for the successful implementation rests with the region. (Quoted in NWDA 2000b: 2)

NWDA's economic strategy is not unique. In fact, the eight RDA strategies are very similar in tone and intent and seem to have adopted the 'lowest common-denominator' approach, where little attempt is made to address the underlying weaknesses of the local and regional economy and its institutional supports (Robson *et al.* 2000). While there may be some value in promoting the discourses of regional entrepreneurialism and its focus on 'exploiting tourism', 'cashing in on culture', and dancing to the tunes of a 'knowledge-based economy' or 'informational age', we argue that *England's North West* is in danger of ignoring many of the region's deeply-entrenched socio-economic problems, not least the declining skills base, a lack of jobs, and the lack of innovative firm starts. These issues are highlighted in a commentary on the North West contained within a hard-hitting OECD report:

> There is a chronically weak demand for certain key skills and knowledge, inadequate incentives and overwhelming obstacles to investment in skills and knowledge by individuals and employers. These inhibitors arise out of the product strategy of some of the region's traders, the way in which the region's labour markets operate and the way in which many employers manage work and workforces. (OECD 1997: 35)

It is, moreover, doubtful whether the promises of welfare state reform, increasingly seen to be a pivotal feature of many regional economic strategies (DETR 1997b), will adequately address these shortcomings. Too often in the North West, 'welfare reform' has meant trimming entitlements and de-registering claimants, in a context in which the supply of new jobs has typically been quite inadequate. So, between September 1993 and February 1997, unemployment in Manchester fell by 53,600, although total employment only increased by 19,100. This meant that for 'every 100 leaving the unemployment register over this four year period there were only 36 new jobs created (all being part time)' (Peck and Tickell 1997: 1). In short there remains a *real* jobs gap (see Giordano and Twomey, this volume). And the real problem is that it is difficult to see this being effectively addressed by RDAs which are – constitutionally and financially speaking – virtually powerless to intervene in the local economy, as the experience with the restructuring of Rover in the West Midlands has demonstrated (Guthrie 2000).

Furthermore, the skills agenda – something that is central to all forms of economic development (see Lovering 1999) – remains one of the policy battles that RDAs have lost to the Department for Education and Employment. The Labour Party, when in opposition, criticised the ability of the Training and Enterprise Councils (TECs) to address market failure and bring about a 'skills revolution'. It was thus of little surprise when the government announced that, from April 2001, the functions of TECs in England would be transferred to 47 Local Learning and Skills Councils. But it is difficult to see exactly where these new institutions can actually succeed where TECs failed: as with the latter, the success of these new structures ultimately rests on the goodwill of employers and they do not possess the regulatory mechanisms to bring about collective private-sector action. The age-old practice of rogue behaviour, whereby firms are able to poach skilled labour, looks set to continue (Jones 1999a).

Democratic renewal?

With an eye to these concerns, the North West's co-ordinated response to the Government's original consultation on RDAs (DoE 1997) made a recommendation for three key 'co-ordination and commissioning of functions' (NWRA and NWP 1997: 3). These relate to: business and enterprise support; labour supply and demand; and the business support functions of the Department of Trade and Industry (DTI). In some respects though, there are growing regional concerns that the projected strategic capacity originally promised by the Labour Party (1995, 1996) might never materialise. Recent research has revealed that the North West Development Agency's budget of £176 million is equivalent to just 0.29 per cent of regional Gross Domestic Product (Robson *et al.* 2000: table 10). Furthermore, over 90 per cent of this budget is committed to *existing* regeneration programmes inherited from the Government Offices for the Regions, English Partnerships and the Rural Development Commission (Jones 1999b). The quotations below would seem to indicate a collective disappointment over the limited institutional and financial capacity of the NRDA, and cast some serious doubts about its regional legitimacy:

> RDAs are the smallest possible initiative towards regionalizing decision making about economic development that can possibly be given without them being absolutely invisible. I mean it is completely ridiculous isn't it? In the North West the RDA will have about £200-250 million, which is about one sixth of what all the stakeholders asked for. (Higher education sector representative, 1998)

> These people said that they are serious about regions. They weren't serious, they are not giving up any significant central power and can you think of a time when any political party did give away any central power? It goes against the grain of historical experience. (Business community representative, 1998)

> [Ministers] talk about 'building up the regional voice' ...You can believe [them] if you want to. I don't. I am all for building from the grass-roots, so why didn't they do things as we suggested? Why didn't they give us enough leverage to make an impact?. (Senior councillor, local government, 1998)

With such limitations in regional strategic capacity, one notable issue concerns the political power and the institutional integrity of England's regions when comparisons are set against the devolutionary packages awarded to Wales and Scotland. For instance, during 1996-97, Regional Selective Assistance amounted to £152.24 million for Scotland, £106.94 million for Wales, but only £13.10 million for the North West. Such asymmetries in the geography of regional selective assistance are likely to become a key focal point in the future agenda of Britain's governance (Phelps and Tewdwr-Jones 2000) – and indeed in its broader constitutional order (Nairn 1997).

All of which invites one to consider the possibility of England's regions engaging in a 'hostile brothers' scenario (Peck and Tickell 1994). In this, cities and regions feverishly attempt to compete in the global market-place by resorting to 'beggar-thy-neighbour' strategies and the selling of place through an advertisement of low regulation of business and cheap labour.

Such pressures were certainly evident in the recent struggle between Wales, Scotland and the North East to capture a Korean electronics plant (Phelps and Tewdwr-Jones 2000). The future governance of a 'warring regional dilemma' represents one of many complexities facing the territorial governance of England. Such concerns are not lost on the national body responsible for co-ordinating urban property redevelopment, English Partnerships, which has argued that in many spheres, effective regional governance is in large measure dependent upon some form of 'national integrity' and the retention of some 'national functions on a permanent basis'. In the view of English Partnerships: 'If different regions utilise different standards or levels of subsidy/investment, each region will be played off or bid up or down one against the other' (quoted in Environment, Transport and Regional Affairs Committee 1997: 144).

John Bridge, an adviser to the Labour Party and now Chair of the One North East, has also indicated that:

> If we allow all 12 regional development agencies to compete freely, the level of competition in two or three years' time will be ridiculous. The in-fighting could actually put off the overseas investor. It is a situation the government cannot countenance. (Quoted in Parsley 1997: 7)

These are indeed very serious issues, which are made exceedingly complex in the North West where intense sub-regional rivalries exist over the attraction of inward investment (see Deas and Ward, this volume). Throughout the 1990s, INWARD, the region's inward investment body funded by the DTI, was continually forced to balance sub-regional demands for inward investment. Because INWARD sought to steer foreign investment towards greenfield sites located outside Manchester's metropolitan boundaries, Manchester City Council has actively been supporting the Manchester Investment and Development Agency (MIDAS) and Marketing Manchester to protect the interest of the city-region. According to Deas and Ward's analysis, 'The formation of MIDAS and Marketing Manchester is emblematic of the desire for territorial coalition building at a scale *different* to that of the standard region' (2000: 285, emphasis added). With the introduction of the NWDA, the scene is set for some interesting sub-regional territorial politics around the location of economic development and this could prove to be a very interesting object of academic analysis.

Turning more specifically to the question of regional representation and accountability, a number of issues have surfaced. Throughout the UK, it would seem to be the case that tensions are mounting over the collective 'ownership' of respective regional economic strategies (Robson *et al.* 2000). RDAs are 'ultimately accountable to Ministers' (DETR 1997b: 54) through boards that draw their social base primarily from the business sector at the expense of civic leaders, co-operative and community enterprise bodies, the voluntary sector and trade unions. This threatens much of the capacity to enliven an integrated network of public-private and civic associationalism (compare Straw *et al.* 1996). Indeed, in some important respects, it would appear to be the case that the central state is once again dictating the terms of the emergent regional institutional forms and that the resultant networks are decidedly 'thin' (see Tickell *et al.* 1995). Again, this scenario is quite out of step with the evidence of many successful regions, the very institutional 'thickness' of which is often afforded a significant role in accounts of economic vitality (see Amin 1999).

Notwithstanding these limitations, it would be imprudent to imply that the introduction of RDAs provides no possibility for democratic renewal and associative democracy in England's regions (Hirst 1997). From April 1998, the North West Partnership and the North West Regional Association merged to form a shadow North West 'Regional Chamber'. This represents a significant development to address the economic and democratic deficit in the region. In July 1999, this shadow Chamber was also to provide the platform for the North West Constitutional Convention – a forum devised to lobby for regional government. The North West Regional Chamber possesses 80 seats – 56 occupied by elected local councillors and 24 occupied by business leaders mainly within BLT networks – and its aim is to influence the various strategies and agendas being produced by the NWDA.

The danger, of course, is that this regionally-grounded form of mobilisation will clash with the centrally-orchestrated character of the whole RDA project; 'ownership' of RDA strategies ultimately rest with the respective Secretaries of (the central) State. One possible outcome of this might see a process of creative tension where regional voices are given a genuine hearing. Another more pessimistic scenario is that the tight control demonstrated by the government in Wales and London will backfire and lead to some regional backlashes (Dungey and Newman 2000). These sentiments filter through from certain stakeholders close to the development of the North West Regional Chamber.

[There] is one notion of a Regional Chamber, a non-statutory body *without* any visible signs of financial support. At the meeting that this was approved by the North West Partnership, the representative of the North West Business Leadership Team who was in the chair [...] kept describing the chamber as a deliberative or consultative body and yet this constitution was passed with the most cursory discussion. Nobody brought out the obvious complete divergences of view, nobody mentioned reality; like, for instance, the fact that whatever money the RDA has a handle on, the lines of accountability for public money are bound to flow through various Secretaries of State ... *They are bound to do this, as it is the British constitution.* (Higher education sector representative, 1998)

This analysis is to be compared with more calculated political statements, although tensions will remain around the final programme of action to be taken by New Labour on directly elected English regional government.

There's a lot of money being spent in the regions and there need to be proper lines of accountability. They must be responsible to this department as the Scottish Development ... was responsible to the Scottish Secretary of State. Let's not waffle around this. We're managing change. We're heading for regional government, but we're not there yet. That's the reality. (Richard Caborn, former Minister for the Regions, quoted in Richards 1998: 5)

What we will have to do is bring forward enabling legislation to enable referendums to take place. We are doing that at the moment. We *will* have a referendum. (Hilary Armstrong, Minister for the Regions, quoted in Hetherington and White 2000: 12, emphasis added; compare with Labour Party 1995, 1996)

Economic governance or political mobilisation?

This chapter has sought to provide an analysis of the ongoing attempts to develop meaningful regional economic governance within the North West of England. From our analysis, the introduction of RDAs can be viewed as an endeavour to initiate a particular brand of new regionalism, but one that is ensnared by a series of tensions. Not least among these is that the particular form of regional coalition-building has been dictated by *central government* political imperatives. The RDAs do not display the kind of organic institutionalisation that has underpinned the success of many North American and European regional powerhouses. Rather, the powers of RDAs are restricted to those functions inherited from central government. Beyond this, the influence of RDAs as yet remains unclear because 'ownership' of the regional strategy is retained within the nation-state scale, 'with no significant financial implications for central government' (HMSO 1997: 4). In a sense, then, RDAs represent a particularly weakened form of devolved institutional capacity, and their impacts on economic development are uncertain. What this also shows, we would argue, is the need for new regionalist analysis to be more circumspect about the intricate connections between the resurgence of regional forms of governance and the social properties of the state. The continuing vulnerability both of the North West's regional economic institutions and its putative regional economic project reveal how far this region remains dependent upon *external* political concessions and funding streams. If this is the 'new regionalism', it has a depressingly familiar ring to it.

Notes

The authors would like to thank the editors for their comments on this chapter. Martin Jones would like to thank the University of Wales, Aberystwyth, for a College Research Fund grant titled 'The new regionalism: building the regional development agencies'. An earlier and longer account of some of the arguments presented here can be found in an article entitled 'Towards a regional renaissance? Reconfiguring and rescaling England's economic governance', *Transactions of the Institute of British Geographers*, 24 (1999), 295–313.

1 The NWRDA covers the counties of Cumbria, Lancashire and Cheshire, and the unitary authorities of Sefton, Wirral, Liverpool, Knowsley, St Helens, Wigan, Bolton, Bury, Rochdale, Oldham, Salford, Manchester, Tameside, Trafford and Stockport.

I I

Poor Manchester:
old problems and new deals

DEAN HERD AND TERRY PATTERSON

> The Government's Welfare to Work programme has provided a major
> stimulus, and the City Pride Partnership has been accepted as the appro-
> priate delivery unit for the New Deal. Previous programmes have relied on
> persuasion and exhortation as a means of tackling unemployment. The New
> Deal is fundamentally different in the critical mass of activity that it will
> generate. This programme will provide a further impetus to the work of the
> Partners to address local joblessness, which is incompatible with our vision
> of creating sustainable and competitive communities. (City Pride Strategic
> Planning Group 1998a: 23)

THE marketed image of Manchester is of a thriving, successful city
built on a combination of entrepreneurial skills and 'can-do' partnerships (City Pride Strategic Planning Group 1994, 1998a, 1998b, 1999b).
The regeneration of Castlefield, Hulme and Moss Side, as well as the
city centre itself following the IRA bomb in 1996; the expansions of
Metrolink and the airport; the creation of new facilities such as the
Bridgewater Hall and the Nynex (now MEN) arena; and the high profile
bids for the Olympic and Commonwealth Games are trumpeted as signs
of a prosperous and booming regional capital - the 'power house of the
region's economy' (City Pride Strategic Planning Group 1998a: 4). This
regeneration strategy calls for a 'feel-good' promotion of the city as a
centre for investment, in an era of competitive regionalism. However,
despite promotional hype, Manchester remains a much divided city.

In the late 1990s, local research revealed formidable levels of severe
deprivation existing in 64 small areas found across Manchester (Griffiths
1998), alongside 138 further areas of notable deprivation and a large
number of poor people elsewhere in the city. These most deprived
neighbourhoods lie only a few miles from the prosperous city centre and
suburbs. This pattern mirrors a national trend. Whereas in the 1980s the

sharpest economic differences were often between the old industrial areas of the North and the South East, the story of poverty from the 1990s is much more complicated and is characterised by deprivation concentrated in tight geographical areas lying in close proximity to relative affluence (Green 1996; TUC 1998, 1999; Turok and Edge 1999). While unemployment has fallen steadily in recent years, many of the high unemployment areas have gained least or actually shown little change. The lack of improvement in these areas of Manchester points to the long-standing structural nature of the problem here and raises many questions over the supply-side emphasis of the recently introduced welfare-to-work initiatives.

This chapter, therefore, offers a critical appraisal of the largest New Deal for Young Unemployed People (18–24), drawing early lessons from the City Pride unit of delivery. It argues that, despite early praise from both national and local partners, New Deal has still to prove it is more than a quick-fix solution and that it can provide sustainable improvements in individual circumstances. Furthermore, New Deal must be seen as more than just another employment and training programme. It is part of an ongoing process which is transforming the welfare state, shifting it from one based on entitlement, in theory providing a safety net for all in times of hardship, to one rebuilt around the work ethic and rights and responsibilities. Unlike previous years, the local response in Manchester is increasingly aligned with national policy. Therefore, evaluation of the local programme provides not only an understanding of the type of New Deal some of Manchester's poorest residents are being offered, but also offers an insight into the future of welfare itself.

The chapter is divided into four sections. The first sets out the local context and reveals a divided city suffering entrenched poverty. The extent and the longevity of the problems suggest that New Deal will find it difficult to provide lasting solutions. Section two explains what New Deal intends to achieve and the philosophy which underpins it. The third section examines the early implementation of the New Deal locally in the 'City Pride' area, including a detailed snapshot in early 2000. It provides a critical overview of welfare-to-work policies. As their 'success' is largely dependent upon the state of the local labour market, this raises serious worries as to how effective the programme can be in Manchester. The chapter concludes by speculating on the lasting significance of New Deal nationally. Having been granted more money and a permanent role under the Spending Review 2000, the 2001 Budget confirmed a policy shift away from youth unemployment towards 'harder to serve' groups such as the long-term unemployed, disabled people and lone parents. As

New Deal 'Mark 2' evolves, this final section suggests that a major rethink of current strategies is needed if inequalities are to be seriously addressed.

Poverty politics

According to the 1998 National Index of Local Deprivation, 'the world's first modern city' (City Pride Strategic Planning Group 1998a: 46) is ranked as the third most deprived local authority district in England – a position which has hardly shifted in the last decade. By the government's own figures Manchester local authority area is recorded as having one of the lowest employment rates in Great Britain (HMSO 1999). On all existing measures of deprivation, Manchester scores badly, and on many its situation has been actually deteriorating throughout the 1980s and 1990s. *Poverty in Manchester: The Third Investigation*, published over a decade ago, found that nearly a third of the city's residents experienced a way of life which is 'drab and falls below average expectation' (MCC 1989: 29). Ten years on and Dave Haslam (1999: 28) unearthed a city of 'unsettled, rarely united communities', still full of ideas and 'dreamers' but in the face of 'recurrent uncertainty and poverty, random violence and suffocating preconceptions from out of town'.

The Labour-controlled City Council, local partners and community groups have keenly attempted to address the city's problems, albeit boxed-in by national policy. The period 1979 to 1997, under successive Conservative Governments, saw a trebling of child poverty and a brutalisation of daily life for many hundreds of thousands in the UK (Andrews and Jacobs 1990; Oppenheim and Harker 1996). The Council stood opposed to the Thatcherite orthodoxy of the 1980s that 'there is no such thing as society'. The local commitment, intensified throughout 1984–87, was to prioritise front-line services and anti-poverty drives and included pledges that 'Manchester City Council Won't Say Farewell to Welfare'. Despite an ambitious anti-poverty programme, the Council predicted a further erosion in the quality of life for Manchester's poorer residents due to the extensive social security changes of 1988 and trends towards social exclusion. It endorsed a comment that 'economic regeneration will leave a lot of people on the sidelines' (MCC 1989: 29).

A local study of the area noted that 'the return of popular anxiety in regard to poverty in the 1980s was clearly associated, in particular, with fear of job loss' (Taylor *et al.* 1996: 166). Benefit cuts for young people in 1988 brought a visible new generation of street homelessness and public begging, while the 1990s witnessed a multi-faceted slump of 'low demand' housing and the appearance of frequent localised street hostility and fear of crime. With industrial decline Manchester lost over a fifth of its population between 1971 and 1996 and at the turn of the twenty-first century the spectre was again raised of the need for fresh housing clearances within the 'vitality and resilience' of other regeneration efforts (Cole *et al.* 2000; Power and Mumford 1999).

The pivotal Labour defeat in the 1987 general election led to a judicious compromise strategy in Manchester (Quilley, this volume). The local response was a difficult course of new pragmatism in public–private partnership, embracing a business agenda of regeneration projects, alongside the continuing commitments to anti-poverty work and a gradual embrace of the emerging 'rights and responsibilities' path. Mapping local poverty became an ever-more important tool both for planning and for bids for investment. The 1986 *Poverty in Manchester* report had noted a major increase in local poverty since the City Council's first report in 1978. It cited a near trebling of unemployment and a greater extent of low pay as key factors. Subsequent reports have charted the rise of poverty and the impact of 'harmful' national policies and have helped to set benchmarks by which local services have been designed and their progress monitored.

A Profile of Poverty and Health in Manchester by consultant Steve Griffiths, commented that:

> Manchester City Council's Planning Studies Group has made Manchester arguably the most advanced in the country in creating an infrastructure of data, service analysis and mapping to enable it to target initiatives and services to people most under pressure. (1998: 1)

The report explored the 'deterioration of fabric and morale' for many of the social groups in the city, including a critique of the damage caused by national policy decisions – for example, in introducing the stricter medical tests for benefits in 1995 and cuts to entitlements for asylum seekers in 1996. In supporting work to 'rebuild sustainable communities', the report retained a vision of redressing material discouragement and strengthening the social fabric. Manchester has also received widespread recognition for its efforts at regeneration, with Hulme most frequently held up as an example of best practice (Harding 1997). It has been successful in winning various European and Government monies and much of the city is now covered by Single Regeneration Budget Challenge Funds.

The fact remains, though, that despite their energies and best efforts the old problems appear to be as entrenched as ever. Unemployment is widespread. While the headline level has fallen in Manchester as else-where in the country, the city has remained with higher levels than Greater Manchester and the North West at more than double the national average of 4.3 per cent. In February 2000, there were 15,598 people or some 9.1 per cent recorded as unemployed and claiming benefit. How-ever, this high figure masked even starker variations at the ward level. The highest unemployment rate was found in Hulme, with 19.2 per cent of economically active people unemployed. Ardwick and Moss Side had levels of 18.7 per cent and 16.4 per cent respectively. Recent studies have shown that there are also increasing numbers of hidden unemployed – those seeking work but no longer included as unemployed in govern-ment statistics (Beatty et al. 1997). In the 1998 Budget statement the government estimated the number wanting to work was more than double the official estimate of unemployment. It put the figure at around 12 per cent of those of working age or four and a quarter million as opposed to the recorded figure at the time. On this basis we can estimate the real unemployment rate in the city of Manchester at that time to be around 19 per cent. Hidden unemployment tends to be highest where recorded unemployment is highest, so the figure could be higher still (Martin et al. 1999; Giordano and Twomey, this volume).

For those without work, life on benefits is increasingly harsh. The extent and effect of poverty in the late 1990s was formidable. The 'Manchester Healthy City' initiative in 1999 noted that mortality in Manchester was the '[h]ighest in England and rising fast!' Manchester was the worst suicide black spot in the country, according to a 1998 official analysis of deaths recorded between 1982 and 1996, while indica-tors of mental health problems were notably high. The Mental Illness Health Needs Index (MINI), for example, identifies Manchester as having the second highest mental health needs by English district (HMSO 1998). Manchester has also had a comparatively low percentage of young people staying on at school at age 16, suggesting widespread deficits, literacy problems and underachievement. Since the uprating of social security benefits was changed to prices in 1980, their real level has declined by a fifth. This has been a significant factor in the rise of numbers of poor and marginalised. In early 1999, for example, 30 per cent of the population of Manchester were claiming, or dependent upon, Income Support, while a staggering 43 per cent of all households in the city were in receipt of Housing Benefit (MCC 1999a).

Even if work is secured, the escape from poverty is far from complete and this raises important questions about the 'work-first' focus of welfare-to-work. Greater Manchester Low Pay Unit's (GMLPU) annual survey of vacancies in Greater Manchester Job Centres found that for the year 1998, 94 per cent of all Job Centre vacancies and 89 per cent of full-time jobs were paying less than the benefit level for a couple with two children (GMLPU 1999). Facing such low wage levels, even with the introduction of the National Minimum Wage, the best people can expect is to work and continue to claim means-tested benefits or the new income-based tax credits. As the report concludes, while falls in unemployment are to be welcomed, it remains the case that there are far more people looking for work than there is work available in Greater Manchester. Add to this that the jobs that are available are increasingly low paid and insecure and we begin to get a picture of large segments of the city's employed as 'working poor'.

There are serious concerns too about the recorded levels of both unemployment and vacancies. Research carried out by the Manchester Economy Group (MEG) highlighted the emergence of a dangerous 'job gap' in the city (Peck and Tickell 1997), while more recent research has questioned the accuracy of the vacancy statistics themselves. Greater Manchester Low Pay Unit found official Job Centre figures to be much higher than the actual number of jobs on display (GMLPU 2000). While the Office for National Statistics has discontinued using the data believing it to be 'unreliable', the Chancellor has returned to a narrow definition of numbers officially unemployed and claiming benefits, maintaining that in an economy with one million unemployed and one million vacancies, work-first measures are an appropriate policy response (HM Treasury 2000). The figures, though, are flawed on both sides of the equation and simply do not add up. There are *more* people seeking work than the official statistics reveal and there are *fewer* vacancies than the recorded level shows. In this economic environment – with under-recorded unemployment, over-recorded vacancy statistics, declining opportunities for full-time work, and both poverty-pay (subsidised by government) and insecurity at work – the residents of Manchester are as much in need of a new approach as anybody. The next section explores what the government's largest New Deal has offered them.

New Labour, New Deals

Since their election in June 1997, New Labour has established an extensive range of programmes and initiatives to address the causes and consequences of poverty and social exclusion. Education Action Zones, Health Action Zones and New Deal for Communities are all active in Manchester. These initiatives have been broadly welcomed as positive and participatory, albeit modest, attempts to extend local partnerships and develop a cross-departmental, bottom-up approach to solving entrenched social problems. New Labour has adopted an annual report into poverty and social exclusion which will track thirty-two indicators in three broad categories (HMSO 1999). These relate to incomes, wider aspects of welfare such as education, housing, health and local environments and others to capture the risk of experiencing poverty in later life, such as teenage pregnancy and truancy.

The long-established links between poverty, ill-health, poor education and unemployment are at last recognised – a significant transformation from previous government policy. Indeed, the Prime Minister has set the judgement of his administration by this goal – 'I believe in greater equality. If the next Labour government has not raised the living standards of the poorest by the end of its time in office it will have failed' (Tony Blair 1996, quoted in *Guardian*, 16 December 1998: 17). Two strategies have been to the fore in attempting to realise this goal. Barriers to employment are being addressed through the welfare-to-work programme and work is being made more 'attractive' through tax and benefit reforms. For example, the various New Deal programmes seek to get 400,000 people into work in two years, the National Minimum Wage should benefit some two million people and the Working Families Tax Credit guarantees a minimum income of just over £200 a week for a family with a child. The real character of this administration, though – its big idea – has undoubtedly been expressed in its desire to remould the welfare state and the uncompromising manner in which it has set about the business of welfare reform.

At the centre of the welfare-to-work policy programme lies the New Deal for 18–24 year olds. It was the first policy announcement on day one of the Blair government, and has remained one of the most substantial elements of it. The proceeds of the one-off £5.2 billion Windfall Tax were divided up so that £3.6 billion went to various New Deals, of which £2.6 billion, or 73 per cent of the total was earmarked for the 18–24 programme (HMSO 1998). The commitment of such resources is of course to be welcomed, as it signals the intent to bring issues of youth unemployment and exclusion to the centre of the political debate. It is not clear, however, whether the model of reform adopted is the best way to raise the standard of living amongst the poorest communities.

New Deal is central in terms of cost, then, but also in terms of the direction of change. Two recent developments serve to underline this. First, the introduction of ONE pilots, a single work-focused Gateway programme, means that most new claimants will be compelled to attend an interview with a personal adviser within three days of making a claim or be liable to lose benefits. Their adviser will work with them, establish their individual needs and help them become 'independent'. This is an essential element in welfare reform and attempts to move the culture away from a passive benefit payment. New Deal pre-dates ONE in its use of personal advisers for each participant and in building upon the Jobseeker's Allowance (JSA) legislation of 1996, to accelerate the rise of local experimentation in welfare initiatives. Second, the decision to merge the Employment Service and the Benefits Agency into a new service for people of working age, with Jobcentre Plus offices piloted locally from October 2001, graphically highlights the extension of this ethos of 'activation': accelerating its reach from those registered to receive JSA, to those in receipt of a wide range of benefits. As the social security secretary observed, this is the 'logical conclusion of the government's welfare policy' (Darling, quoted in *Guardian*, 17 March 2000: 15).

New Deal, now followed by ONE and Jobcentre Plus, marks the latest step in a gradual transition which is witnessing the genesis of a new kind of welfare across a range of Western economies, most notably the UK and US (Peck and Theodore 2000a). These economies are casting aside traditional, passive, welfare settlements which regulated labour at a time of full employment. Such institutions are now seen as the causes of, not the solutions to, poverty and dependency. Instead there is a shift to social contracts, 'rights and responsibilities' and a more active 'workfare' regime. Here, 'workfare' is understood as a complex range of interconnected programmes and processes which remove universal entitlement to welfare and replace it with less welfare (both in terms of reduced eligibility and levels of support); the extension of compulsion to participate in education and training programmes and low-paid 'make-work' schemes; and an increased surveillance of the activities of those receiving benefits (Peck 1998).

The New Deal for 18–24 year olds is a compulsory programme focusing on young people who have been signing as unemployed for six months or more. Some, such as ex-offenders, can choose to enter the programme early. Although there is local flexibility in terms of design and delivery, the programme is fundamentally a national one. The framework that was handed down from central government begins with an intensive period of guidance, counselling and advice known as the 'Gateway'. The chief aim of this element is to move people into unsubsidised work. While contractual arrangements for the New Deal have been handled locally by the Employment Service (ES), Gateway services are operated by a range of providers in each locality, either individually or in partnership. Those who fail to move into work during this period, which is intended to last up to four months, must choose one of four options:

- a job with an employer, including at least one day a week in education or training, working towards an accredited qualification; employers are offered up to £60 a week for up to 26 weeks to contribute to the costs of recruiting and employing, as well as £750 towards the costs of training; this option now includes provision for self-employment;
- a placement for six months in the Environmental Task Force, which includes day-release for education and training towards accredited qualifications;
- a placement for six months with a voluntary sector organisation, again including day-release education or training towards accredited qualifications;
- a twelve-month placement in education or training leading to a qualification, usually capped at NVQ Level Two.

Since the launch of New Deal, ministers have repeatedly stressed that young people who refuse to take up a placement will have 'no fifth option' of continued full benefit. The final component of New Deal is the 'follow-through'. Clients who have failed to secure permanent work will be offered further active support as part of an individual action plan to achieve this.

New Deal has several positive differences to previous employment programmes. A broad range of local partners, including Employment Service, local authorities, Training and Enterprise Councils, the new Learning and Skills Councils and the private sector have been recruited to help design and deliver the programme. There is greater local flexibility for these partnerships to achieve client-centred solutions to unemployment. The different local models adopted are intended to feed competition and breed innovation in solutions that will sweep away institutional barriers to getting the unemployed to work. That said, in other ways it closely resembles the range of employment programmes, tried in the 1980s and early 1990s, which were constructed in the belief that the major cause of unemployment was that too many people were unable or unwilling to work. The ultimate objective of New Deal is to improve the employability of the unemployed and the programme seeks to achieve this by focusing on quality and individual choice. It concentrates on the attitudes, work orientations and basic job skills of young unemployed people in order to maximise flows into available jobs in the local labour market. So, the programme is 'active' on the supply side of the labour market while being almost entirely 'passive' on the demand side. It is this imbalance that raises some of the greatest concerns about its effectiveness.

In the last two decades, Britain has increasingly focused on supply-side initiatives that the New Deal typifies. This approach is untypical in Europe as a whole where supply-side measures have been adopted along with targeted job-creation measures, such as the adoption of Intermediate Labour Markets at the local level. There is scope for this within New Deal, but the priority lies with the centralised imposition of a programme framework and philosophy which locates the cause of unemployment with individual levels of employability. Two economic theories underpin the welfare-to-work approach to tackling long-term unemployment (Webster 1997). On the one hand, it is felt that being unemployed makes people less employable (the 'withering flowers' hypothesis of Sir Alan Budd, Chief Economic Adviser to the Treasury). On the other, people are believed to remain unemployed for longer because social security benefits give them an incentive to do so (the 'replacement ratio' hypothesis set out by Professor Richard Layard of the London School of Economics). This theoretical diagnosis of the causes of long-term unemployment has led to the New Deal's emphasis on employability, delivered within the 'tough love' of compulsion (Peck and Theodore 2000a). The logic runs that because unemployment is due to the existence of a pool of 'unemployable' people, a one-off programme to raise their employability, funded by a one-off windfall tax, will permanently reduce unemployment. The focus has fallen on the young because it is believed that in stopping them becoming unemployable the economy carries less 'unemployables', thus leading to the end of long-term unemployment. In turn, in an ideal scenario, this will release funds to be spent on improving public services.

Local labour market results, however, are very difficult to evaluate accurately because it is virtually impossible to disentangle the impact of the New Deal from other influences in the economy. For example, by the summer of 1999, the total number of unemployed 18–24 year olds was at the lowest level since July 1974 and between April 1997 and April 1998, claims amongst this client group fell by a third. After the New Deal was rolled out nationally in April 1998, it fell by over 40 per cent to around 71,000. Credit for this fall was claimed on behalf of the New Deal, but this trend can be traced back many months before New Deal was operational. Evaluation is hampered further because Government has introduced a system which is far from transparent. For example, 'sustained' jobs are recorded as outcomes of New Deal intervention.

'Sustained' jobs, in fact, are those which last for at least thirteen weeks. While this represents an improvement on the measure under the previous administration which made no distinction at all between sustained and unsustained jobs, it remains a very low threshold.

Nationally, to the end of April 2001, almost 300,000 jobs had been filled through New Deal (Employment Service National Returns, June 2001). However, over 67,000 individuals returned to claim benefit within thirteen weeks and there is no way of knowing how many of the rest lasted only a few weeks more. Nowhere in the government analysis is there a concept of 'additionality' or 'value added'. All jobs are simply claimed as successful New Deal outcomes, even those that would have been taken anyway. It is accordingly impossible for Government to be sure how much, if any, saved revenue will be available to be diverted to public services, let alone when this may prove possible. Major research by the National Institute of Economic and Social Research (1999) has revealed that about 4 in every 5 young people acclaimed as finding work through the New Deal would have found work anyway, albeit perhaps more slowly. The report described the New Deal as having a 'modest positive effect.'

Academics are divided over the merits of welfare-to-work programmes (Cressey 1999), and while there is little conclusive evidence either way, two points are significant here. First, successful programmes operate under favourable local labour market conditions. Various studies of the impact of American reforms have shown that where programmes have proved successful, unemployment numbers fall more due to business cycle effects than welfare-to-work strategies (see, for example, Blank 1997; Katz and Carnevale 1998; Ziliak et al. 1997). Indeed, Ziliak and his colleagues found that as much as 78 per cent of the reduction of American unemployment between 1993 and 1996 was attributable to business cycle conditions and only 6 per cent to active labour market measures. The very areas that need these programmes to work most therefore – those urban areas with the highest and most entrenched unemployment levels – tend to perform worst. Second, it is not clear whether savings are made. Indeed, some programmes that achieve the best results end up spending more per welfare recipient (House of Commons Social Security Committee 1998). This raises the thorny question of whether welfare-to-work is about reducing unemployment or redrawing the boundaries of social regulation?

There are serious question marks too as to whether New Deal will be able to achieve significant reductions in UK unemployment *however* much is spent. As Turok and Webster (1998) argue, the rate of long-term unemployment is closely related to the overall rate of unemployment. Indeed, since 1993, when long-term unemployment in Britain peaked at 4.4 per cent of the labour force, it fell steadily without the intervention of New Deal to be around 2 per cent in 1998. While there are always going to be some within the labour market who face difficulties, for whatever reason, in securing and holding down work and therefore need support, this contradicts the view that the majority of long-term unemployed are so unemployable that a sufficiently strong recovery will not pick them up. Turok and Webster also found that the regional distribution of New Deal target groups closely matched that of total unemployment and that an almost perfect fit exists between the loss of manufacturing jobs and total unemployment. These findings again reinforce the need for demand-side measures to be given more prominence.

While there is clearly a need to increase the skills of some in the labour market, there are dangers in continuing to focus primarily on individual and cultural, as opposed to community and structural, causes of unemployment. Such an approach assumes that given more skills, the market will automatically adjust and expand to create employment opportunities. This neglects labour market discrimination, structural weaknesses of local labour markets and the uneven distribution of jobs. Inheriting this legacy, New Deal almost completely neglects the fact that there is insufficient demand for labour in many parts of the country where the largest concentrations of unemployed live. Therefore, the people and the places that have most need of a New Deal may well continue to experience the greatest discrimination and the imbalance of supply and demand in local labour markets will continue to expand.

City Pride and welfare-to-work

New Deal in Manchester is delivered as part of the City Pride partnership that lies at the heart of Greater Manchester and covers a population of 1.1 million people. As well as the City of Manchester it includes parts of the City of Salford, Tameside and Trafford. Locally, New Deal has been enthusiastically welcomed by partners:

> The recent decision by Government to base the delivery of New Deal Welfare to Work on the City Pride area, is a welcome recognition of the strength of our partnership in this area. The partners look forward to tackling the causes, and not just the effects, of deprivation and disaffection within the grain of Government policies and priorities. (City Pride Strategic Planning Group 1998a: 3)

As other chapters in this volume outline, the history of successful partnership bidding in Manchester meant that a broad and inclusive partnership was readily assembled. A combination of partnership strengths and the economies of scale afforded by the large size of the unit has led to significant innovation in design. This, indeed, had to be the case. As an interviewee put it:

> You can probably get away with delivering pure New Deal in Norfolk, bits of North Devon and places like that, but in the big urban areas it's not a programme that will work without significantly more thinking on the part of local partners. (Member #1, City Pride Strategic Planning Group, 1999)

In City Pride, that extra thinking has stamped a distinctive local shape on the programme. 'Localisation' is evident in two ways: those measures which are the result of a pick 'n' mix from a national menu and those which are the product of genuine bottom-up innovation. Changes which fit into the first category include: the establishment of minimum wage rates of pay in the employer option even for those who wouldn't qualify for it normally; the extension (where possible) of the employer option beyond 26 weeks; the desire to take only temporary vacancies which could be proven to be of sufficient quality to be beneficial; and the packaging of extra funding to extend the FTET option to beyond NVQ level two, a limit the partners vehemently opposed.

There is, though, also evidence of bottom-up innovation. One example is the sectoral Gateway for the construction industry which is now part of national thinking about how to improve the Gateway element and make it more work-relevant. Another, one of the most prized innovations to emerge locally, is the Community and Environmental Employment option. From the outset, there was a strong feeling that the third and fourth options should be merged into a single range of *waged* opportunities. Nationally the Voluntary Sector and Environmental Task Force were to be quite distinct, usually paying only benefit plus £15. Locally, however, partners wanted them to be viewed as equal to the Employer option and be as close to working in the open labour market as possible. Therefore a cocktail of funding – Employment Service, Training and Enterprise Council, Local Authority, Single Regeneration Budget Challenge Fund and European – was put together and since April 1998 a merged option has run as the Community and Environmental Employment (CEE) programme. This incorporates an Intermediate Labour Market model which supports local organisations delivering community and environmental services and is designed to create real jobs, provide training and improve the employability of participants.

The model provides financial assistance/support for the sponsoring employer, including the cost of employing and training additional staff. By offering a merged provision it was felt that a more co-ordinated and effective policy which built up local capacity could be offered. The partners wanted to ensure that this did not end up as a sink option and so all positions were to be waged, 'real jobs'. The only difference with the employment option, then, would be that these jobs would be of social benefit and more likely to be temporary.

Expectations, however, have been raised well beyond what local New Deal partnerships were ever realistically going to deliver. As a senior partner put it:

> [the] rhetoric of New Deal is about eliminating unemployment amongst 18–24 year olds. In a city like Manchester it's never going to do that for a whole variety of reasons, but what it can do is reduce the problem and reduce it to a point where it doesn't have a disproportionate impact ... If it doesn't tackle unemployment in Manchester and Sheffield and such places then ultimately in terms of the problems it's tried to address it will have failed. (Member #2, City Pride Strategic Planning Group, 1999)

It is too soon to judge the effectiveness of City Pride New Deal on the early data presented here, let alone to argue that it has failed. However, it is possible to comment on a number of issues and highlight programme responses, which reflect the way the problems are being perceived locally: first, the size and type of the client group locally; second, the nature of the City Pride labour market; finally, the extension of sanctions and compulsion when both national and local partners maintain New Deal is part of a co-ordinated approach to address poverty and social exclusion.

The welfare-to-work client group is largest in precisely those parts of the country where the labour market is weakest. Around half of the 18–24 year old client group were in 18 of the 471 local authority districts (Simmonds and Bewick 1997) and one-third of the client group in five cities (London, Birmingham, Glasgow, Liverpool and Manchester). The sheer size of the problem in these places has created huge problems of programme delivery, especially in terms of sufficient quality and capacity. Table 11.1 reveals wide gaps between forecasts and outcomes in the programme's first year.

In City Pride between April 1998 and January 2000, over 10,000 participants joined the local Gateway. Almost 6,000 joined in the first year making City Pride New Deal 18–24 one of largest programmes in the country, and many of these were considerably disadvantaged and facing multiple barriers to work.

Table 11.1 City Pride New Deal 18–24 forecasts and performance (all participants)

	1998/99 (forecast)	1998/99 (performance)	1999/2000 (forecast)
Eligible clients	10,708	7,933	5,257
Gateway entrants	8,963	5,943 (75)	3,942 (75)
Joining options	5,378	1,273	2,000
Subsidised employment	2,460 (46)	389 (31)	500 (25)
Full time education & training	1,918 (35)	591 (46)	900 (45)
Community & environmental employment	1,000 (19)	293 (23)	600 (30)

Source: City Pride Strategic Planning Group (1998a), City Pride Strategic Planning Group (1999b)
Note: The figures in brackets are percentages

It is no surprise, therefore, to learn that in Manchester the 'challenge faced by strategic and delivery partnerships in City Pride has … been immense and … there have been many successes and many harsh lessons learned' (City Pride Strategic Planning Group 1999a: 4). Given the huge volume of clients and a completely new programme to make operational – with contracts to sign, staff to train and capacity of sufficient quality to build – problems were as anticipated. Less than a sixth of the expected subsidised jobs and less than a third of education, training and community or environmental places were delivered. The rushed nature of delivery and outdated original information partly explain this and reflect the ideological urgency of the programme for the New Labour Government. By the end of the first year, less than 25 per cent of Gateway entrants had taken up an option in the City Pride area, instead of the 60 per cent predicted. The limited number of subsidised jobs delivered meant that the second year forecast, in percentage terms, was revised down to little over half of the initial year prediction. The other options were clearly viewed as more achievable.

The client profile in City Pride is very similar to the national picture in terms of gender (73 per cent are male), ethnicity (15 per cent are from minority ethnic groups) and disability (12 per cent are disabled). The high proportion of young males compared to young females reflects not only the dearth of jobs for young working-class males with the collapse of traditional manual jobs, but also the labour market discrimination and wider social pressures which make it harder for women to maintain a claim. There are significant differences from the national pattern, though, in the depth and range of barriers to work that these groups face locally. While the partners had a far from complete knowledge initially, they expected that around 16 per cent would have qualifications at NVQ level 2 or equivalent, 1 per cent would have problems speaking English, 6 per cent would have problems writing English, 4 per cent would have numeracy problems, 6 per cent health problems and 8 per cent other problems (Manchester TEC 1998). The entrenched local structural difficulties have produced a client group which local partners have rapidly discovered is far more seriously disadvantaged than was first thought, with, for example, 47 per cent having no qualifications and 25 per cent having never worked (City Pride Strategic Planning Group 1999b). Furthermore, the local intake may understate potential 'need' because some groups, such as people recently arrived from abroad, are now generally disentitled or discouraged from claiming the qualifying benefit.

The City Pride labour market has experienced massive and sustained job losses through much of the last two decades. Ongoing shifts in the structure of the wider economy and the nature of employment have led to an increasingly segmented and polarised labour market that includes privileged, high-wage non-manual workers and the underprivileged, part-time, temporary, low-waged and unemployed (Giordano and Twomey, this volume). Such new employment structures have led to increased insecurity and cities like Manchester have performed worse than the rest of the country both in periods of recession and periods of recovery. Turok and Edge (1999) found the difference in labour market conditions between urban and non-urban areas to be widening, with cities continuing to lose jobs. Indeed, the largest twenty cities have lost around half a million jobs since 1981, while the rest of the country has gained over three times that many. Although services have grown, this has been nothing like large enough to compensate for manufacturing losses.

By the end of January 2000, some 22 months into the programme, the City Pride area had a significantly higher proportion of young people still on the Gateway (58 per cent) than the national average (50 per cent). Entry into the subsidised employment and environmental options were comparable at around 25 per cent and 17 per cent, but much greater use was being made of the education and training option nationally (42 per cent compared to 32 per cent) and the voluntary sector option locally (27 per cent compared to 17 per cent). This unevenness reflects a potential strength of New Deal (namely its ability to provide local flavour), but also reveals how participant choice is severely limited depending on local labour market characteristics.

Table 11.2 Destination of New Deal 18–24 clients leaving Gateway, January 1998–January 2000

	City Pride	*Great Britain*
Total	8,324	35,7100
	%	%
Unsubsidised jobs	27	26
New Deal options of which	33	42
subsidised jobs	20	19
FTET	47	45
VS	24	19
ETF	9	18
Other benefits	11	8
Other known	9	8
Other unknown	20	20

Source: Employment Service National Returns, March

Key differences also emerge between local groups as participants move into options. While one in five of males at this stage entered the voluntary sector element, 44 per cent of females did. The environmental element shows the exact opposite with much lower levels for females (5 per cent) than males (21 per cent). Minority ethnic participants enjoyed similar levels of subsidised employment placements (24 per cent) – although the numbers are very low (with only 33 participating at that time) – but are over-represented in the voluntary sector option (35 per cent compared to 27 per cent) and under-represented in terms of access to environmental placements (9 per cent compared to 17 per cent) (Employment Service National Returns 2000). These differences raise the worry that referrals to options are less to do with client choice than with the pigeon-holing of certain groups into particular activities. Not only does this accentuate labour market discriminations, which these groups already face, but it also neglects the range of opportunities that the local CEE option has sought to offer in an attempt to break away from the stigma of previous 'sink' options.

Most attention has, justifiably, been focused on outcomes. Table 11.2 provides information on the destination of clients who have left Gateway. It shows that young people leaving locally took up open market employment at just above the national rate. National planning targets assumed that 40 per cent of New Deal clients would enter unsubsidised jobs from Gateway. While City Pride is some way short of this target (27 per cent), it has fared slightly better than Great Britain (26 per cent). Strikingly, however, only 33 per cent have entered the various local options. This compares to 42 per cent in the country as a whole. Local numbers moving on to other benefits were notably up for women, disabled clients and people from minority ethnic communities. Other unknown destinations were consistently higher for all local groups too.

Government has quoted research that maintains as many as 57 per cent of those recorded as moving into unknown destinations have actually found jobs. This figure, though, is somewhat misleading. By the time they were interviewed, 55 per cent were actually unemployed again (Convery 2000). This high figure raises worries about the impact of the programme on the most excluded.

Central to this concern is the operation of a more stringent sanctions regime. While no data are available for City Pride, information supplied by Employment Service nationally, reveals that the North West had the highest incidence of sanctions in the option stage of New Deal in the first year. Just over 8,000 people in Great Britain were sanctioned in the option stage, with almost 1,300 of these based in the North West. Some 10,800 people had sanctions applied in the first year of the programme as a whole. To March 1999, there was a dramatic increase in the number of young people sanctioned. Nationally, the figure almost quadrupled over a six-month period. Particularly worrying is the fact that 23 per cent of New Dealers on the Environmental Task Force in the North West region have been sanctioned, meaning that a significant number of people are unwilling or unprepared to enter this option. This raises questions as to the quality of some programmes and the real choice that is being offered clients. By comparison, very few people were sanctioned for refusing to try subsidised employment. Problems of exclusion are compounded by the large numbers trapped outside the programme. While government set a target of placing 250,000 young unemployed back into the labour market, the extent of the problem is much greater. In fact, some 500,000 16–24 year olds are missing from the unemployment register, but are not in education, training or work (Bentley and Gurumurthy 1999). For every young person claiming Jobseekers' Allowance, another has slipped through the system. Around 200,000 of those missing from the registers have no qualifications and this number includes 130,000 16–17 year olds who have had their benefit rights removed and 125,000 over 18 who are looking for work but not claiming benefits.

Problems of exclusion have been anticipated for several groups. For example, Wyler (1999: 1) describes the New Deal generally as having 'by-passed those who are homeless' in its first year of operation, despite the achievements of small-scale projects such as those run by the Big Issue in the North West. Manchester City Council estimated that over 500 young people entering New Deal faced average rent shortfalls of £20 a week because of Housing Benefit restrictions in 1998/99. They commented that it 'is therefore highly likely that the Employment Service will use a greater number of benefit sanctions with this group than others, adding further to a vicious circle of difficulties' (MCC 1999a: 25–6). Further Manchester-based research found early problems for the image of New Deal with young people as well as early experiences of poor quality, lack of choice and false hope (Faichnie 1999). Key partners delivering the New Deal in Manchester mark out a sharp learning curve with a mixture of local confidence and ill preparation, as borne out in the following quotes:

> We took it further and said that the employment should be sustainable and should be developmental. It causes problems for the central model of 'a job's a job'...What we were trying to do was say we will be selective – certainly about the jobs that had funding support, the subsidised jobs, that they should have training and development content. (Member #3, City Pride Strategic Planning Group 1999)

> We had some ideas about what we thought was going to happen and then the exact opposite happened. So, when we're talking about planning for next year we can't use the first year as a typical year. We can't say this happened so this is what we'll expect in the future. Year one was not typical. We had an incredibly steep learning curve, we were dealing with the majority of the clients, some of the toughest clients who had been unemployed for a long, long time, at a time when we weren't geared up to do it. (Member #4, City Pride Strategic Planning Group 1999)

> There will be more diagnosis when people arrive at Gateway. There's been some concern in the past where people have been referred to Gateway services from advisers who said this person needs motivation and confidence building, psychometric tests etc and they arrive at Gateway to find that maybe they need counselling or they're still taking drugs or have dyslexia. (Member #5, City Pride Strategic Planning Group 1999)

A final concern is the extension of compulsion, which necessitates a greater use of sanctions. Arguments against compulsion are philosophical and practical. Compulsion is understandable in that it is easier to design and manage programmes when exact numbers are known. Mandation for this client group – the youngest – is generally easier to win support for than others such as lone parents. City Pride partners, including the voluntary sector and trade unions, have supported the use of compulsion as the counterbalance to a wider range of quality options. However, they have remained acutely aware of the tensions inherent in operating a mandatory programme.

Compulsory programmes prove difficult to operationalise locally and take responsibility away from participants because they take away the choice of participating. Voluntary programmes work because participants are self-selecting and more enthusiastic and this allows advisers and resources to focus on the most motivated. There is also a risk that mandation creates sink provision and those most in need of help are trapped into poor quality options with no realistic opportunity of progression into good jobs. Answers to Parliamentary questions have underlined this worry. They revealed that only one in ten of those entering the education and training option complete it before leaving New Deal and that Government neither knows how many nor what type of qualifications are being gained by participants (*Observer*, 2 April 2000: 5). High drop-out rates have been an unsatisfactory feature of many New Deal education and training options in Manchester. Information and Communications Technology, English for Speakers of Other Languages, Childcare, Construction and Printing are amongst popular local courses bringing improved prospects. However, many of the students successfully completing a course under the New Deal had already been studying part-time whilst on benefit. The drop-out rate suggests difficulties ahead in the drive to improve basic literacy and numeracy skills for all participants on New Deal. The failure to quantify educational goals and attainments has represented a glaring weakness and inefficiency in the political ambition of the programme; although it is due to receive attention under New Deal 'Mark 2'.

In effect, New Deal is primarily reordering the job queue, with the most able pushed closer to the job market. For those who are least job ready, and according to local estimates in City Pride that is 51 per cent of the client group (City Pride Strategic Planning Group 1999b), the thrust of programmes offers little more than rotation between various education, training and work options which for most participants serve to exaggerate existing labour market discriminations. As Peck and Theodore (2000b) argue, the fact that demand for jobs exceeds supply in these areas means that access to the employment option is effectively rationed and it is employer and adviser definitions of who is most employable which are paramount. In this way, New Deal could exaggerate the labour market discriminations experienced by the most disadvantaged groups – the minority ethnic, disabled, and ex-offenders – and simply end up cherry-picking the most employable. There is already intense competition for limited jobs in these areas and wages could therefore fall further at the lower end of the labour market to absorb higher employment. The reality in this scenario is not an increased market of 'employables' creating a self-sustaining environment with the creation of more jobs, but rather the displacement of lower-paid workers, yet greater pressure on wages to fall and further workplace insecurity. Already enduring an understandable degree of 'scheme-fatigue', this group is marginalised further and New Deal ends up subsidising insecure work and providing a workforce for it.

Research findings point to the fact that if the opportunities on offer are of sufficient quality then they will attract the vast majority of unemployed who are seeking work. One such study of young unemployed in four British cities reaffirmed that the overwhelming majority have a strong desire to secure jobs, and most were actively looking. They felt that harsh JSA regulations were irrelevant in shaping this outlook. It found that they wanted the security of a full time permanent job with a 'living wage' and, given their experience of previous programmes, they were cynical of schemes that were used just to get numbers off the unemployment register (Finn *et al.* 1998). Ultimately, it may prove necessary to accept that there will always be a small number not interested and mandatory programmes turn these into 'option conscripts' who just go through the motions. This wastes the time of providers and participants who have volunteered, the valuable resources available and threatens to undermine the role of personal advisers who need to build up trust with the client if the relationship is to work. The whole programme ethos should not be constructed around the small numbers who are recalcitrant. Instead, these should be given a more supportive framework that is in keeping with the philosophy of social inclusion.

Viewed in this light, changes locally driven by the need to see quicker movement, take on a far greater significance. For example, City Pride Gateway changed in 1999/2000 to become attendance based, requiring Employment Service New Deal Personal Advisers to mandate clients to Gateway provision for a specific period of time each week. It is also moving towards a programme which offers 'intensive support in applying for specific vacancies with certain employers and work with those employers to develop Gateway services which meet their particular needs' (City Pride Strategic Planning Group 1999b: 12). The danger evident here is that Gateway will become little more than a recruitment and selection process for individual companies and will shift their training costs to the public purse. While in some ways this is what employment programmes of this type do anyway, this reconstruction significantly alters the two central features on which New Deal was sold. First, it raises the issue about a potential loss of choice as Gateway in practice recognises a hierarchy amongst the four options and centres on pushing participants into any local jobs to meet employer needs. Second, it jeopardises the goal of employability as generic skills that may raise long-term prospects are subsumed by the specific skills needed by prominently positioned large local employers in the short term.

Proud, but still poor

New Deal represents a central part of New Labour's plan to 'make work pay' because for the Chancellor and the Prime Minister, work remains the central way that Government can help the poor. As a result, what emerges is a reworking of the historical moral line built around the notion of a 'deserving' working poor and an 'undeserving' unemployed poor (Bauman 1998). The 1999 and 2000 Budget statements have made this clear with a range of tax incentives and credits as the carrots of encouragement for the former, and a yet more punitive welfare for the latter. For example, the 1999 Budget announced that those remaining in New Deal Gateway for more than three months would face greater pressure from the Employment Service to move off the unemployment register. As the Treasury explained, this was 'to reinforce the message that there is no option of continuing on benefits' (*Financial Times*, 10 March 1999: 6). Building on this, the 2000 Budget signalled the extension of Trailblazer Gateway, which intensifies the initial element and focuses on the 'work-ethic' of participants. Furthermore, the compulsory nature of the New Deal for Young People is now to be replicated for those on the New Deal for 25-plus. This kind of populist 'Welfare Crackdown' (*Daily Mail*, 10 February 1999: 1) runs counter to the reality that those who are still on Gateway after this time either face significant barriers to work or are situated in labour markets which have high unemployment and few opportunities of work.

New Deal, though, is not just part of a welfare-to-work strategy which seeks to make the poor work for their benefits. In redesigning welfare, it is also resocialising welfare recipients and making them ready for the kind of contingent work which is increasingly all that is on offer. This creates an institutional legacy which is not only shaped by the flexible labour market but which shapes it too, thus facilitating the transition to even greater numbers in contingent work. At this wider level, it represents an attempt to regulate flexible labour markets and to make them work. New Deal, therefore, is of paramount significance both to the unemployed and the employed. It marks a key moment in a systemic change where policy-makers believe that a new labour market structure requires a new institutional order. The new focus is on individualised, Personal Adviser direction, with extended compulsion and a likely enhancement of target-driven conditionality. Experimentation will be rewarded on a 'can-do' basis, where innovation and competition will lead to continuation of the local models or projects, which best comply with this national agenda.

City Pride innovations are part of the process of looking for localised solutions in a context of diminishing welfare – a test bed for new ideas within national constraints. Localisation, however, is a double-edged sword. Devolving responsibilities and targets gives degrees of local autonomy, but with funding restraints and strict legislative control, central political power is enhanced, while local partners generally face political blame for any underachievement. The initial returns nationally, but especially locally, point to an overstatement of what could be quickly achieved. The most job-ready young unemployed advanced most promptly and the most socially excluded remained outside the system, in the Gateway, dropped out, or departed to unknown destinations. The education and training option, accounting for almost half of all option places, has proved much too limited, resulting in high rates of non-completion. It has glaringly lacked evaluation of skills gained. Serious alternative strategies should also be considered, including significantly improved financial support for study and training and the removal of penalties and obstacles for those seeking to study whilst on benefit. Partial steps such as the introduction of Education Maintenance Allowances and Learning Direct are welcome. However, they remain insufficient to address the current institutional discouragement to study for those on low income.

It will prove impossible to address poverty fully without greater consideration of demand-side factors. Like many other large cities, Manchester suffers from not having enough jobs that both pay at a high enough level and are of sufficient duration to lift the working poor out of poverty. Of those who remain without work, welfare-to-work programmes to date provide training that is inadequately resourced to provide sufficient skills to escape poverty wages. The exceptions are those who would generally have escaped as the local labour market expanded anyway. Equally, the social service and skills development elements of programmes are subservient to the work-first, register reducing function and so are generally under-resourced and of insufficient time to address

genuinely participants' needs. Many Manchester localities have collap-
sed into poverty, dragging down the life-chances and expectations of
residents because there is too little public assistance in areas which the
market has abandoned. New community-based social investment programmes are a commendable improvement but remain too modest and
too fragmented.

Despite the gloss of New Labour's approach, there is a danger that
their emphasis on macho policy rhetoric creates an environment where
all welfare is seen as bad. The 'ending welfare as we know it' process is
likely to lead to a pattern of individual Job Accounts and responsibility
firmly placed on individuals to sort out 'employability' options, using a
privatised system of credits for purchase, with very limited recourse to a
safety net of benefits. In this way the legacy of the New Deal may well
be to shift the UK closer to the limited, prejudiced American models of
social support and away from the more solidaridistic, demand-side
conscious approaches of much of continental Europe. If the future is to
be one of 'trainingfare' or 'schemefare' (Jones 1999a), with the New
Deals expanded and made permanent, then it is crucial that such programmes are properly resourced and are genuinely person-led and
flexible. They also need to offer relevant qualifications of a sufficiently
high standard and exhibit enough quality and choice so that they can be
presented as voluntary programmes. Furthermore, they need to be
offered in tandem with urban and industrial policies that are genuinely
bottom-up, coupled with a more generous welfare to ensure that
participants are not kept in hardship or poverty traps. Fresh thinking is
needed both on the natural rewards of work and on publicly supported
jobs in the form of small-scale Intermediate Labour Market projects
which need greater prominence and sufficient time and resources to be
properly evaluated.

I 2

Hypocritical city: cycles of urban exclusion

ROSEMARY MELLOR

I know very well that this hypocritical plan is more or less common to all great cities ... I have never seen so tender a concealment of everything that might affront the eye and the nerves. (Engels 1844)

THE classic presentation of Manchester is still that of Engels, who over a hundred and fifty years ago as a young man used his insights as a migrant to industrialising England to present a critique of the industrial capitalist order. As an outsider, from a craft-workshop industrial town in the Rhineland, he was able to develop his observations and the surveys and commentaries of his contemporaries – doctors, scientists and businessmen – into an analysis of city and society. *The Condition of the Working Class in England* was written between September 1844 and March 1845, and first published in England in 1892; it is both a founding Marxist text and the first attempt at an analysis of industrial urbanisation.

What Engels pinpointed was not the factory system, but the conditions of living and association in the new-style city. These included the city-centre slums, notably Little Ireland; the terraced cottages, short leasehold property built with single brick walls on bare earth; the expansion of the commercial buildings in the urban core over both slums and Georgian houses to form a distinct business district; the migration of the 'money aristocracy' to the suburban villas outside the dense knot of districts housing the 'operatives'; the system of road-building which allowed the monied to come in and out of the city centre 'without ever seeing that they are in the midst of the grimy misery that lurks to the left and right'. That the elite of Manchester, the liberal manufacturers, could be so assured that the working class was 'doing famously' while in such squalor indicated a hypocrisy in 'the matter of this sensitive method of construction' (Engels 1969: 79–81).

Central Manchester was then and for many decades subsequently the nerve centre of a regional production system – hence its designation as 'Cottonopolis'. City and region have gone through several phases since. In Engels' own lifetime the business core was to expand over the city-centre slums as it maintained its monopoly over world trade in cotton. Only thirty years after his death did this control ebb so that ultimately the production of cotton textiles in North West England became negligible, and the warehouses and merchants' offices in the city centre redundant. Similarly, improvements to public health were soon to be enforced and the worst of the workers' houses were demolished or improved before 1900. The extension of powers to local authorities and the levying of increased local rates enabled extensive reforms to the infrastructure of the city and ultimately its wholesale rebuilding in the twentieth century. The great gain was the extension of right of access to decent housing and suburban living to the 'operatives' through the mandatory provision of housing by local authorities after 1919. But, by the close of the millennium, the transfer of responsibility from the 'liberal bourgeoisie' castigated by Engels (themselves, and many of their wives and families, devoting much money, time and attention to the amelioration of living conditions) to the local authorities had resulted in a far greater detachment of ordinary people from investment decisions and policy-making.

The great gains of the past century and a half must not be understated. Indications of poverty now include lack of self-contained dwelling, no television or refrigerator, as well as frustration of children's expectations of toys, trips and treats. If the surveys conducted for the Ministry of Housing and Local Government in Oldham in the 1960s are re-read, or the photographs of inner Manchester or Salford at the same time are re-viewed, then it is obvious that poverty now is a very different everyday experience. It is less a matter of survival (hypothermia, damp, chronic malnutrition), more a question of comfort in the home, proper family life and inclusion in the society's common existence. If Manchester is a 'dual' city, one likened by a national newspaper's property correspondent (Clark 2000) to a 'Third World city' in its juxtaposition of inner city poverty and abandonment with the concentrated investment in the central area, then its dualism is of a different quality to that observed by Engels.

A counter-theme to this broad tide of progressive reform, peaking after the two world wars, and reconsidered since 1979, is to be found in the cycles of expansion, recession and restructuring which have characterised the industrial economy. These have resulted in a regional economy which confers affluence on a minority, sufficiency if not comfort for the majority, in most cases without the rigours of lifelong industrial labour. Manchester, assessed either as city or city-region, has long ceased to be preponderantly industrial. But it still has, as in Engels' days, a reservoir of unskilled and under-employed people, very often debilitated by generations of poverty and hardship, many concentrated in the urban core districts. With the renaissance of the city centre, some are at work in the low-paid casual jobs generated by the leisure economy, some on a career path, but the differential is unmistakable. Much has shifted, but social inequalities are still concentrated in the city – and the dualism is pronounced.

In the light of this, can it be said that Manchester of the new millennium evinces any of the hypocrisy of the raw years of capitalist urbanisation castigated by Engels? After all, for decades, both the Council and national leadership have been pledged to the improvement of the city for *its* people. The argument here is that the priorities for the post-war reconstruction of Manchester have indeed showed selectivity and bias which can be deemed insensitive if not hypocritical. This was most conspicuous in the clearance of the slums after 1955 and the comprehensive redevelopment schemes that destroyed the old working-class city. In these, absolute priority was given to improvement of city-centre accessibility by road. In consequence, the arterial roads through Salford and South Manchester scythe through old neighbourhoods, destroying their local centres, and the replacement housing was stacked up in forbidding tower blocks since rejected by conventional households. Britain led the world in public-sector redevelopment (Mellor 1977), but the new building was presented in terms of 'punctuation of the skyline' or 'new towns for old', that is, revamping and modernisation to attract investment or secure business rank for that town or city. It also perpetuated the schism between the poor and the others: only the poorest were unable to live in cottage-style houses, not flats constructed in a forbidding style. To justify this renewal programme in terms of modernisation showed social ignorance as deep as that of the first phase of Manchester's development. People's health and comfort were improved, but at a cost.

More recently, and conspicuously, in the 1990s there was a renewed attempt at remaking Manchester. This time there was a business–leisure agenda in which the cosmetic presentation of the city centre was crucial. In this the poorer people of Manchester (whose only centre it is) have no role. To the investors they represent what a city should not be – untidy, shabby, without money, liable to crime. This reclamation of the city centre for a lifestyle whose motifs are boats (on the Irwell), bars and bistros, supplemented by boutiques and balls (in St Ann's Square), is typical of city centres throughout the developed economies; Manchester is one among many. The peculiarities of Manchester are the scale of the poverty-belt enveloping the urban playground, the reality of it being the home of last resort for the entire city-region and beyond, and also its 200-year history.

The presentation in this chapter of this latest phase in the city's modernisation is in three parts. First it covers the reconquest of the centre for leisure before it moves on to examine the value of a city-centre location to the regional business economy and third, it ends on the continuing denial of the city to the poor.

Consuming Manchester

The refashioning of the city centre stems from its local plan whose publication in 1980 coincided with the calamitous downturn in the region's industrial economy in 1979–82. The city centre of Manchester had dominated commercial labour markets in the conurbation. There were 167,000 employed in its 1.5 square miles in 1961, approximately 14 per cent of the employment total of Greater Manchester. This had fallen to 98,000, 8.6 per cent of the total, by 1977 (MCC 1980a). There was then evident a massive erosion of the urban core economy. The basis of the decline was fivefold: the city had ceased to be the nerve centre for world trade in cotton textiles; its role as provincial business centre was diminishing; it was no longer host to wholesale food markets; its industries were closing; and it was ceasing to be the town centre for the local population, which itself was much depleted by clearance (MCC 1980b). The labour force was to retract further as printing presses, warehouses and insurance companies decentralised in the next decade: for example, *Manchester Evening News* closed its printworks in Deansgate and relocated its work to Trafford Park.

The one comparative study of regional centres concluded that the Manchester region, with few affluent residents in the inner core, no effective public transport system serving the central area, and 'strong' suburbanisation of office development, did pose particular problems for the city centre (Greater Manchester Council 1985). Subsequent policies have been framed within this context of European disadvantage. The new thinking switched attention to exploiting the city centre's heritage as the cradle of the industrial revolution and its legacies as 'the last and greatest of the Hanseatic towns – a civilisation created by traders' (Taylor 1976: 208). During the 1980s the major achievements were the establishment of the museums at Castlefield and the promotion of an

urban heritage park, the reconstruction of Central Station as an exhibition centre and mass forum (G-MEX), the reopening of the two oldest
theatres, investment in city-centre hotels, and the tourist attraction at
Granada Studios. Later, on recovery from the crash in the commercial
property market in 1990–91, there were to be two subsidised 'landmark'
developments – at Victoria Station and the Bridgewater development on
the south side – before the concerted efforts to rebuild the core to the
retail district and extend it northwards after the IRA bomb in 1996
(Williams, this volume). There have also been more hotels, leisure complexes on Deansgate and Oxford Road, the creation of a 'gay village'
and a burst of investment in city-centre housing. The city centre is now
an esteemed model for the renaissance of British cities (Rogers 1999).

First, a heritage industry (Hewison 1987) was implanted in the city
centre, then an economy with the panache of a holiday camp (or
Mediterranean resort) was promoted in the archaic shell of the old city
centre. Archaeology – the reconstruction of the Roman fort, industrial
history – the conversion of the world's oldest passenger station and its
warehouses into a fine industrial museum, architecture – the renovation
of the palatial mercantile headquarters of the textile firms into hotels,
and the ambience of canal and riverside – have all been promoted as
conferring an aura of historic particularity on an otherwise inaccessible
and uninviting environment. Local enthusiasts were vital in the early
stages in demonstrating the palatability of 'heritage'; as decisive were
the activities of local entrepreneurs, such as Tom Bloxham at Urban
Splash, with a passion for revitalising the old city. They showed what
was possible, that there was a market for the artefacts and ambience
derived from the past. Eventually, as tides of property capital swept
through all city centres, this enthusiasm was lost in the presentation of
Manchester as the city of the new millennium.

The interests in regeneration of the city centre were diverse. There
was Central Government, pledged to the social and political reclamation
of the inner cities; the construction industry deterred by the cost of
greenfield sites and finding access to them slowed by planning controls;
the financial institutions with substantial long-term investments in city-
centre property; individuals and trusts adding to their property
portfolios; businesses (including the banks) with freehold or long leasehold interests at stake. There was a business community fearing for its
future as second-tier centre in Britain. As well, there was the local
authority, deprived of central government support, facing diminished
local revenue and influence. By 1989 there was a fledgling coalition of
public agencies and private interests generating an alternative vision of

urban life and labour in a modernised city. As the agenda was set by the need to regenerate markets in property it inevitably marginalised those whose access to markets was restricted.

All the efforts of the 1990s were to represent the city as in the Commonwealth Games bid as one of 'Europe's most exciting and energetic places' (City Pride Strategic Planning Group 1994). Since the initiation of the first Olympic bid in 1985 by a group from the business sector (Cochrane *et al.*, this volume) and the establishment of the Development Corporation in 1988, there was then endorsement of a property-led regeneration strategy by the City Council. Subsequently, the submissions for the Olympics and other global sporting competitions attracted much media attention. A vocabulary and policy prescription for the city's regeneration has percolated public opinion and become accepted as *the* commonsense appraisal of the way forward. This 'script', articulated by the local authority, is 'shared and adhered to by actors in all aspects of urban regeneration: a script which crosses institutional and departmental lines' (Quilley, this volume). It keeps the city 'on the move' and legitimises its destiny, and it aligns with recent sociological writing in which it is argued that the status and future health of cities depend on the emerging pattern of information flows (Castells 1994, 1997; Lash and Urry 1994). This script enables fusion between the strategies of cultural promotion and business reinvestment; it is also reflected in the emphasis on a small-scale mesh of public spaces in the re-planning of the bomb-damaged retail core. The ideas are widely disseminated: 'the future of the city is very much tied up with information, with events and happenings, and with the city's information base' (Robson, B., quoted in *City Life*, June 1997).

The most remarked feature of Manchester's transformation has been the ascendancy of the leisure industry. It is evident in the promotion of the arts and the cultural industries. Over two decades public initiative has moved from the serious-minded recreation of Castlefield to the construction of a single building – the 'Urbis Centre' – simulating the grand sweep of urban endeavour in history. Dominating public perception is the idea of the 24-hour city, first floated tentatively by architects and developers at the beginning of the 1990s, received with suspicion by many (including the police), then, with the relaxation of licensing and the encouragement of residential developments, becoming the leitmotif of urban regeneration. A philosophy of urbanity, in which the city district (or quarter) should offer everything needed for daily existence, was to frame the policy guidelines. Work and leisure, private and public life, day and night, were to be synthesised; all the accepted break-points and boundaries cast away. Cumulatively this pointed to a civilised lifestyle and the presentation of Manchester as 'Glamchester' (*Vogue*, November 1997), and a model for urban regeneration in Europe.

All this had been presaged by the French philosopher-sociologist, Henri Lefebvre, who three decades ago observed the construction of the Pompidou Centre on the site of Paris's food markets. He wrote then: 'leisure is becoming an industry of prime importance. We have conquered for leisure the sea, the mountains and even the deserts. There is now a process of reintegration of space at the heart of the cities' (Lefebvre 1970: 265). But the regional centre of Manchester cannot emulate Paris. It has neither the cultural wealth of French heritage, nor the undisputed status of a national business centre. So, whereas in Paris leisure investment has to compete for space in the city with either business or heritage interests, in Manchester leisure uses are increasingly the only contenders for what were once prime positions. The centre is being transformed into a series of playgrounds; the development sequence vindicates Harvey's claim that cities are subject to 'the capitalisation of spaces of representation ... constructed spaces for ritual enjoyment in the crowd' (Harvey 1990: 262). And yet for all the emphasis on 'fun and games', on cultural promotion as the basis of the renaissance, there is another aspect: that of the symbiosis of business and leisure. If Manchester is to retain its role as regional centre (and its claim to Euro-city status) the conversion of the semi-derelict buildings and vacant spaces into something appealing, if not glamorous, must be promoted.

One development symbolises the complementarity of interests, and also their limitations. The Bridgewater complex is the flagship for the business community and new home for the city's orchestras, including the Hallé, for so long a symbol of Manchester's worth as a city. Designed by a London architect, with sculpture commissioned from a Japanese, offices and concert hall cluster round a relic from the past, a canal basin reclaimed from a wasteland car park. It was crucial in the reorientation of the 'half-square mile' of the business centre southwards and in attracting further investors. But even this, initiated by property developers and the managing partner of the largest law firm, only went ahead after years of negotiation, three-way subsidy from the EU, Whitehall and the City Council for the concert hall and a package occupancy agreement by leading professional firms. In the property market the demand is for shopping and leisure for regional mass markets, not commercial offices, nor elite culture (Williams, this volume).

In all this there was inconsistency and incongruency with everyday realities. First of all there was tension between the promotional rhetoric and the capacity to realise the setting for this urbane lifestyle. The city's infrastructure was old, the revenue of the statutory agencies limited and commercial investors hesitant. There was also a mythical element in the promotional campaigns: this urbane vision presents plazas as more important than motorways, cafés than conference catering, and life in the crowd as more significant than private transactions. The designation of defunct tracts in the city centre as public arenas was to be the rationale for regeneration strategies that had to reincorporate a degraded environment into a modern society. Urbanity masks the development realities: expensive land, high costs of renovation or site recapture and marketing difficulties.

The transformation of the sunken giant, a sad relic of Britain's imperial and industrial past, into the 'cool' or 'vibrant' playground is a manifestation of a general process of reconquest of space in the urban cores and their regrading. In the cycle of urban property investment the moment has come for reclamation of previously developed land and buildings: a rent-gap has opened between potential, or speculative, values of prestigious new buildings and the values conferred by previous use. The partnership between business community and state agencies depended on a consensus that 'bricks and mortar' regeneration, 'flagship developments and place marketing' (Quilley 1999: 244) would facilitate this 'reimagineering' (Rutheiser 1996) which will further the restructuring of the regional economy. It is ever more the case that the priorities of finance capital, realised in and through the speculative development process, dominate the uses made of cities (Harvey 1977).

City-centre businesses

Manchester's business community comprises specialised financial and professional services, many of which are not available elsewhere in the North West. Some firms, such as the major accountancy or insurance companies, provide the skills needed 'in-house'; others rely on a network of referrals for complementary services. This can be termed the 'business-service complex', following the discussions of Andy Leyshon (1989) and Saskia Sassen (1994, 1996). All of these emphasise the crucial role of such complexes in contemporary cities. They are regional (if not national or global) facilities; they retain central city bases (for reasons which are discussed below).

In Manchester the business-service complex is not especially important in sustaining the gloss and glamour of the city centre. Partners and staff undoubtedly do use lunchtime facilities, but most of the younger staff take sandwiches to their desks, and very few indeed go to the concert hall, the theatres, or participate in the nightlife. Many do the greater part of their 'choice' shopping in the outer suburbs where they expect to live. Although the purchasing power of the business service professionals is high, the city centre captures relatively little of it. The working hours are too long, the work too demanding to encourage more central-city use or residence.[1] The business-service complex does occupy 'City' style buildings, especially the newest ones, giving that aura of commercial prosperity to the regional core. Rhetorically, could Manchester present itself as a significant city without the imposing office buildings it now has? Would hotel towers and apartment blocks substitute?

Nor is there direct benefit to the business-service firms or their workforce from the promotion of the glamour city. Accessibility suffers, car parking charges increase, cherished venues for lunch or after-hours' sociability disappear to be either redeveloped or remodelled, nearly all the workforce live elsewhere, and the better qualified have neither the time nor inclination to spend the valued hours outside work in the city centre. The leisure developments feed off mass popular culture rather than elite tastes (the Hallé has struggled to survive financially). Arts and corporate business do not feed off each other as in New York or Los Angeles (Davis 1990; Harvey 1990; Zukin 1988). But the second tier American cities, such as Detroit, Atlanta, St Louis, Pittsburgh or Philadelphia, present a ghastly vision of what could happen to the accumulated investment in central business districts if there were no decisive action. The American experience was of office towers enveloped in urban wastelands or ravaged ghettoes, urban core economies abandoned as business and people trickled to the suburbs. In contrast, there has been the happier European precedent of carefully-tended buildings and spaces for well-groomed people in urbane settings, all this as the setting for business.

The business community of cities such as Manchester is not large enough to make full use of existing buildings, much less generate the investment for polished rebuilding. One of the world's major industrial regions can no longer sustain its business centre on that scale: something has to supplement it in the urban core. If the cluster of professional business and financial services that constitute the business community were to retain its city-centre status, then there had to be an eclectic strategy for the rebuilding of the city centre. Only thus could the regional economy retain what the prominent urban theorist, Castells (1994: 27) termed 'the economic engine of the city in the informational global economy'. The designation is misleading, however, in that the business-service complex is not the 'engine' of the city but the region. Within the North West its influence is disproportionate to either its employment capacity (although that in the professional firms has increased greatly since 1995) or its direct contribution to regional wealth. There is no clear rationale for its being in the city, at its centre. The conditions that brought it into being in the first half of the nineteenth century – poor communications and the need for face to face contact in mastering volatile global markets – have evaporated.

The following discussion considers its role as this regional 'engine', and the issue of its central location within Manchester. Why is it that so much of the region's business is facilitated by firms in the urban core – as it was in Engels' day – when accessibility and communication are so different? The interview data that the following discussion draws on are derived from a survey conducted in 1998 in which thirty-four senior partners of professional firms in six sectors of the business–services complex, as well as ten representatives of the professions and key spokespeople, were interviewed. The six sectors were those of commercial law, accountancy, business finance, advertising and design, the actuarial profession and architecture. In addition there were seventy interviews with employees in the firms headed by these partners or directors. The themes discussed here constituted one section only of the interviews (see Devine *et al.* 2000). Opinions were expressed vigorously, with skill and fluency; cumulatively a most illuminating presentation was given of working life in the business community, and its prospects.

Manchester is unusual in that it was once a world city; moreover, one which had in its hinterland a world industrial region – northern England. The retraction of the business centre has been lengthy – its heyday was 1920; the city has long lost its global significance as a transactional centre. Similarly, the attrition of provincial autonomy – fully operational since the beginning of the nineteenth century – has continued. Metropolitan dominance, that is, the golden circle of London, is pervasive. It affects the location of headquarters (70 per cent of those in the UK are located in the South East), access to finance, and the location of the business-service professions. There is also the threat of the 'edge' city (Garreau 1991): the business parks and office developments of the suburbs, airport or satellite towns so much more accessible to workforce and clients than the old urban core. With the investment in infrastructure – motorways, rail link to the airport and the expansion of the airport itself – so the pressure to suburbanise Manchester intensifies. However, it is still of inestimable significance to the regional economy – fostering its development and maximising its potential for growth. Its value is evident in four respects – investment, know-how, wealth and careers.

Finance

The city has the headquarters of all the locally active financial institutions with the power to make significant decisions and assemble financial syndicates, and they can call on all the associated services to do so. The business–services complex mediates much investment from within and without the region. It is the skills of the professionals which speed up business transactions, their knowledge that smoothes over the difficulties, their commitment that effects the deal. They are responsive to the needs of local business because it is from their strength that future fee income will derive (Pritchard 1997: 323–55); they are promoters of entrepreneurship.

Know-how

Through the 1990s, the concentration of professional, specialised services at the urban core was the node for the restructuring of the regional economy, building on innovation within it, and for the promotion of business efficiency. Globalisation opened up opportunities for this business–services complex; not only has the attention of London firms been diverted internationally but the regional firms can act as mediators and facilitators for regional entrepreneurs. There is a distinct interest in promoting the effectiveness and the profitability of their business. Those with local orientation are taking a wider view of possibilities and a longer-term commitment to the business they had initiated. In sum, 'good quality financial and business services play a major role as catalysts, helping to ensure that economic opportunities are identified, structured into fundable projects and supported by high quality advice and services' (Wood and Clifford 1993: 5). So the commercial lawyers, accountants and venture capitalists have a direct hand in furthering the development of new technologies and maximising the returns from skilled industrial management (Leyshon 1989).

These activities are as crucial to the viability of the region as they are to promotion of the regional core as a European business city. The region is being incorporated into extra-regional circuits of capital, even globalised, but while there is a strong local complex of business services the locally generated economy has potential.

Wealth

Many of the UK's most wealthy people live in the region, which is important for local economies. However, the impact of this wealth is diffused in that the demand of the professional workforce is for rural, small town or suburban living. Consumption is directed away from the urban core and it is not a major element in its regeneration.

Careers

There is the direct reward of employment in the sector – highly paid professionals, graduate trainees, and white-collar support staff, many highly experienced. The business services sector provides opportunities for the 'creme de la creme', the educated entrants to the labour force, to stay in their chosen region so checking the brain drain to London. More of the universities' output can be absorbed, as well as the aspiring young people of the region.

The distinguishing feature of Manchester as a business centre is its vitality at the turn of the millennium. In the interviews conducted in 1998 there was satisfaction that participants in the city business nexus had done more than hold the established complex of services against competition from either London or other regional centres: they had actively rebuilt it. A common estimation was that the regional core had established a competitive, intensely working, respected and profitable array of business services increasingly dominated by the large firms. There was considerable evidence of increased salaries and partners' fees, extra recruitment, increase in turnover, extension of services and up-grading of offices, and investment in new buildings. The spokespersons for the business community argued that it had the skills, resources and capacity to cater for the business needs of the immediate region of almost seven million people, this in itself exceeding that of several of the member-states in the EU. The current consensus was that, as in other regions, dependence on London was diminishing and the city was now a full-service centre able to tackle a much greater complexity of business than ten years previously. The long shadow of London is paler – though difficult to remove entirely because Manchester remains a regional business centre in a national economy that is closely integrated.

To an extent, therefore, Manchester is a factor in the new regionalism evident throughout Europe. If the supremacy of the national capitals is being dented then there may be a 'renewal of the role of regions and cities as loci of autonomy and decision making' for 'major cities throughout Europe constitute the nerve system of the economy and the political system of the Continent' (Castells 1994: 27–8). Castells' argument, echo-ing that of many others, relates as much to the cultural and political assertiveness seen in cities such as Bacelona and Bilbao, Thessalonika or

Frankfurt, as the balance changes between national centres and their regional satellites in the provision of business services. However, if there is a 're-regionalisation' in England or the North West in a long-centralised nation-state, it is based on much shallower foundations than elsewhere (Jones and MacLeod, this volume). Nor has the evaluation of the international business community yet shifted. The realistic assessment from the Manchester Business and Professional Forum is still:

> In that sense, whatever the expertise of this eccentric who happened to live in the city, however good he was, he would be the exception rather than the rule, and the disdain they have for their colleagues in Lille, Marseilles or Bordeaux or wherever, would be shared by those in London. Therefore, in fact, they could only choose people of their standing. (Director, Association of European Financial Centres, 1998)

The conventional explanation of clustering in central locations revolves round double access to a central place: that of firms to a specialised labour force and clients to firms. These were not the explanations given by the majority of respondents in these interviews. Access to staff was mentioned, for example by the manager of a large actuarial unit in an insurance company, situated next to a central railway station. Others referred to the ease of finding white-collar support staff. However, it was commonly agreed that the accessibility of the city-centre is poor and that although city-centre location could be attractive to support staff and graduate recruits, more senior staff hated their journey to work, frequently lengthening their working day by travelling early or late in an attempt to avoid rush hour. It was admitted that congestion deters clients too and one aspect of the sensitivity to the demands of clients is willingness to travel to them. In some interviews it was evident that there was ongoing discussion within firms as to whether a central location was worthwhile.

The reasons expressed for maintaining a relatively expensive and sometimes inconvenient base for the firm were those of: *convenience* – access to clients, to place of work (Law Courts), central area institutions (government offices or Town Hall), or technical services; *concentration* – the cluster of interdependent professional firms in a given area, expressed either as 'the community', or even 'the village'; *conviviality* – the opportunities for chat, conversation or more systematic cultivation of information; and *credibility* – firms would lose standing in their sector of activity if they located outside the urban core. Not only would they be seen to be detaching themselves from the networks of information, but from association with the key participants in their sector.

For many firms, although it may be convenient to be within walking distance of associate firms there is something more at stake. One accountant who considered moving out to Salford Quays chose to stay in the more expensive Manchester city centre location in part due to the 'belief that we should be near the bankers, the solicitors'. They went on to add, 'We have a lot of contacts in Manchester City Council, a lot of bankers out there, head offices out there, all the solicitors are here. We just felt we ought to be in the business community' (Accountant, private-sector corporation, 1998). Another accountant reinforced the sense that being 'in and amongst it' has broad material and non-material returns to corporations: 'It's just a perception I suppose that Manchester is a main centre that keeps professionals concentrated within the area. Not just accountants – there are bankers, lawyers. It basically has a financial centre here. It is a necessity to be attached to that, because of the need to benefit from meeting other professionals' (Accountant, private-sector corporation, 1998).

The reiterated, overarching theme is that of '*being* in the business community'. There is an intricate structure of referral work; not only does each firm in each sector have its regular co-referees, 'little circuits of activity', they will from time to time need specialised consultants. With technical refinement there is ever-greater need of interpretation and mediation between professions.[2] In principle this advice and consultation need not be in the city centre; in practice, in commercially driven competitive markets, being at the centre, in this community, is seen as crucial.

It has been something of a mystery why the 'new production complexes' such as Manchester's are maintained in the city centre. As Sassen says, 'according to standard conceptions about information industries, the rapid growth and disproportionate concentration of producer services in central cities should not have happened' (Sassen 1994: 65–6). She advances a succinct rationale in terms of 'the joint production of certain service offerings', the 'needs and expectations of the people likely to be employed in these new high-skill jobs' and the nature of the production of these services that requires 'multiple simultaneous inputs and feedbacks'. In a regional centre the emphasis has to be shifted: first, to take account of the mutual support and trust necessary in the more vulnerable setting: all gain advantage from the co-operative proximity of mutually servicing firms. And second, to give recognition to the social dynamics which underpin locational choices. These affect all, employees, partners and firms, irrespective of the intensity of gaining a contract, servicing a client or doing a deal.

Manchester's professional firms are gaining advantage because they work together; they can do so because of the spatial convenience, the years of chance encounters and the more formal social occasions. They know their associates, and know they can trust them. And that trust is underpinned by sharing the same city location: 'I think there is also the psychology. If we suddenly told all the professionals we were moving out of Manchester ... they'd say "Oh, that's nice for you. Have a nice short journey to work" and they'd never speak to you again' (Senior banker, corporate finance, 1998). Equally, within this business–services complex, firms seek competitive advantage through their contacts and their cultivation of the local information circuits. The clustering in a relatively limited tract of the regional core aids the cultivation of often-fragile connections. Hence the awareness of the casual contact:

> If you walk the streets at lunchtime and you go into various watering holes you can bump into people which you don't outside the city centre. ... Being near each other and bumping into people, it's more of a social than a real business need. ... But there is an argument for seeing people, you bump into them, you lunch with them and so on. (Actuary, 1998)

Also, paradoxically, the new entrepreneurialism, breaking up domination by institutions or monopoly firms, accentuates localism. Whether firms are breaking into a field or struggling to hold their position, there is the acute need for information. As one executive in a venture capital firm, recruited to establish a Manchester office the year before the interview, acknowledged:

> The investing end of our business is increasingly getting more and more of a local game ... It's hard to do it from 200 miles away, and it's a hell of a lot easier if you're on the doorstep, you get to see things you wouldn't other-wise see and you get to see things earlier. (Senior executive, venture capital corporation, 1998)

Conviviality, being a member of a business community, becomes all the more necessary for firms exposed to risk. Absent from accounts focusing on the global centres such as London is this dimension of competition in actively contested and re-framed markets.

Moreover, if we are to understand central city domination of professional business services, then we have to engage with the corporate culture in which centrality signifies success. It is evident in the reluctance of overseas or London client firms to deal with North West business-service firms away from the centre of the region. So a law firm relocating from Stafford saw its move as due to pressure from clients stressing that 'it was important to them for us to be in Manchester and this echoes what many of our national clients want'. Another firm moving from Liverpool justified its decision in similar terms. The social referencing is as evident in the choice between more accessible sites in the suburbs, or at Salford Quays, and the increasingly gridlocked city centre:

> If we want to be a commercial player we have to be here and none of us would think of going anywhere else now and taking the firm anywhere else, it wouldn't work, we wouldn't be seen to be seriously interested in commercially based work. (Banker, corporate finance, 1998)

The social gravitational effect of the elite firms has not changed. At the core of the corporate culture is the mystique and excitement of the major transaction, the deal which generates a whirl of documents rushed by hand from office to office, the late evening working in the lawyers' offices on transactions and the resulting profit. Something of the success and the excitement is experienced vicariously by the other associated activities in the cluster. Even if few can attain or contribute to the major deals, maintaining this proximity, marked by the same postcodes, is essential to the firm's reputation in its own field. 'I think for as long as we are here (in the city centre) any of the other major firms will want to be where we are. Not because we're "X" but because we are one of the major players' (Senior partner, large law firm, 1998). The interesting question is why lead firms not only stay but take on new and costly premises on lengthy leases in city-centre locations which clients and staff find it arduous to reach. The answer is straightforward:

> It was quite deliberate in transferring our profile within the cities and moving to more spectacular and prestigious offices and to make more of an impact within the city and to show the direction of the firm, that we're not just a small local firm but a national firm with offices to rival the London firms ... We are number fourteen in the top twenty national law firms so we don't want to portray an image that says we are a small regional firm. (Managing partner, large law firm, 1998)

The message is clear: if global and national business–services firms cluster at the core of the world's transactional centres, then so must the key firms in the regions. The corollary of that principle is that Manchester must look and feel good to outsiders. However, in a city with an extended commercial core dating from a period of dominance in markets beyond the region, the more compact business–services sector whose operations are largely limited to the regional economy cannot alone reinvigorate the city centre. Investment must be sought from other sectors of the economy. In Britain's regional centres at the turn of the millennium, this tends to mean the retail and leisure industries. In consequence business and play coexist. The principal stockbroker will have offices over a smart café-bar and fashion shop, and glossy offices tower over shopping arcades. The intensively working world of highly regarded professions is cheek by jowl with the appealing life of active streets and newly engineered public spaces. It is also in sight of the inner city whose residents' visibility in the city centre is resented, feared and disliked.

Excluding the poor

There is the city enveloping the revitalised core – poor Manchester, a city of uncertain employment, lifetime poverty, chronic ill-health and educational disadvantage. The urban core is notoriously poor; the local authority is repeatedly at the head of the national league for the proportion of children living in poverty, those born to unsupported mothers, indicators of welfare support, and death-rates (Herd and Patterson, this volume). Much of this is concentrated in a poverty belt around the city centre, the same districts internationally notorious for their ill-health a century ago and, because of their rebuilding in slum clearance programmes, now taking on the additional stigma of 'inner city'. The linkage between the two is long-standing: as regions industrialised, the slums in and around core business districts housed the poorest of the poor looking for employment to depots and warehouses, gasworks and building sites, laundries and public services – all rough manual labour. These notoriously unhealthy neighbourhoods, densely built, tightly occupied and heavily polluted, had therefore a symbiotic relationship with the regional centre – a relationship which was broken by the withering away of the central economy. Its restructuring from the handling of goods to information, along with the decline in routine jobs in shops and offices, disadvantages the unskilled, men and people of colour.

Currently every stratagem is being deployed to tie the city centre into a cosmopolitan circuit of work and play intended to maximise its appeal to investors, so enhancing its image as the front stage for the region. The functional relationships of the inner city are, however, very different: it constitutes a regional pool of low-cost housing, a staging post for newcomers to the city, a place where poor people feel at home, and the site of informal industries such as drug-dealing and prostitution, as well as – more formally – the cheap labour industries of food-processing and clothing. The circumstances that brought this stigmatised space in proximity to the city centre have gone. While some of this space may be integrated into the 'Euro-city', the discontinuity between cosmopolitanism and poverty will be accentuated.

Yet both cosmopolitan and poor are users of the central city, and indeed the latter depend on it. The only accessible banks, principal shopping centre, market-place, sources of entertainment and relaxation, even the venue for marriages, are there. For many it is the only place to sit out, to be part of public life, to be in the turbulence of the crowd. For the many who never holiday it gives a window on another life. So the seats in the shopping streets and public gardens are sought after by the elderly, hopeless, extended families and the lonely. And, as well, there are the shoplifters, pickpockets, 'plastic' fraudsters and the professional car-thieves staking out the car parks. (The indicators of notoriety for the city include 'staggeringly' high retail crime, use of stolen credit cards and car theft.) And, too, there are the underground (and not poor) networks centring on the city's nightclubs and bars.[3] Menacingly, hoodlums also target lone men in the 'gay village' and revellers leaving the clubs. All these are as much an element of the 'showcase city' as the smartly dressed crowds, night or day. The urban core is open to all comers; it does not have the defensible space of the purpose-built shopping mall, leisure centre or country club.

Efforts have been made to provide for this poor city, but does a Ferris wheel in Piccadilly Gardens or a small fair in Albert Square compensate for the redevelopment of the old market, the loss of cheap retail outlets, or the paucity of sitting-out space? Upgrading the look of the city means reinvestment from the private sector and therefore a change of clientele and the dispossession of those with the lowest consumer potential. Also, revealingly, it means the sacrifice of its heritage to 'abstract' space, that is, 'merchandised' and homogeneous (Lefebvre 1979: 293). Changes in designation and design of three places in the city centre indicate the inevitability of dispossession. The first is the conversion of the Corn Exchange after it was shattered by the IRA bomb in 1996. Before, alternative traders and craftspeople clustered there with their stalls, popular with 'drop-out' youth; now, refurbished in style, and with an ultra-modish plaza outside, it is renamed 'The Triangle', and marketed for expensive boutiques. Second, there is the dismantling and meticulous rebuilding of the two pubs from Shambles Square in an entirely different location and the associated loss of the public space as an unnoticed suntrap for casual drinkers. Third, there is the scheme proposed for 'putting the pride back into Piccadilly' (MCC 1999b), redesigning the Gardens so as to enhance the market value of the units in the adjoining property complex (so losing popular cheap shops), and rescuing it from its 'sordid' image (Coleman 1987). In this last controversial deal the predominant considerations are those of recouping previous investment and 'creating a welcoming first impression' (City Council leader Richard Leese, quoted in Manchester City Council 1999b). So another facet of the city's heritage is diminished and the poor are further marginalised. The different interests are not reconcilable: in the view of the modernisers, Manchester's poor city people should not be there. But, unlike, say, French or German cities, there is nowhere else for them to be in public. The old shopping roads (the same decried by Engels as concealing the poor districts behind their facades) were destroyed in the blitzkrieg of slum-clearance. Their cinemas, snooker or dance halls, boys' clubs, pubs, churches, banks and shops were then replaced by parkways enhancing the approaches to the business city. Trees there are aplenty, but the institutional foci of local life were obliterated.

If the poor are to lose 'their' city centre then do they gain in other respects? Each of the three developments listed above is hailed as bringing jobs and opportunities, however short-term these may be. There are two issues here – the nature of the jobs provided, and the criteria used for selecting employees. Nationally as much as locally, it is known that the predominant characteristics of work in the retail sector and all branches of the leisure industry are those of low skill, low wage, part-time or casual employment. These overwhelmingly outnumber skilled or managerial jobs. Many agree that those who live in the stigmatised inner city do not have access to this work (postcode discrimination) and those who are categorised as black, irrespective of skill or qualifications, find barriers. The city-centre workforce of Manchester, like that of Liverpool, unlike that of London, is conspicuously white. Selective, exclusionary, segmented labour markets are the norm. Racism is one element; enhancing the quality or impact of 'service' by style and accent is another. Whereas rough labour was valued in the centre of 'Cottonopolis', presentational gloss governs selection in 'Glamchester'.

Cities such as Manchester with its regional core economy of business and leisure demonstrate the power of social divisions of labour which empower some and hinder others in the scramble for legitimate work. In the leisure sector with its clubs, café-bars, hotels, boutiques, entertainment venues and shopping malls, city-centre employers may put a premium on acceptability of manner, dress and accent and not skills. Typically, the employee represents the firm or organisation; the position is a public one. In the business-professional sector, where much of the service work is backstage, priorities are different. The critical parameter is the availability of alternative recruits, especially school pupils and students from the 50,000 strong higher-education sector. If employers can pick and choose, they (can) exaggerate the skill, education, and experience requirements of their jobs. They use diplomas, or colour, or personal histories as convenient screening devices. Therefore inner city residents, even 'true' Mancunians, living within sight of the city-centre towers, may be debarred from much of the work in the urban core.

The problem of Manchester's poverty cannot be resolved by the makeover of its city centre. Even if there were not these barriers to employment and there were surer routes to self-advancement, poor Manchester would still be there. Assessment of the impact of regeneration policies has been hampered by failure to realise that the reserve of poor people in the city is replenished by migration. With the exception of the southern student corridor, mobility rates are highest in the poor districts. If and when a household experiences some success, so it moves somewhere better, usually closer to the suburbs, so relinquishing housing or school places for the next wave of poor. The inner cities now constitute a national reserve of undesired housing (Power 1999). It is therefore essential to distinguish between the 'stock' of urban poor, its so-called 'underclass', and this 'flow' in and through the city's poor housing (see Ward 1988: 65 for a perceptive discussion). No 'landmark' strategy can succeed if there is not the matching comprehensive investment to anchor the city's population. This should include provision and support for the region's small and medium-sized enterprises rather than privately built housing or supermarkets (as at Hulme). 'Spot' treatment of the fabric and services of the city can be rapidly nullified (as clinics, schools and nurseries subject to arson, theft, ram-raids or vandalism know well). And to magnify the old discontinuities between city centre and inner city is to jeopardise the security and therefore economic viability of the privileged spaces and glossy facades of the region's centre.[4]

A just city?

To say that contemporary Manchester is characterised by hypocrisy is not to say that the needs of the poor are disregarded at all times and by everybody. There are private charities which fund hostels for the helpless and many voluntary organisations supporting families in the poorest districts such as Ancoats or Moss Side, the young homeless, drug addicts and others. Charitable fund-raising mobilises sociable activity in the business community as in the suburbs. Since the early 1980s there has also been substantial public expenditure on the comprehensive reconstruction of districts such as Miles Platting and Ordsall, then Hulme, and now East Manchester.[5]

Nevertheless, this consideration for the disadvantaged is not evinced in the promotion of the entrepreneurial city-region serviced by the business community, property capital, the construction industry and public authorities in the city centre. There is more to a city than 'hot' money, investment fervour, image on some ill-defined international stage or the latest fashion in civic design. The majority live in the city out of necessity, not choice; the poor cannot and should not be exiled from their city's public spaces at the dictat of speculative developers or the reluctance of the majority to countenance their existence.

As the urban core – the city centre, the canals, Salford Quays – is transformed into a showcase for the region, so the poorer residents (which include most young people and children) are edged out of sight. A small example, but a telling one, is the limitation of fishing and swimming; another is the exclusion of skateboarders; another is day-time drinking in the open. Authoritative institutions react to the threat of the poor's visibility and their use of public, that is, common space. In the planners' estimation the generative tide of investment has to be sustained if cities such as Manchester are to overcome the incubus of the past. But cities have always been the home of the poor, and their city centres, at least in Britain, have been notable for their openness as places of congregation. Whatever city is promoted has to take account of this if its planning is to escape the charge of hypocrisy.

Notes

1 This assessment runs counter to the statements made by Sassen (1991, 1994) and the research by Zukin (1988) from which derive arguments about gentrification. It is based on interviews with employees in the professional business firms, which confirm the findings by Wynne and O'Connor (1996) that it is middle-ranking public-sector employees and those making a lifestyle choice who predominate in Manchester's city-centre housing market, not the professional-business elite.

2 An example was given by a venture capitalist who in a recent deal had needed the advice of a management consultant, actuary, environmental consultant and planner as well as the usual accountancy and law firms.

3 More than one club has had to close at police insistence, most notably its 'star', the Hacienda.

4 This assessment is more sceptical about the sustainability of city-centre investment than that of the *Economist* (1998) which in other respects is similar. The conclusion was that 'with the modern-day mixture of civic pride, entrepreneurship and seemingly intractable social problems Manchester has recovered much of the mix that once made it the most commented-on city in the world'.

5 Though the input from public funds is trivial compared to the private investment in the city centre itself. Government input into Hulme has been £32.5m over five years; that proposed for East Manchester totals £78.6m over seven years. In the city centre the Great Northern scheme in Deansgate alone was presented as being £100m, that for the Printworks site £55m, and so on.

Bibliography

AGMA [Association of Greater Manchester Authorities] (1997), *Strategic Planning Framework for Greater Manchester*, Wigan, AGMA.

Amin, A. (1999), 'An institutionalist perspective on regional economic development', *International Journal of Urban and Regional Research*, 23, 365–78.

Amin, A. and N. Thrift (1994), 'Living in the global', in A. Amin and N. Thrift (eds), *Globalisation, Institutions, and Regional Development in Europe*, Oxford, Oxford University Press.

Andrews, K. and J. Jacobs (1990), *Punishing the Poor: Poverty under Thatcher*, London, Macmillan.

Bailey, N. (1995), *Partnership Agencies in British Urban Policy*, London, UCL Press.

Bauman, Z. (1998), *Work, Consumerism, and the New Poor*, Buckingham, Open University Press.

Beatty, C., S. Fothergill, T. Gore and A. Herrington (1997), *The Real Level of Unemployment*, Sheffield, Centre For Regional Economic and Social Research, Sheffield Hallam University.

Beesley, I. and P. de Figueiredo (1988), *Victorian Manchester and Salford*, Halifax, Ryburn Publishing.

Bentley, T. and R. Gurumurthy (1999), *Destination Unknown: Engaging with Problems of Marginalised Youth*, London, DEMOS.

Beynon, H., D. Elson, D. Howell, J. Peck and L. Shaw (1993), 'The remaking of economy and society: Manchester, Salford and Trafford 1954–1992', *ICLS Working Paper* 1, International Centre for Labour Studies, Manchester University.

Blank, R. M. (1997), *What Causes Public Assistance Caseloads to Grow?*, Evanston, Illinois, Northwestern University Press.

Boddy, M. and C. Fudge (eds) (1984), *Local Socialism: Labour Councils and New Left Alternatives*, London, Macmillan.

Bradford, M. and A. Steward (1988), Inner city refurbishment: an evaluation of private–public partnership schemes', *CUPS Working Paper* 2, School of Geography, Manchester University.

Brenner, N. (1998), 'Global cities, global states: global city formation and state territorial restructuring in contemporary Europe', *Review of International Political Economy*, 5, 1–37.

Brenner, N. (1999), 'Globalisation as reterrritorialisation: the re-scaling of urban governance in the European Union', *Urban Studies*, 36, 431–51.

Briggs, A. (1963), 'Manchester: symbol of a new age', in A. Briggs, *Victorian Cities*, London, Odhams Press.

Burch, M. and I. Holliday (1993), 'Institutional emergence: the case of the North West region of England', *Regional Politics and Policy*, 3, 29–50.

Canniffe, E. and T. Jefferies (1997), *Manchester Architecture Guide*, Manchester, Manchester Metropolitan University.

Castells, M. (1994), 'European cities, the informational society and the global economy', *New Left Review*, 204, 18–32.

Castells, M. (1997), 'An introduction to the information age', *City*, 7, 6–17.

Chaloner, W. H. (1962), 'The birth of modern Manchester', in C. F. Carter (ed.), *Manchester and its Region*, Manchester, Manchester University Press.

Christie, I., M. Carley and M. Fogarty, with R. Legard (1991), *Profitable Partnerships: A Report on Business Investment in the Community*, London, PSI Publishing.

City Pride Strategic Planning Group (1994), *City Pride: A Focus for the Future. Manchester, Salford and Trafford from the Present into the Twenty-First Century*, Manchester, City Pride Strategic Planning Group.

City Pride Strategic Planning Group (1998a), *City Pride 2: Partnerships for a Successful Future. Manchester, Salford, Trafford and Tameside from the Present into the Twenty-First Century*, Manchester, City Pride Strategic Planning Group.

City Pride Strategic Planning Group (1998b), *Welfare to Work New Deal for 18–24 Year Olds Delivery Plan 1998/99*, Manchester, City Pride Strategic Planning Group.

City Pride Strategic Planning Group (1999a), *Reform of the EU Objective 2 Structural Funds 2000–2006: The Case for the Manchester City Pride Area*, Manchester, City Pride Strategic Planning Group.

City Pride Strategic Planning Group (1999b), *Welfare to Work New Deal Delivery Plan 1999/2000*, Manchester, City Pride Strategic Planning Group.

Clark, R. (2000), 'Manchester disunited – the new and the old', *Daily Telegraph* (22 January).

CMDC [Central Manchester Development Corporation] (1990), *Development Strategy*, Manchester, CMDC.

Cochrane, A. (ed.) (1987), *Developing Local Economic Strategies*, Milton Keynes, Open University Press.

Cochrane, A. (1988), 'In and against the market? The development of socialist economic strategies in Britain 1981- 1986', *Policy and Politics* 16, 159–68.

Cochrane, A. (1989a), 'The future of local economic strategies', *Local Economy*, 3, 132–41.

Cochrane, A. (1989b), 'Restructuring the state', in A. Cochrane and J. Anderson (eds), *Politics in Transition*, London, Sage.

Cochrane, A. (1993), *Whatever Happened to Local Government?*, Buckingham, Open University Press.

Cochrane, A. (1994), 'Restructuring the local welfare state', in R. Burrows and B. Loader (eds), *Towards a Post-Fordist Welfare State?*, London, Routledge.

Cochrane, A. (1995), 'Searching for a new local politics of growth: public-private partnership and municipal Labourism in Sheffield', unpublished paper, Faculty of Social Sciences, Open University.

Cochrane, A. and A. Clarke (1987), 'Investing in the public sector: the enterprise board experience', in A. Cochrane (ed.), *Developing Local Economic Strategies*, Milton Keynes, Open University Press.

Cochrane, A., J. Peck and A. Tickell (1996), 'Manchester plays games: exploring the local politics of globalisation', *Urban Studies*, 33, 1319–36.

Cole, I., S. Kane and D. Robinson (2000), *Changing Demand, Changing Neighbourhoods: The Response of Social Landlords*, Sheffield, Centre for Regional Economic and Social Research, Sheffield Hallam University.

Coleman, W. (1987), 'Where there's muck there's Manchester', *Guardian* (20 August).

Convery, P. (2000), 'Assessment of the New Deal after two years', paper presented to the Centre for Local Economic Strategies conference, London, 30 March.

Cooke, P. and K. Morgan (1998), *The Associational Economy: Firms, Regions and Innovation*, Oxford, Oxford University Press.

Cooper, D. (1994), *Sexing the City: Lesbian and Gay Politics Within the Activist State*, London, Rivers Oram Press.

Cox, K. and A. Mair (1988), 'Locality and community in the politics of local economic development', *Annals of the Association of American Geographers*, 72, 307–25.

Cressey, P. (1999), 'New Labour and employment, training and employee relations', in M. Powell (ed.), *New Labour, New Welfare State*, Bristol, Polity Press.

Dalby, S. (1993), 'Just the tonic for Eastlands', *Financial Times* (23 June).

Davenport-Hines R. P. T. (ed.) (1990), *Business in the Age of Depression and War*, London, Frank Cass.

Davis, M. (1990), *City of Quartz: Excavating the Future in Los Angeles*, London, Verso.

DEA [Department of Economic Affairs] (1965), *The North West: A Regional Study*, London, Department of Economic Affairs.

Deas, I. and B. Giordano (2000), 'Competitiveness in English conurbations:

assets and outcomes', unpublished working paper, Centre for Urban Policy Studies, Manchester University.

Deas, I., J. Peck, A. Tickell, K. G. Ward and M. G. Bradford (1999), 'Rescripting urban regeneration, the Mancunian way', in R. Imrie and H. Thomas (eds), *British Urban Policy and the Urban Development Corporations*, 2nd edn, London, Sage Publications.

Deas, I. and K. G. Ward (2000), 'From the "new localism" to the "new regionalism"? The implications of regional development agencies for city-regional relations', *Political Geography*, 19, 273–92.

Deben, L., S. Musterd and J. Weesep (1994), 'Urban revitalisation and the revival of urban culture', *Built Environment*, 18, 84–90.

DETR [Department of the Environment, Transport and the Regions] (1997a), 'Partnerships for prosperity in the English regions', *Press Notice 489/ENV*, London, Department of the Environment, Transport and the Regions.

DETR (1997b), *Building Partnerships for Prosperity: Sustainable Growth, Competitiveness and Employment in the English Regions*, Cm. 3814, London, HMSO.

DETR (1998), *Regional Development Agencies: Draft Guidance on RDAs' Strategies*, London, Department of the Environment, Transport and the Regions.

Devine, F., J. Britton, R. Mellor and P. Halfpenny (2000), 'Economic restructuring, globalisation and the professions: case studies from Manchester's financial business sector', *Work, Employment and Society*, 14, 521–40.

Dicken, P. (1998), *Global Shift: Transforming the World Economy*, 3rd edn, London, Paul Chapman.

Dicken, P. and P. E. Lloyd (1976), 'Geographical perspectives on United States investment in the United Kingdom', *Environment and Planning A*, 8, 685–705.

Dicken, P. and P. E. Lloyd (1978), 'Inner metropolitan industrial change, enterprise structures and policy issues: case studies of Manchester and Merseyside', *Regional Studies*, 12, 181–97.

Dicken, P. and A. Tickell (1992), 'Competitors or collaborators? The structure and relationships of inward investment in Northern England', *Regional Studies*, 26, 99–106.

Dicken, P., J. Peck, and A. Tickell (1997), 'Unpacking the global', in R. Lee and J. Wills (eds), *Geographies of Economies*, London, Edward Arnold.

DoE [Department of the Environment] (1989), *Strategic Planning Guidance for Greater Manchester*, RPG4, London, HMSO.

DoE (1993), *Annual Report 1993: The Government's Expenditure Plans 1993–94 to 1995–96*, Cm. 2207, London, HMSO.

DoE (1997), 'Regions invited to have their say', *Press Notice 214*, London, Department of the Environment.

DTI [Department for Trade and Industry] (1998), *Regional Competitive Indicators*, London, Department for Trade and Industry.

Dunford, M. and G. Kafkalas (1992), 'The global-local interplay, corporate geographies and spatial development strategies in Europe', in M. Dunford and G. Kafkalas (eds), *Cities and Regions in the New Europe: The Global-Local Interplay and Spatial Development Strategies*, London, Belhaven.

Dungey, J. and I. Newman (eds) (2000), *The Democratic Region*, London, Local Government Information Unit.

Dunning, J. H. (1983), 'Changes in the level and structure of international production: the last 100 years', in M. Casson (ed.), *The Growth of International Business*, London, Allen & Unwin.

Dyos, H. J. and M. Wolff (1973), *The Victorian City*, London, Routledge & Kegan Paul.

Economist (1998), 'Britain's provincial cities. In London's shadow' (1 August), 24–5.

EDAW (1996), 'Manchester Urban Design Competition: second round bid', London, EDAW.

Eisenschitz, A. and J. Gough (1993), *The Politics of Local Economic Policy: The Problems and Possibilities of Local Initiatives*, London, Macmillan.

Engels, F. (1969; 1st publ. 1844; 1st pub. in English 1892), *The Condition of the Working Class in England*, London, Panther Books.

Environment, Transport and Regional Affairs Committee (1997), *Regional Development Agencies: First Report*. London, HMSO.

Evans, R. (1997), *Regenerating Town Centres*, Manchester, Manchester University Press.

Faichnie, C. (1999), *Rhetoric and Reality: Young People and the New Deal*, Manchester, Greater Manchester Low Pay Unit.

Fazey, I. (1995), 'Survey of European regional finance centres', *Financial Times* (20 February).

Fenton, H. (1983), 'Structure planning in a metropolitan context – Greater Manchester', in D. T. Cross and M. R. Bristow (eds), *English Structure Planning*, London, Pion.

Finn, D., M. Blackmore and N. Nimmo (1998), *Welfare to Work and the Long Term Unemployed: They're Very Cynical*, London, Unemployment Unit and Youthaid.

Fitzsimmons, J. (1998), *City Centre Living: A Study of the Residents of Central Manchester*, M.T.Pl. dissertation, School of Planning and Landscape, University of Manchester.

Flage, H. (1998), *Urban Design Policy and Practice*, M.T.Pl. dissertation, School of Planning and Landscape, University of Manchester.

Florida, R. (1995), 'Toward the learning region', *Futures*, 27, 527–36.

Fox, A. (ed.) (1995), *Arena: The Building of the Nynex Arena*, Manchester, Len Grant Photography.

Friedmann, J. (1986), 'The world city hypothesis', *Development and Change*, 17, 69–83.

Friedmann, J. (1995), *Cultural Identity and Global Process*, London, Sage.

Fröbel, F., J. Heinrichs and O. Kreye (1980), *The New International Division of Labour*, Cambridge, Cambridge University Press.

Garreau, J. (1991), *Edge City: Life on the New Frontier*, New York, Doubleday.

Glancey, J. (2001), 'The wonder years', *Guardian* (7 May).

Gordon, A. (1997), 'Issues and problems in conducting economic impact analysis: a case study of the IRA bombing of Manchester city centre, 1996', unpublished M.A. dissertation, Town and Regional Planning, Leeds Metropolitan University.

Greater Manchester Council (1985), *Comparative Study of Conurbations*, Manchester, Planning Department.

Greater Manchester Low Pay Unit (1999), *Jobwatch '98: A Survey of Vacancies in Greater Manchester Jobcentres*, Manchester, GMLPU.

Greater Manchester Low Pay Unit (2000), *Job Vacancy Statistics in Greater Manchester*, Manchester, GMLPU.

Green, A. (1996), 'Aspects of the changing geography of poverty and wealth', in J. Hills (ed.), *New Inequalities: The Changing Distribution of Income and Wealth in the United Kingdom*, Cambridge, Cambridge University Press.

Griffiths, S. (1998), *A Profile of Poverty and Health in Manchester*, Manchester, Manchester Health Authority and Manchester City Council.

Guthrie, J. (2000), 'England's Regional Development Agencies: Rover casts its shadow', *Financial Times* (11 May).

Gyford, J. (1985), *The Politics of Local Socialism*, London, George Allen and Unwin.

Hall, P. (1998), *Cities in Civilization: Culture, Innovation, and Urban Order*, London, Weidenfeld & Nicolson.

Hall, T. and P. Hubbard (1998), *The Entrepreneurial City*, Wiley, Chichester.

Harding, A. (1997), *Hulme City Challenge: Did it Work?* Liverpool, European Institute for Urban Affairs.

Harvey, D. (1977), 'The urban process under capitalism', *International Journal of Urban and Regional Research*, 2, 101–31.

Harvey, D. (1985), *The Urbanization of Capital: Studies in the History and Theory of Capitalist Urbanization*, Oxford, Basil Blackwell.

Harvey, D. (1989), 'From managerialism to entrepreneurialism: the transformation of urban governance in late capitalism', *Geografiska Annaler*, 71, 3–17.

Harvey, D. (1990), *The Condition of Postmodernity*, Oxford, Blackwell.

Haslam, D. (1999), *Manchester, England: The Story of the Popcult City*, London, Fourth Estate.

Healey, P. (1997), *Collaborative Planning: Shaping Places in Fragmented Spaces*, London, Macmillan.

Hebbert, M. and I. Deas (2000), 'Greater Manchester – "up and going"?', *Policy and Politics*, 28, 79–92.

Hetherington, P. (1999), 'The gritty city goes lookie-feely', *Guardian* (4 April).

Hetherington, P. and M. White (2000), 'Ministers rebel over English assemblies' *Guardian* (26 May).

Hewison, R. (1987), *The Heritage Industry*, London, Methuen.

Hill, C. R. (1992), *Olympic Politics*, Manchester, Manchester University Press.

Hill, C. R. (1994), 'The politics of Manchester's Olympic bid', *Parliamentary Affairs*, 47, 338–55.

Hirst, P. (1997), *From Statism to Pluralism: Democracy, Civil Politics and Global Politics*, London, UCL Press.

HM Treasury (2000), *The Goal of Full Employment: Employment Opportunity for All Throughout Britain. Trends in Regional and Local Vacancies and Unemployment*, London, Stationery Office.

HMSO (1997), *Regional Development Agencies Bill*, London, HMSO.

HMSO (1998), *New Ambitions for Our Country: A New Contract for Welfare*, Cm. 3804, London, HMSO.

HMSO (1999), *Opportunity For All – Tackling Poverty and Social Exclusion: First Annual Report*, Cm. 4445, London, HMSO.

Holden, A. (1999), 'Manchester first! Entrepreneurial strategies and enterprising narratives in the construction of a local hegemonic project', unpublished Ph.D. thesis, School of Geography, University of Manchester.

House of Commons Social Security Committee (1998), *Social Security Reform: Lessons from the United States of America*, HC552, London, HMSO.

Howell, D. (1990), *Made in Birmingham: The Memoirs of Denis Howell*, London, Macdonald.

Hudson, R., M. Dunford, D. Hamilton and R. Kotter (1997), 'Developing regional strategies for economic success: lessons from Europe's economically successful regions', *European Urban and Regional Studies*, 4, 365–73.

Hulme City Challenge (1994), *Rebuilding the City: A Guide to Development*, Manchester, Hulme Regeneration Ltd.

Imrie, R. and H. Thomas (1993), 'The limits of property led regeneration', *Environment and Planning C: Government and Policy*, 11, 87–102.

Jacques, M. (1994), 'The erosion of the Establishment', *Sunday Times* (16 January).

Jessop, B. (1994), 'The transition to post-Fordism and the Schumpterian workfare state', in R. Burrows and B. Loader (eds), *Towards a Post-Fordist Welfare State?* London, Routledge.

Jessop, B., J. Peck and A. Tickell (1999), 'Retooling the machine: economic crisis, state restructuring, and urban politics', in A. E. G. Jonas and D. Wilson (eds), *The Urban Growth Machine: Critical Perspectives Two Decades Later*, New York, SUNY Press.

Jones, M. (1999a), *New Institutional Spaces: Training and Enterprise Councils and the Remaking of Economic Governance*, London, Jessica Kingsley.

Jones, M. (1999b), 'The regional state and economic regulation: regulation, re-generation or political mobilisation?', *Mimeograph*, Institute of Geography and Earth Sciences, University of Wales, Aberystwyth.

Jones, M. and G. MacLeod (1999), 'Towards a regional renaissance? Recon-figuring and rescaling England's economic governance', *Transactions of the Institute of British Geographers*, 24, 295–314.

Jones, M. and K. G. Ward (1998), 'Grabbing grants? The role of coalitions in urban economic development', *Local Economy*, 13, 29–38.

Katz, B. and K. Carnevale (1998), *The State of Welfare Caseloads in America's Cities*, Washington, DC, Center on Urban and Metropolitan Policy, Brookings Institute.

Kearns, G. and C. Philo (eds) (1993), *Selling Places: The City as Cultural Capital, Past and Present*, Oxford, Pergamon.

Keating, M. (1998), *The New Regionalism in Western Europe: Territorial Restruc-turing and Political Change*, Cheltenham, Edward Elgar.

Kelly, P. F. (1999), 'The geographies and politics of globalisation', *Progress in Human Geography*, 23, 379–400.

Kennedy, M. (1960), *The Hallé Tradition: A Century of Music*, Manchester, Manchester University Press.

King, A. D. (1983), 'The world economy is everywhere: urban history and the world system', *Urban History Yearbook*, 7–18.

King, A. D. (1990), *Global Cities: Post-Imperialism and the Internationalization of London*, London, Routledge.

Kitchen, T. (1996), 'The future of development plans: reflections on Manchester's experiences 1945–1995', *Town Planning Review*, 67, 331–53.

Kitchen, T. (1997), *People, Politics, Policies and Plans: The City Planning Process in Contemporary Britain*, London, Paul Chapman Publishing.

Knox, P. and P. Taylor (1995), *World Cities in a World-System*, Cambridge, Cambridge University Press.

KPMG Management Consulting (1993), *Manchester 2000: Economic Benefits and Opportunities of the Olympic Games*, London, KPMG Management Consulting.

Krugman, P. (1994), 'Competitiveness: a dangerous obsession', *Foreign Affairs*, March–April, 28–44.

Labour Party (1995), *A Choice for England: A Consultation Paper on Labour's Plans for English Regional Government*, London, Labour Party.

Labour Party (1996), *A New Voice for English Regions: Labour Party Statement on Regional Economic Policy*, London, Labour Party.

Lansley, S., S. Goss and C. Wolmar (1989), *Councils in Conflict: The Rise and Fall of the Municipal Left*, London, Macmillan.

Lash, S. and J. Urry (1994), *Economies of Signs and Spaces*, London, Sage.

Law, C. (1988), 'From Manchester docks to Salford quays: a progress report on a redevelopment project', *Manchester Geographer*, 9, 2–15.

Law, C. (1992), 'Property-led urban regeneration in Manchester', in P. Healey, S. Davoudi, S. Tavsanoglu, M. O'Toole and D. Usher (eds), *Rebuilding the City: Property-Led Urban Regeneration*, London, E. & F. N. Spon.

Law, C. (1994), 'Manchester's bid for the Millennium Olympic Games', *Geography*, 79, 222–31.

Lawless, P. (1990), 'Regeneration in Sheffield: from radical intervention to partnership', in D. Judd and M. Parkinson (eds), *Leadership and Urban Regeneration: Cities in North America and Europe*, London, Sage.

Le Corbusier (1927), *Towards a New Architecture*, New York, Brewer and Warren.

Lefebvre, H. (1970), *La Revolution Urbaine*, Paris, Gallimard.

Lefebvre, H. (1979), 'Space, social product and use value', in J. Freiburg (ed.), *Critical Sociology*, New York, Irvington.

Lefevre, C. (1998), 'Metropolitan government and governance in western countries: a critical review', *International Journal of Urban and Regional Research*, 22, 9–25.

Levine, M. V. (1989), 'Urban development in a global economy: the cases of Montreal and Boston', in R. V. Knight and G. Gappert (eds), *Cities in a Global Society*, London, Sage.

Leyshon, A. (1989), 'Financial and producer services within British financial centres', *Progress in Planning*, 31, 151–229.

Lloyd, J. (1988), 'The crumbling of the establishment', *Financial Times* (16 July).

Lloyd, P. E. (1980), 'Manchester: a study in industrial decline and economic restructuring', in H. P. White (ed.), *The Continuing Conurbation: Change and Development in Greater Manchester*, Aldershot, Gower.

Lloyd, P. E. and P. Dicken (1979), 'New firms, small firms and job generation: the experience of Manchester and Merseyside', 1966–1975', *North West Industry Research Unit Working Paper* 2, School of Geography, University of Manchester.

Lloyd, P. E. and C. M. Mason (1977), 'Manufacturing industry in the inner city: a case study of Greater Manchester', *North West Industry Research Unit Working Paper* 1, School of Geography, University of Manchester.

Lloyd, P. E. and C. M. Mason (1978), 'Manufacturing industry in the inner city: a case study of Manchester', *Transactions of the Institute of British Geographers*, 3, 66–90.

Lloyd, P. E. and D. E. Reeve (1981), 'Recession, restructuring and location: a study of employment trends in North West England, 1971–1977', *North West Industry Research Unit Working Paper* 11, School of Geography, University of Manchester.

Lloyd, P. E. and J. Shutt (1985), 'Recession and restructuring in the north west region, 1974–1982: the implications of recent events', in D. Massey and R. Meegan (eds), *Politics and Method: Contrasting Studies in Industrial Geography*, Cambridge, Cambridge University Press.

Lloyd-Jones, R. and M. J. Lewis (1988), 'The business community and political economy in Manchester, c. 1815–1825', in R. Lloyd-Jones and M. J. Lewis (eds), *Manchester and the Age of the Factory*, Beckenham, Croom Helm.

LOCB [London Olympic 2000 Campaign Board] (1991), *London Olympic 2000*, London, London Olympic 2000 Campaign Board.

Loftman, P. and B. Nevin (1996), 'Going for growth: prestige projects in three British cities', *Urban Studies*, 33, 991–1019.

Logan, J. and H. Molotch (1987), *Urban Fortunes: The Political Economy of Place*, Berkeley, University of California Press.

Lovering, J. (1999), 'Theory led by policy? The inadequacies of the "new regionalism" in economic geography, illustrated from the case of Wales', *International Journal of Urban and Regional Research*, 23, 379–95.

Lynch, T. (1993), 'An ideal climate for records', *Financial Times* (23 June).

Mackintosh, M. and H. Wainwright (eds) (1987), *A Taste of Power: The Politics of Local Economies*, London, Verso.

MacLeod, G. (2000), 'The learning region in an age of austerity: capitalizing on knowledge, entrepreneurialism and reflexive capitalism', *Geoforum*, 31, 219–36.

MacLeod, G. and M. Goodwin (1999), 'Space, scale and state strategy: rethinking urban and regional governance', *Progress in Human Geography*, 23, 503–27.

Manchester Commonwealth Bid Committee (1995), *Manchester 2002: Commonwealth Games Bid*, Manchester, Manchester Commonwealth Bid Committee.

Manchester Friends of the Earth (1996), 'Planning for real for the heart of Manchester: September 21st '96, Shambles Square M4 3AQ', Manchester, Manchester Friends of the Earth, Manchester LA 21 Forum, Neighbourhood Initiatives Foundation and Royal Town Planning Institute.

Manchester Investment and Development Agency Service [MIDAS] (1998), *Trafford Park: Manchester*. Manchester, MIDAS.

Manchester Olympic Bid Committee (1993), *The British Olympic Bid: Manchester 2000*, Manchester, Manchester Olympic Bid Committee.

Manchester TEC (1998), *Characteristics of the New Deal Client Group: A Study by Manchester TEC for the City Pride New Deal Strategic Planning Group*, Manchester, Manchester TEC.

Mandelson, P. and R. Liddle (1996), *The Blair Revolution: Can New Labour Deliver?*, London, Faber and Faber.

Marketing Manchester (1996), *The Manchester Image Process: The Consultation Project*. Manchester, Marketing Manchester.

Marketing Manchester (1997a), *The Marketing Manchester Initiative*, Manchester, Marketing Manchester.

Marketing Manchester (1997b), *Marketing Manchester Annual Review 1996–97*, Manchester, Marketing Manchester.

Martin R., C. Nativel and P. Sunley (1999), 'The local impact of the New Deal: does geography make a difference', paper presented at the Annual Conference of the Institute of British Geographers, University of Sussex, 4–7 January.

Martin R., P. Tyler and M. Baddeley (1997), 'If jobs matter, softly softly is the right way to go for Emu', *The Observer* (16 November).

Massey, D. (1984), *Spatial Divisions of Labour*, London, Macmillan.

MCC [Manchester City Council] (1980a), *Draft Local Plan*, Manchester, MCC Planning Department.

MCC (1980b), *Housing and Urban Renewal*, Manchester, MCC Planning Department.

MCC (1986), *Poverty in Manchester*, Manchester, Manchester City Council.

MCC (1984a), *City Centre Local Plan*, Manchester, Manchester City Council.

MCC (1984b), *Economic Briefing Note*, no. 11, Manchester, Manchester City Council.

MCC (1984c), *Review of Corporate Economic Strategy*, Manchester, Manchester City Council.

MCC (1986), *Work: A Strategy for Employment*, Manchester, Manchester City Council.

MCC (1989), *Poverty in Manchester: The Third Investigation*, Manchester, Manchester City Council.

MCC (1992), *Economic Development Strategy: Executive Summary and Financial Statement*, Manchester, Manchester City Council.

MCC (1995), *Development Guide for Manchester*, Manchester, Manchester City Council.

MCC (1999a), *Manchester Matters: Economic, Unemployment and Welfare Benefits Bulletin*, 10, Manchester, Manchester City Council.

MCC (1999b), *Update 4/2*, Manchester, MCC Planning Department.

MCCTF [Manchester City Centre Task Force] (1996a), *Manchester City Pride, A Focus for the Future: International Urban Design Competition*, Manchester, Manchester City Centre Task Force.

MCCTF (1996b), *International Urban Design Competition: Second Round Guidance*, Manchester, Manchester City Centre Task Force.

McKenzie, F. A. (1902), *The American Invaders*, London, G. Richard.

Mellor, R. (1977), *Urban Sociology in an Urban Society*, London, Routledge.

MMTF [Marketing Manchester Task Force] (1997), *First Implementation Plan*, Manchester, MMTF.

MMTF (1998), *Second Implementation Plan*, Manchester, MMTF.

MMTF (1999), *Third Implementation Plan*, Manchester, MMTF.

Murphy, P. and R. Caborn (1996), 'Regional government – an economic imperative', in S. Tindale (ed.), *The State and the Nations: The Politics of Devolution*, London, Institute for Public Policy Research.

Nairn, T. (1997), 'Sovereignty after the election', *New Left Review*, 224, 3–18.

New Statesman (1998), 'Sowing the seeds of English devolution', *New Statesman*, Special Supplement (26 June).

Newsco (1997), *North West PLC 1997/98*, Manchester, Newsco in Association with English Partnerships.

NWDA [North West Development Agency] (2000a), *England's North West: A Strategy Towards 2020*, Warrington, North West Development Agency.

NWDA (2000b), 'Launch of regional strategy spells out NWDA's vision for the North West region in the millennium', *Press Notice*, Warrington, NWDA.

NWP [North West Partnership] (1996), *Sustainable Regional Economic Strategy for North West England*, Wigan, North West Partnership.

NWRA and NWBLT [North West Regional Association and North West Business Leadership Team] (1993), *Regional Economic Strategy for North West England, Prepared by PIEDA*, Wigan, North West Regional Association.

NWRA and NWP [North West Regional Association and North West Partnership] (1997), *Regional Development Agencies: Response of the North West Regional Association and the North West Partnership*, Wigan, North West Regional Association.

OECD [Organisation for Economic Co-operation and Development] (1988), *The Newly Industrializing Countries: Challenge and Opportunity for OECD Industries*, Paris, OECD.

OECD (1997), *Skills, Training and Regional Competitiveness*, Paris, OECD.

Ohmae, K. (1995), *Triad Power: The Coming Age of Global Competition*, New York, The Free Press.

Oppenheim, C. and L. Harker (1996), *Poverty: The Facts*, 3rd edn, London, Child Poverty Action Group.

Parkinson, M. (1989) 'The cities under Mrs Thatcher: the centralisation and privatisation of power', *Centre for Urban Studies Working Paper* 6, Liverpool, University of Liverpool.

Parkinson-Bailey, J. (ed.) (1996), *Sites of the City: Manchester. Essays on Recent Buildings by their Architects*, Manchester, Manchester Metropolitan University.

Parsley, D. (1997), 'Regional warfare threatens UK plc', *Sunday Times Business Section* (12 October).

Parsons, W. (1988), *The Political Economy of British Regional Policy*, London, Routledge.

Paxman, J. (1991), *Friends in High Places: Who Runs Britain?*, London, Penguin.

Peck, J. (1995), 'Moving and shaking: business elites, state localism and urban privatism', *Progress in Human Geography*, 19, 16–46.

Peck, J. (1998), 'Making space for welfare-to-work: Assessing the prospects for Labour's New Deal', *SPA Working Paper* 41, Manchester, School of Geography, University of Manchester.

Peck, J. and P. Dicken (1996), 'Tootal: internationalisation, corporate restructuring and "hollowing out"', in J.-E. Nilsson, P. Dicken and J. Peck (eds), *The Internationalization Process: European Firms in Global Competition*, London, Paul Chapman.

Peck, J. and M. Emmerich (1992), 'Recession, restructuring and the Greater Manchester labour market: an empirical overview', *SPA Working Paper* 17, Spatial Policy Analysis, School of Geography, University of Manchester.

Peck, J. and N. Theodore (2000a), 'Work first: workfare and the regulation of contingent labour markets', *Cambridge Journal of Economics*, 24, 119–38.

Peck, J. and N. Theodore (2000b), 'Beyond "employability"', *Cambridge Journal of Economics*, 24, 729–50.

Peck, J. and A. Tickell (1994), 'Searching for a new institutional fix: the after-Fordist crisis and global-local disorder', in A. Amin (ed.), *Post-Fordism: A Reader*, Oxford, Blackwell.

Peck, J. and A. Tickell (1995), 'Business goes local: dissecting the "business agenda" in Manchester', *International Journal of Urban and Regional Research* 19, 55–78.

Peck, J. and A. Tickell (1997), 'Manchester's job gap', *Manchester Economy Group Working Paper* 1, Manchester, Manchester Economy Group.

Phelps, N. and M. Tewdwr-Jones (2000), 'Scratching the surface of collaborative and associative governance: identifying the range of social actions in institutional capacity building', *Environment and Planning A*, 32, 111–30.

Pike, A. (1997), 'Where partnership is not just a buzz word', *Financial Times* (30 June).

Porter, M. E. (1990), *The Competitive Advantage of Nations*, London, Macmillan.

Power, A. (1999), *Estates on the Edge*, Basingstoke, Macmillan.

Power, A. and K. Mumford (1999), *The Slow Death Of Great Cities? Urban Abandonment or Urban Renaissance*, York, Joseph Rowntree Foundation.

Pritchard, J. (1997), *The Legal 500: The Clients' Guide to UK Law Firms*, 10th edn, London, Legalease.

Quilley, S. (1997), 'Constructing Manchester's new urban village: gay space and the entrepreneurial city', in G. B. Ingram, A.-M. Bouthillette and Y. Retter (eds), *Queers in Space: Communities, Public Places, Sites of Resistance*, Seattle, Bay Press.

Quilley, S. (1998), 'Manchester first: from municipal socialism to the entrepreneurial city', *International Journal of Urban and Regional Research* 24, 601–21.

Quilley, S. (1999), 'Entrepreneurial Manchester; the genesis of elite consensus', *Antipode*, 31, 185–211.

Randall, S. (1995), 'City Pride – from "municipal socialism" to "municipal capitalism"', *Critical Social Policy*, 43, 40–59.

Ravetz, J. (2000), *City Region 2020: Integrated Planning for a Sustainable Environment*, London, Earthscan.

Redford, A. (1934), *Manchester Merchants and Foreign Trade: volume 1 1794–1858*, Manchester, Manchester University Press.

Reich, K. (1986), *Making it Happen: Peter Ueberroth and the 1984 Olympics*, Santa Barbara, Capra Press.

Richards, S. (1998), 'An evangelical DIY salesman', *New Statesman*, Special Supplement, June 26, 4–5.

Robinson, F., K. Shaw and M. Lawrence (1994), 'It takes two to quango: UDCs and their local communities in the North East', *Northern Economic Review*, 21, 47–60.

Robson, B. T. (1988), *Those Inner Cities: Reconciling the Economic and Social Aims of Urban Policy*, Oxford, Oxford University Press.

Robson, B., M. Bradford, I. Deas *et al.* (1998), *The Impact of Urban Development Corporations in Leeds, Bristol and Central Manchester*, London, Department of the Environment, Transport and the Regions.

Robson, B., J. Peck and A. Holden (2000), *Regional Development Agencies and Local Area Regeneration*, Bristol, Policy Press.

Rodgers, H. B. (1986), 'Manchester: metropolitan planning by collaboration and consent, or civic hope frustrated', in G. Gordon (ed.), *Regional Cities in the United Kingdom 1890–1980*, London, Harper and Row.

Rogers, H. B. (1980), 'Manchester revisited: a profile of urban change', in H. P. White (ed.), *The Continuing Conurbation: Change and Development in Greater Manchester*, Aldershot, Gower.

Rogers, R. (1999), *Towards an Urban Renaissance: The Urban Task Force*, London, E. & F. N. Spon.

Roth, A. (1997), 'Blair's first days: Old Labour left-overs join Blairites in power', *Guardian* (6 May).

Rowthorn, R. E. and J. R. Wells (1987), *Deindustrialization and Foreign Trade*, Cambridge, Cambridge University Press.

Rutheiser, C. (1996), *Imagineering Atlanta: The Politics of Place in the City of Dreams*, London, Verso.

Sassen, S. (1991), *The Global City: New York, London, Tokyo*, Princeton, Princeton University Press.

Sassen, S. (1994), *Cities in a World Economy*, London, Sage.

Sassen, S. (1996), 'Rebuilding the global city, economy, ethnicity and space', in A. D. King (ed.), *Re-Presenting the City*, Basingstoke, Macmillan.

Schlosser, E. (1998), 'Saturday night at the Haçienda', *Atlantic Monthly*, October, 22–34.

Seyd, P. (1990), 'Radical Sheffield: from socialism to entrepreneurialism', *Political Studies* 38, 335–44.

Simmons, D. and T. Bewick (1997), 'Employability in the local economy', *Local Work* 1, Manchester, Centre for Local Economic Strategies.

Simson, V. and A. Jennings (1992), *The Lords Of The Rings: Power, Money and*

Drugs in the Modern Olympics, New York, Simon and Schuster.

Smythe, H. (1994), *Marketing the City: Flagship Developments in Urban Regeneration*, London, E. & F. N. Spon.

South Cityside Steering Group (1996), *Partnership for Regeneration in South Manchester (PRISM)*, KPMG, Manchester.

Stewart, M. (1994), 'Between Whitehall and town hall: the realignment of urban policy in England', *Policy and Politics*, 22, 133–45.

Storper, M. (1997), *The Regional World: Territorial Development in a Global Economy*, New York, Guilford.

Straw, J., D. Henderson and D. Foster (1996), *New Politics, New Britain: Restoring Trust in the Way We are Governed*, London, Labour Party.

Stringer, G. (1994), 'The need for faith in the inner city', *Guardian* (30 September).

Taylor, A. J. P. (1976), *Studies in English History*, Harmondsworth, Penguin.

Taylor, I., K. Evans and P. Fraser (1996), *A Tale of Two Cities: Global Change, Local Feeling and Everyday Life in the North of England. A Study in Manchester and Sheffield*, London, Routledge.

Thomas, N. (1996), 'Supply side socialism, the political economy of New Labour', *New Left Review*, 216, 37–54.

Thornley, A. (1993), *Urban Planning Under Thatcherism*, 2nd edn, London, Routledge.

Thrift, N. J. (1990), 'Doing regional geography in a global system: the new international financial system, the City of London and the south east of England', in R. J. Johnston, J. Hauer and G. A. Hoekveld (eds), *Regional Geography: Current Developments and Future Prospects*, London, Routledge.

Tickell, A. and J. Peck (1996), 'The return of the Manchester Men: men's words and men's deeds in the remaking of the local state', *Transactions of the Institute of British Geographers* 21, 595–616.

Tickell, A., J. Peck and P. Dicken (1995), 'The fragmented region: business, the state and economic development in North West England', in M. Rhodes (ed.), *The Regions and the New Europe*, Manchester, Manchester University Press.

Tocqueville, A. de (1958), *Journeys to England and Ireland*, trans. G. Lawrence and K. Mayer, London, Faber and Faber.

TUC [Trades Union Congress] (1998), *Jobs in the Regions: The New Regional Divide*, London, TUC.

TUC (1999), *Reinforcing the New Deal*, London, TUC.

Turok, I. and N. Edge (1999), *The Jobs Gap in Britain's Cities: Employment Loss and Labour Market Consequences*, Bristol, Policy Press.

Turok, I. and D. Webster (1998), 'The New Deal: jeopardised by the geography of unemployment?' *Local Economy*, 13, 309–28.

Tye, R. and G. Williams (1994), 'Urban regeneration and central–local government relations: the case of east Manchester', *Progress in Planning*, 42, 1–97.

Tym, R. and Partners (1981), *Capital of the North: The Business Service Sector in Inner Manchester/Salford*, Manchester, Roger Tym and Partners.

UNCTAD (1998), *World Investment Report, 1998*, New York, United Nations.

Wagstyl, S. (1996), 'Nice work if you can get it', *Financial Times* (18 December).

Wainwright, H. (1987), *Labour: A Tale of Two Parties*, London, Hogarth Press.

Wainwright, M. (1999), 'Manchester: the gritty city goes lookie-feelie', *Guardian* (14 April).

Wannop, U. (1995), *The Regional Imperative: Regional Planning and Governance in Britain and the United States*, London, Jessica Kingsley.

Ward, C. (1988), *Welcome Thinner City*, London, Bedford Square Press.

Ward, K. G. (2000a), 'State licence, local settlements and the politics of "branding" the city', *Environment and Planning C: Government and Policy*, 18, 285–300.

Ward, K. G. (2000b), 'From rentiers to rantiers: "active entrepreneurs", "structural speculators" and the politics of marketing the city', *Urban Studies*, 37, 1093–108.

Webster, D. (1997), 'Welfare to work: why the theories behind the policies don't work', *Working Brief* (10–11 June).

Whiteley, P. (1983), *The Labour Party in Crisis*, London, Methuen.

Williams, G. (1995a) 'Manchester City Pride – a focus for the future', *Local Economy*, 10, 124–32.

Williams, G. (1995b), 'Prospecting for gold: Manchester's City Pride experience', *Planning Practice and Research*, 10, 124–32.

Williams, G. (1996), 'City profile–Manchester', *Cities*, 13, 203–12.

Williams, G. (1998), 'City vision and strategic regeneration: the role of City Pride', in N. Oatley (ed.), *Cities, Economic Competition and Urban Policy*, London, Paul Chapman.

Williams, G. (1999), 'Greater Manchester', in P. Roberts, K. Thomas and G. Williams (eds), *Metropolitan Planning in Britain: A Comparative Study*, London, Jessica Kingsley.

Williams, G. (2000), 'Rebuilding the entrepreneurial city: the master planning response to the bombing of Manchester City Centre', *Environment and Planning B: Planning and Design*, 27, 485–505.

Wood, D. and B. Clifford (1993), *A Survey of Financial, Professional and Business Services in UK Regions*, Manchester, Manchester Business School.

WTO [World Trade Organisation] (1995), *Annual Report*, Geneva, World Trade Organisation.

WTO (1998), *International Trade: Trends and Statistics, 1995*, Geneva, World Trade Organisation.

Wyler, S. (1999), *New Deal, Big Deal? The Experience of Homeless Young People in the First Year of the Government's New Deal*, London, Centrepoint and Crisis.

Wynne, D. and J. O'Connor (1996), *From the Margins to the Centre*, Aldershot, Ashgate.

Ziliak, J. P., D. N. Figlio, E. F. Davis and L. S. Connolly (1997), *Accounting for the Decline in AFDC Caseloads: Welfare Reform or Economic Growth?*, Madison, Wisconsin, University of Wisconsin-Madison, Institute for Research on Poverty.

Zukin, S. (1988), *Loft Living*, London, Hutchinson.

Index